RUSSIAN FEDERATION

MONGOLIA

HSTAN

STAN

Lake Balkhash

● Alma Ata

KIRGHIZIA

● Turpan

● Aksu

SINKIANG

Kashi ●

EAST-TURKESTAN

Yarkant ●

Hotan ●

CHINA

KASHMIR

Central Asia

TIBET

ORIENTAL RUGS
Volume 5
TURKOMAN

ORIENTAL RUGS
Volume 5
TURKOMAN

Uwe Jourdan
Introduction to the English Edition by
Ian Bennett

ANTIQUE COLLECTORS' CLUB

First published 1989
Battenberg Verlag, Augsburg
© Weltbild Verlag, Augsburg
English translation © Antique Collectors' Club Ltd.
World copyright reserved

ISBN 1 85149 136 8

British Library Cataloguing-in-Publication Data
A catalogue record for this book is available from the British Library

Printed in England by the Antique Collectors' Club Ltd., Woodbridge, Suffolk
on Consort Royal Satin from Donside Mills, Aberdeen, Scotland

CONTENTS

ACKNOWLEDGEMENTS

The author and publisher are grateful to all the people mentioned on page 63 who have loaned colour photographs for the carpet illustrations, as well as to all the companies and individuals who have contributed to this book with criticism, advice and assistance. Special thanks go to:

Mr Gert Nagel of the auction house Dr Fritz Nagel, Stuttgart, who provided most of the colour illustrations and, giving up his private time, was essential to the success of this book; Ms Doris Eder, who collated numerous pieces of relevant information during her dedicated cataloguing of the colour illustrations loaned by auction house Nagel.

I am grateful to Robert Pinner for his kind permission to reprint the article on pages 26 and 27, Mr Li Zuding (Great Wall of China Ltd./ Hamburg/Shanghai) and to Mr Ian Bennett (i.e. Mosaik-Verlag/Munich) for allowing me to reprint the drawings in fig.78 (*Patterns from the Carpets*) and figs. 26, 27 and 28-33 (*Carpets of the World*).

Fig. 1

INTRODUCTION TO THE ENGLISH EDITION

This is the fifth in the series of specialist monographs published by the Antique Collectors' Club on Oriental carpets, a series which began with a volume on Caucasian rugs in 1981. Like that first volume, this book on Turkoman weavings is largely reliant for its illustrations on pieces sold by the German auction house of Dr Fritz Nagel in Stuttgart. Unlike the Caucasian book, however, this volume has been augmented by illustrations of a number of rare weavings garnered from various sources; all of the latter are acknowledged in the relevant captions and the reason for this 'diversification' is given below.

Another difference between the English editions of the first and latest volumes in the *Oriental Rugs* series is that *Turkoman* is a translation of the text written by Uwe Jourdan for the German edition (Battenberg Verlag, München, 1989) whereas the text for the English edition of *Caucasian Rugs* is completely different from that of its German counterpart; the former was written by me and that of the German edition by Doris Eder, formerly of Nagel's.

Turkoman weaving is the subject of intense and apparently ceaseless academic study; as such, attributions, dating, nomenclature and so on change frequently and are often the subject of heated debate between various factions of Turkoman specialists. A good example of this is the attribution of a number of weavings previously attributed wholesale to the Yomut tribe. Careful structural analysis has shown them to be the work of at least two different tribes or sub-tribes, apart from the Yomut themselves; represented in this volume by rugs such as that in no.113, they have been given various names during the last few years – Ogurjali, Imreli, Göklan, 'Fine Brown Yomut', etc. However, basing their nomenclature on one of the most distinctive design elements found on several main carpets of these types, the most recent writers to study these weavings, Annette and Volker Rautenstengel and Siawosch U. Azadi, have opted for the non-tribe-specific appellation 'Eagle Group' which, due to certain structural features, they have divided into three sub-groups. Their joint monograph on the subject, *Studien zur teppich-kultur der Turkmen* (privately printed ltd. edn. 500 copies, Hilden, 1990), was published after the German edition of Mr Jourdan's book had appeared and given the widespread acceptance of their principal hypotheses, I have opted for the Rautenstengel-Azadi terminology where relevant.

When reviewing the German edition for *Hali*, the international magazine of fine carpets and textiles, the noted expert on Turkoman weavings, Robert Pinner, remarked favourably on another aspect of this book which links it to its Caucasian predecessor. Because of the large number of readily available colour separations, it was possible in both cases to publish books with an astonishing number of colour illustrations at very reasonable cost.

Additionally, because the principal source of these illustrations was one auction house, the examples covered a very wide range of quality as well as type, although this made any gaps which existed extremely obvious.

The Caucasian volume limited itself to weavings from the late 18th to the early 20th centuries and was thus able to cover the full range of village rugs and bags, both piled and flat-woven, from this period in sufficient depth without having to resort to 'outside' illustrations. With the Turkoman volume, however, it was necessary to augment the available supply of illustrations from Nagel with examples of exceptionally rare and important types which had either not passed through Nagel's rooms or of which no good picture had survived.

The result is a book which has a fair number of masterpieces among a body of illustrations which shows Turkoman weaving in far greater depth and diversity than that of any previously published monograph on the subject. Thus the prospective collector or anyone wishing to learn more about this most complex subject has a chance to study a large number of weavings of the types and qualities most likely to be encountered in galleries and auction houses; some of them are of such humble status as to have made their depiction in colour in any general or even specialist book most unlikely. Therefore, as with the Caucasian book, Mr Jourdan's publication on Turkoman weavings is a remarkably rich, detailed and, above all, useful reference source for students and collectors, no matter what their level of expertise.

Mr Jourdan has read widely and has handled more Turkoman weavings in a few years than most people will see in a lifetime. His text is a distillation of the extensive literature on Turkoman weaving written by an enthusiast with much experience and a good eye. As much attention has been given to cataloguing and describing the least important weaving as it has to the most important, so that readers carefully studying the text and illustrations synchronistically should emerge with a good knowledge of the history and diversity of Turkoman weaving. For the fine tuning, they should then turn to the specialist works listed in the bibliography. I certainly hope and expect that Mr Jourdan's book will become the most convenient and widely used reference source for Turkoman weaving, as the volume on Caucasian rugs has been for some time in its respective field.

Ian Bennett
London

INTRODUCTION AND SURVEY

Geography

West Turkestan is an area of some 700,000 square kilometres with the Caspian Sea to the west, the Mangyshlak Peninsula to the northeast and the Kapet-Dagh Mountains and the outskirts of the Hindukush forming a semi-circle to the south. West of what since 1924 has been the border of the Soviet Socialist Republic of Turkmenia are Afghanistan and the Iranian province of Khorassan. At the eastern side is the huge Chinese province of Xinjiang (Sinkiang), usually referred to in the context of weaving literature as East Turkestan. Thus viewed in simple geographic terms, it is easier to understand the nature of this Eurasian basin, part of the ancient world's dry belt.

To the western side of the region is the Karakum desert and to the east, between the Amu-Darya and Syr-Darya rivers, is the Kyzylkum desert. To the south, in what is now the Soviet Socialist Republic of Uzbekistan, are the important trading centres of Bukhara and Samarkand, the latter having been a major post along the ancient Silk Road, which ran from China through East Turkestan and on westwards, via Tashkent in Uzbekistan, Mary (Merv) in Turkmeniya and Khorasan. Many different ethnic groups have occupied this region for millennia and among those associated with weaving, in addition to the Turkomans themselves, are the Uzbeks, Karakalpaks and Kirgiz.

Historical Research

Serious research into the weaving culture of the Turkomans must, of course, encompass more than aesthetic appreciation. The beauty of such weavings has unquestionably been the most important factor both for historians and collectors but it is the starting point, the motivation for a greater curiosity. The history, genealogy, beliefs and way of life of the Turkoman steppe peoples are all of great importance to their art. Turkoman weavings, therefore, with their distinctive palettes, motifs and compositions, are not merely examples of a strange and exotic 'folk' art but represent a highly complex and historically continuous culture.

This strong historical continuity was made possible by the innate conservatism of Western and Central Asian tribal cultures and, most importantly, by their nomadic, or semi-nomadic, way of life. The Turkomans (who belong to a Western Turkic language group – unlike any other Central Asian peoples) have thus been able to maintain and develop their own special culture.

Because the majority were nomads or semi-nomads, hardly any written sources exist to indicate the origins of the Turkomans but it is clear that they are descended from the Oghuz tribe, whose genealogies list a few names still found in the 19th century.

Other descendants of the Oghuz were the Seljuks and Ottomans, who built great empires from the 11th century onwards, their power and

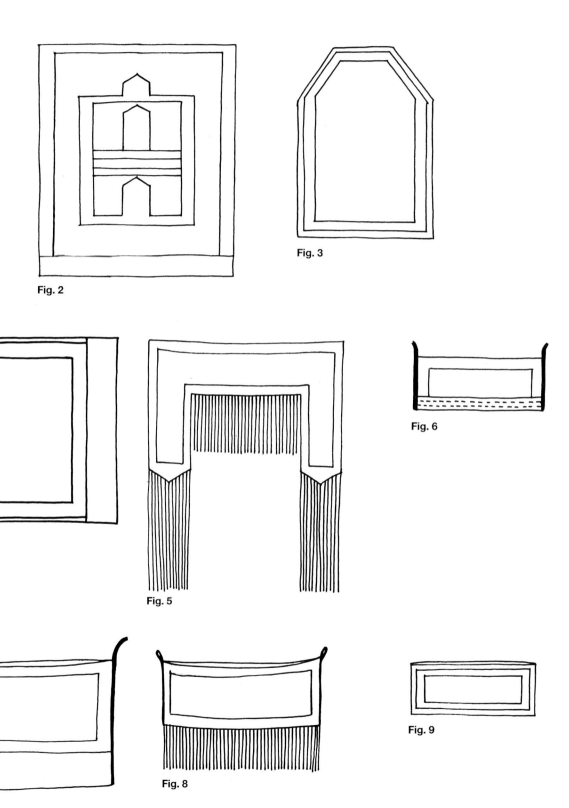

Fig. 2

Fig. 3

Fig. 4

Fig. 5

Fig. 6

Fig. 7

Fig. 8

Fig. 9

territorial expansion creating a Turkic-based culture into eastern Europe, North Africa and Spain. Within this historical context, therefore, it is not difficult to see the importance of the Oghuz and their descendants; and the history of the Oghuz, with all its later political and geographical ramifications, is crucial to a proper understanding of Turkoman weaving, as will become clear.

Way of Life

The earliest researchers into the Turkomans and their weaving culture started from the assumption that the Turkomans had always been nomads and therefore the historical roots of their weaving were to be found in nomadic traditions. That the art of knotting grew out of the practical necessities of a nomadic way of life appears to be a convincing hypothesis. Mobility was an important requirement of this lifestyle and all the nomad's personal property had to be, as far as possible, light, easily transportable and made from readily available raw materials, the most important of which was the wool from their own flocks of sheep. Piled carpets provided protection from the cold underfoot – in these climates, freezing temperatures seep up from the ground at night – and could also be used as covers and blankets.

However, the general opinion today is that although nomads unquestionably played an important part in the development of pile weaving, they may not actually have invented it. In the nomadic environment, it was easier to make felts and flat-weaves. Felting, indeed, is probably among the oldest of textile techniques. No loom is needed and items can be made in a comparatively short time. By contrast, the production of a knotted carpet can take several months, and thus it is hardly a technique suitable for a nomadic way of life.

Whenever carpets are depicted in early art, whether Eastern or Western, they are associated with power and wealth, both religious and secular. From such evidence, it would seem that for a long time pile weavings were the preserve of the upper echelons of the societies which made or imported them. It is therefore more likely that they were produced by settled communities rather than by semi-nomadic ones. The manufacture of rugs by knotting woollen threads on to a net-like ground structure was probably derived from flat-weave techniques. The development from a continuous flat-weave such as *sumak*, through such loose napping as the loop-pile technique to the final refinement of 'knotting' seems logical.

It was not only geography and climate which forced many of the inhabitants of Central Asia into a nomadic way of life. There was also the constant plundering and pillaging which went on between neighbouring groups, the fight for good grazing lands at different times of the year, the struggle to secure access to water supplies and the constant internecine battles between the Turkomans themselves. The origins and development of equestrianism among the steppe nomads, starting with the Scythians around 700 B.C., are also of considerable importance when discussing the history of this region.

The Turkomans were divided into tribes, the number of which it is now hard to estimate; the tribes themselves were further sub-divided into various kinship groups and individual families, much like the large tribal confederations in Iran, many of which are also wholly or in part of Turkic origin. The Turkoman family lived in a distinctive tent, called a *yurt*, which could be erected and dismantled within a few hours. The base of a *yurt* was a lattice-like construction made of willow with a domed roof and covered in felt (see no.134).

Horses were the key to a tribe's power, and served as their major status symbol. The principal source of its wealth was its sheep which provided wool, milk and, on festive occasions, meat. The task of looking after the flocks, as well as weaving, fell to women. Other raw materials for weaving, although to a much lesser extent, were obtained from camels and goats.

Types of Turkoman Weaving

The various types of Turkoman weaving were determined by the nomadic lifestyle – tent dwelling and ease of mobility – and by the raw materials available from which everything was made, from the various types of bag, cradles, rugs and covers, weavings for dividing the space within a tent, entrance covers, bands for concealing the joint between the 'walls' to the 'roof' and so on – in other words a woven 'architecture' and interior design. Both the objects themselves and the manner in which they were made and decorated were the results of a long tradition; many of the designs were handed down from generation to generation and are associated with specific tribes or sub-tribes.

Apart from the large main carpets (*hali* or *khali*), which, like other specific weavings, seem to have been used only on special occasions, the following are some of the most interesting types of Turkoman weaving:

Ensi. Used to cover the entrance to a tent, in other words a woven 'door' (fig.2). Because of the *mihrab*-like design of many *ensis*, some writers have assumed that they were also used as prayer rugs; there appears to be no evidence of this usage and a number of authorities have specifically excluded it.

Namazlyk. A prayer rug, usually with a clearly recognisable *mihrab* (niche) design (see no.51). Turkoman prayer rugs are primarily associated with the Ersari; surviving examples by other tribes are generally late in date.

Salatshak. An hexagonal weaving, the exact function of which is controversial (fig.3). Again, the *mihrab*-like designs of many examples have led some writers to suggest that they are prayer rugs but several specialists in Turkoman weavings, including Siawosch Azadi, have stated that they were made as cot covers. Some examples have a slit at one end, suggesting use as a saddle-cloth. Again, the majority of published examples do not appear particularly old (see also *Tainaktsha*).

Small Rugs. Rugs woven in a small, almost square, format. In the opinion of many writers, they were used as hearth rugs (see fig.4). They do not appear to have a specific name and like the larger main carpets are usually

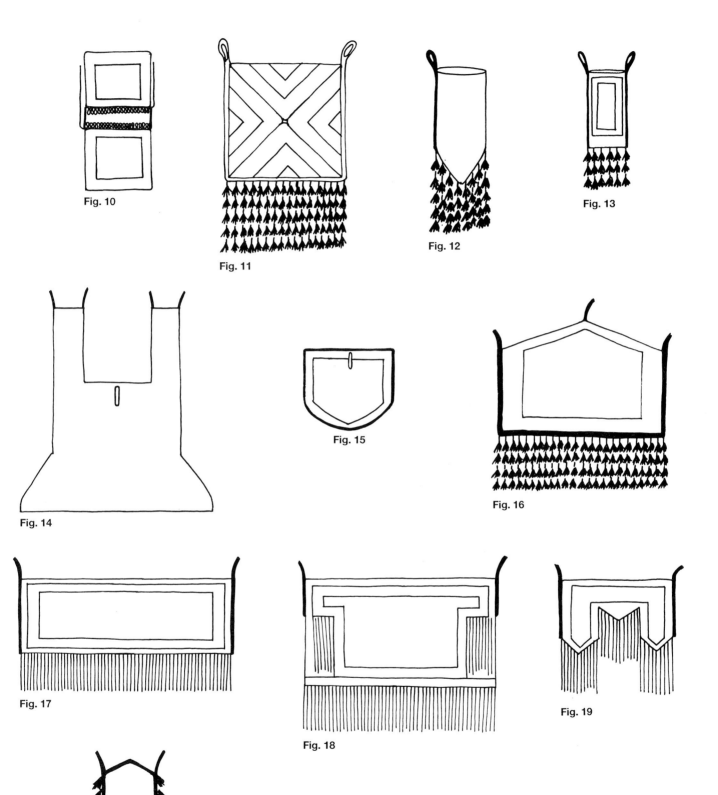

Fig. 10

Fig. 11

Fig. 12

Fig. 13

Fig. 14

Fig. 15

Fig. 16

Fig. 17

Fig. 18

Fig. 19

Fig. 20

called *hali* or *khali*. However, according to the Russian writer V.G. Moshkova, the source of much of the taxonomy of Turkoman weavings now in common use, a small rug with Tekke guls used for the threshold is called a *dip khali*.

Kapunuk. A shaped weaving with two long hanging sides made to hang above the interior of the tent entrance (i.e. above the *ensi*. See fig.5).

Germech. Small pile-weaving, narrow and rectangular in shape, suspended in the tent-entrance on a rod about 25cm. above the ground to keep out dirt and animals (see fig.6). Visually, such weavings are indistinguishable from *torbas* and according to Azadi in *Turkoman Carpets*, only four examples are known.

Jolami. Tent band, usually on a white ground. Usually less than 0.30m. wide by more than 20m. in length. The more usual type has the design piled on a flat-woven ground but there is a small number of highly valued all-pile examples. Most *jolami* are attributed to either the Tekke or Yomut tribes. There are various types of band used within the tent to give strength to the structure; these have different names depending on their function, with the main kind of band described above being called *ak yup* or 'white girth' (see nos.135-137).

Chuval. The largest of the various kinds of Turkoman woven bags with a single face (see fig.7).

Torba. Smaller version of the above (see fig.8).

Mafrash. The smallest format Turkoman single-faced bag which, like *chuvals* and *torbas*, has a flat-woven back, usually in undecorated plain weave, and loop fastenings (see fig.9). The word *mafrash*, it should be noted, appears in various Central Asian languages to describe different types of woven bag. Among the Shahsavan of the Caucasus and northwest Iran, for example, it refers to a large multi-sided bedding bag or woven 'trunk', usually in the *sumak* technique (see fig.10). Some examples of all three types of single-faced bag retain long, free-hanging side-cords and side-tassels.

Bokche. Small envelope-like bags woven in one piece with the four sides forming four triangular shaped flaps (see fig.11).

Okbash. Small pouch-like bags, usually with triangular bases and often retaining long plaited cords decorated with tassels (see fig.12). Apparently used to cover the ends of tent strut-poles. Most old examples are attributed to the Yomut, although at least three by the Tekke are known. There seems to be some confusion between an *okbash* and an *igsalyk* (see below) in the literature, with the leading contemporary Soviet specialist, Elena Tzareva (*Rugs and Carpets from Central Asia, Leningrad and Harmondsworth*, 1984), describing two weavings (Nos. 82-3), which in the West would be called *okbash*, as '*igsalik*'.

Igsalyk, Gashokdan, Chemche Torba, Aina Khalta, At Torba, Dis Torba* (or *Duz Torba*), *Darakbash. Types of small piled containers for specific objects – cutlery, mirrors, etc. *Igsalyks* are of rectangular, almost square, shape with four triangular flaps at the base (i.e. the same weavings as those called *okbash* in the West, see above and also fig.13). According to Soviet researchers, they are used as spindle bags. *Aina khaltas* are small rectangular weavings, approximately 40 x 25cm., used to carry mirrors. *At torbas* are rectangular horse nose-bags and *chemche torbas*, although of very similar shape, were used apparently for carrying long-handled wooden spoons; a *darakbash* is a tiny pentagonal bag for a comb. *Dis torbas* were used for salt and, according to their shape, for other comestibles such as sugar, flour, etc.

Tainaktsha. Large shaped horse blanket, examples of which can be either piled or flat-woven (see fig.14). Many Soviet writers also describe a *salatshak* (see above) as a horse or saddle cover.

Eyerklyk, Tsherlyk. Forms of horse saddle covers. the former has a semi-circular body with or without two long rectangular flaps (see fig.15).

Asmalyk. Camel-flank hangings, presumably always made in pairs (see fig.16). The most usual form is pentagonal but there are some rarer heptagonal examples known. Large rectangular weavings by the Salor with indented 'T'-shaped compositions are also presumed by many Turkoman experts to have served the same function. Rectangular weavings without specific 'T'-shaped compositions but which do not seem to have had backs, are often called *jollars* and are presumed by some writers to have also been used as camel-flank hangings.

Khalyk, Dezlyk. Shaped weavings somewhat similar to *kapunuks* (see above) but smaller and often with an extra rectangular flap at the base of the 'cross-bar' (see figs.17, 18 and 19). Used as decoration for the camel's breast. *Khalyk* is the word favoured by Western writers, modern Soviet researchers preferring *dezlyk* (or *dezlik*).

Diah Dezlyk, Tutash. the former are small pentagonal weavings used to cover the front knees of a camel, usually during festivals and special occasions such as wedding processions (see fig.20). Azadi (*Turkoman Carpets*, Pl.53) illustrates a pair of very similar weavings which he describes as *tutash* or pan-holders, remarking that such pieces were always made in pairs.

The Role of Pile Weaving

The practical importance of weaving to the nomadic way of life undoubtedly led to the development of increasingly sophisticated knotted artefacts as well as to the craft itself becoming an expression of individual identities and beliefs. The skill of Turkoman weavers thus not only demonstrated a desire for comfort and decoration but was also used in specific instances, of which the making of prayer rugs is the most obvious, to illustrate certain aspects of their culture.

A woman's importance, indeed her value, within such a society depended to a great extent on her abilities as a weaver. Men were essential to ensure a particular group's survival, to defend it against attack and to increase its strength and influence by subduing others. The bearing of children and their rearing, the care of livestock and the making of most of the appurtenances of tribal life, including weavings, were the tasks of women. It is understandable, therefore, that weddings were occasions of particular importance and were used by brides to display all their talents as weavers.

Characteristics of Turkoman Weaving

The two most obvious characteristics of Turkoman weavings in general, and of carpets in particular, are their use of geometric ornamentation and their predominantly red to red-brown palette. Red had already achieved considerable symbolic significance in the Neolithic period – the habit of covering skeletons with red ochre was widespread before the 5th millennium B.C. – and during the Bronze Age in Central Asia was associated with the warrior class. Turkoman weavings with white or light ground colours are unusual and were probably used only during weddings and important religious festivals.

The principal motif found on Turkoman weavings is the *gul* (*gül, gol* or *göl*; see below), a geometric, usually octagonal, motif of an emblematic nature. The fields of carpets are usually decorated with rows of 'major' *guls* interspersed regularly with smaller 'minor' *guls* of different shape. This field is surrounded by major and minor borders and although it is unusual to find instances where the 'frame' cuts into the major *guls*, it is not difficult to read the composition of any Turkoman carpet's field as a section of an infinite repeat.

At the ends of carpets and at the bottom of bags and *ensis*, there are usually extra panels, called *elems*. Some, usually by the Tekke, are piled with simple stripes; but generally they are more elaborately decorated, often with different patterns at top and bottom. The *elems* themselves are followed by flat-woven ends (although these are very often missing from older pieces). According to Moshkova the one exception to the general rule is to be found in Saryk carpets which always had large flat-woven ends but never any *elems*.

Degeneration

The ancient traditions of the Central Asian nomads were not able to survive the various encroachments which took place during the 19th century. Continuous warfare plus the growth of central government powers weakened nomadic autonomy and led to increasing poverty. Towards the end of the 19th century, Turkoman weaving became more and more commercialised as the Turkomans themselves fell under Russian domination.

Turkomen weaving changed from being essentially a domestic occupation to being a marketable export. Designs, sizes and colour schemes were adapted to meeting the growing demands of western markets. The consequences of this interference with a traditional tribal art form, epitomised, perhaps, by the increasing use of synthetic dyes, were disastrous. The final death blow came, however, with the introduction of Soviet rule during the 1920s. Old Turkmenistan became a Soviet Socialist

Republic, in which ideological concept the nomadic way of life had no place. Peoples were forcibly settled or resettled under rigid state control.

The Age of Turkoman Weavings

The labels 'old' and 'antique' applied to Turkoman weavings in the international carpet market are intended to be significant historical and stylistic indicators. 'Antique' pieces are those presumed to be more than 100 years old and thus, to a large extent, this class of weaving has little or none of the signs of degeneration referred to above; weavings thought to be from the first half of the 19th century or earlier are especially valued by collectors. However, many 'old' carpets from around the turn of the century are well worth serious consideration, particularly if they, too, have escaped the degenerative process.

Rugs made after the Revolution, mainly in state-run workshops, are of no interest to serious collectors and the new collector should also be wary of imitations and copies made in Pakistan and elsewhere, which are marketed as 'Bukhara'.

Naturally, it is best if the age of a weaving can be determined with some exactitude, especially as the adjectives 'old' and 'antique' begin to lose their relevance as indicators of quality the nearer we get to the 21st century. However, as with all Oriental rugs, the dating of Turkoman weavings is extremely difficult and requires a considerable amount of experience. A number of criteria can be used as aids in the dating process but there is still considerable disagreement, even among experts. Dyes, motifs, materials and condition all have their parts to play and there is also a comparatively small number of dated pieces which have a limited role as pointers.

Dyeing Techniques

One of the most important physical guides in determining a weaving's origin and age is its palette, particularly if this contains synthetic dyes. The first analine dyes began to appear in Eastern weavings during the second half of the 19th century and were initially expensive and available in only a very limited palette; thus the earliest rugs with analine dyes, probably dating from the late 1870s and 1880s, have only small amounts, the most common being a very light-fugitive mauve called fuchsine. Other early synthetic colours include a somewhat lurid orange and various types and shades of red and pink; the reds in particular have a tendency to run if brought into contact with liquids and most early synthetics show signs of fading, especially if the base of the knot is compared with the tip of the pile. Natural colours are far less sensitive to light, particularly over short periods, and if the dyes are properly mordanted, they will not run.

This does not mean, of course, that rugs with no synthetic colours are all antique or even old. Conversely, a rug with small amounts of analine dye could still be antique and in any case, the presence of such dyes does not necessarily destroy the aesthetic merit of a weaving – indeed it could be argued that in the early days, because of their cost, such colours were only

18

Fig. 21

Fig. 22

Fig. 24

1800		1900	
50	1267	00	1318
51	1268	01	1319
52	1269	02	1320
53	1270	03	1323
54	1271	04	1321
55	1272	05	1322
56	1273	06	1324
57	1274	07	1325
58	1275	08	1326
59	1276	09	1327
60	1277	10	1328
61	1278	11	1329
62	1279	12	1331
63	1280	13	1332
64	1281	14	1333
65	1282	15	1334
66	1283	16	1335
67	1284	17	1336
68	1285	18	1337
69	1286	19	1338
70	1287	20	1339
71	1288	21	1340
72	1289	22	1341
73	1290	23	1342
74	1291	24	1343
75	1292	25	1344
76	1293	26	1345
77	1294	27	1346
78	1295	28	1347
79	1297	29	1348
80	1298	30	1349
81	1299	31	1350
82	1300	32	1351
83	1301	33	1352
84	1302	34	1353
85	1303	35	1354
86	1304	36	1355
87	1305	37	1356
88	1306	38	1357
89	1307	39	1358
90	1308	40	1359
91	1309	41	1360
92	1310	42	1361
93	1311	43	1362
94	1312	44	1364
95	1313	45	1365
96	1314	46	1366
97	1315	47	1367
98	1317	48	1368
99	1316	49	1369

0 1 2 3 4 5 6 7 8 9

Fig. 23

1278 = 1861

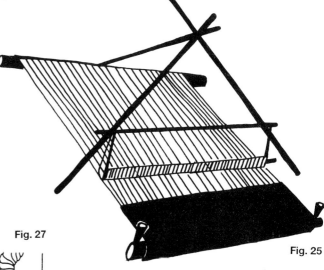

Fig. 25

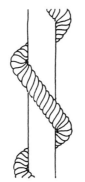

Fig. 26

Fig. 27

used on special weavings.

One natural dyeing agent, indigo, was not found in Turkmenistan but was easily available from both Afghanistan and India. Madder root, which is indigenous and was always available, gives a wide range of colours from deep red, through red-brown and dark aubergine to pale pink, and can also be used in combination with other dyes. Plants such as henna, crossthorn, safflower ("dyer's thistle") and sumak were also indigenous. Extracts from these, as well as madder and indigo, give the basic Turkoman palette – many shades of red, aubergine, blue, yellow, green and brown. By using undyed wool, various shades from cream to deep brown could be obtained. Brown is used to outline designs and motifs on most Turkoman weavings. Black, as opposed to a very dark brown, is usually the sign of a late weaving. In some weavings, the clear white found in small areas is usually cotton.

Red could also be obtained from various species of bark insect, particularly cochineal and lac; the presence of these dyes can also be a help in dating. For the ordinary collector, of course, scientific dye analyses can be difficult and costly to obtain. However, there is some useful published material on the subject, particularly by Professor Mark Whiting of Bristol University, who divides Turkoman weavings into five periods based on their dye content (Mackie and Thompson, *Turkmen*, pp.223 ff.).

The quality of colour as a whole, as well as the palette itself, are helpful in the dating process and enable useful conclusions to be reached without the help of scientific analysis. Comparisons between the colours of rugs within a particular group will often allow us to arrange weavings into a broad chronological sequence.

The Development of Patterns

As the use of colour changed, so did the use of motifs and designs from one generation of weavers to another. It is easy to see, for example, that the *gul* shown in fig. 21 is a much simplified version of the Tekke *gul* seen in fig. 22 and thus it can be argued that clues as to date can be found in the differences which occur in the numerical ratios of vertical to horizontal knots; early pieces, according to this argument, have an equal number of knots in each direction, later pieces having a higher vertical knot count so that the motifs appear flatter or 'stretched' sideways. Thus Tekke main carpets which have the roundest *guls* are considered to be among the earliest; following from this, it is often argued that a squarish format is also indicative of an early date.

There are, however, many problems with such hypotheses as changes occurred only very slowly and in small details. Secondly, carpet knotting in a tribal environment was based on precedent, with designs being handed down from mother to daughter and faithfully reproduced. However, as outside influences increased throughout the 19th century, those weavers who were the most isolated were the last to be affected. Thus what would have seemed the norm to one group of weavers might have seemed archaic to another; the cultural environment which allowed for the smooth linear progression of design was being destroyed during the very period in which most of the surviving tribal Turkoman weavings were made. It is certainly dangerous to argue that simple renditions are necessarily later than complex ones; indeed many writers have suggested, quite logically, that exactly the opposite is true.

Condition

The condition of a weaving is not in itself much guide to age and can only be used as evidence in a supporting role. Very early rugs can sometimes be in astonishingly good condition, especially if they have been in the West for a long period, just as comparatively modern rugs are found in very poor condition both in the East and the West.

One effect of age on weavings of many types and origins is corrosion. Iron oxide was commonly used to achieve a dark brown colour, but this has the effect of making the yarn brittle. Areas which are piled with such wool soon wear down to give an unintentional but sometimes quite pleasing relief effect (see the *elem* panels of the Yomut rug no.99). In general, corrosion does not affect the value of a weaving unless it is very serious and detracts markedly from the piece's appearance. Again, because this effect can occur in quite a short space of time, it does not in itself furnish proof of great age. It can also be artificially induced, as can changes in palette, which can be caused both by chemical 'washing', as well as by prolonged exposure to direct sunlight. This has happened to many rugs from the end of the 19th century onwards, due to Western demand for paler colours.

Dated Carpets

A few Turkoman weavings exist with inwoven dates, although they are quite rare and are all from the end of the 19th or early 20th centuries – i.e. no examples are known from the 'pre-synthetic' period. Thus the amount of knowledge to be garnered in this way is small, though not entirely insignificant. This is also the case with the acquisition dates of certain examples in museums.

Inwoven dates are usually in the Islamic calendar, which begins with the flight of Muhammad to Medina in 622 A.D. (the Hejira). Because the Islamic year is lunar, a formula is needed to convert an Islamic date into a Gregorian one: divide the Hejira date by 33.7, subtract the result from the Hejira date and then add 622. For an approximate equivalent, add 583 to the Hejira date (for Arabic numerals and conversion chart, see figs.23-24).

Great caution must be taken with inwoven dates, however. In some instances, they may not represent the year a rug was woven but some important festival or event which the weaver wished to commemorate. The date could also have been copied from an older rug – most weavers were illiterate and might have understood a date as being simply part of a design. Many rugs also bear entirely false dates or genuine dates which have been 'doctored' – it is, for instance, very easy to change an Arabic 3 into a 2 by removing three or four knots, thereby making the rug appear to be dated a century earlier than it is.

Unfortunately, European paintings, one of our most important sources of information about early carpets from many of the great weaving cultures, is of very little help with Turkoman weavings since the earliest representations of these do not appear until the end of the 19th century.

Early Carpets

Although there is no actual evidence of Turkoman weavings of the types illustrated in this book having been made before the 19th century, many experts date particular examples to the 18th century or even earlier. It is difficult, if not absurd, to believe that pile weaving was born, reached maturity and died among the Turkoman nomads within the space of a few decades in the 19th century; it is now generally accepted that those early weavings are the fruits of an ages-old tradition.

Many assume that Central Asia was where pile weaving began, but we have to admit that there are no obviously archaic forerunners of 18th/19th century Turkoman rugs from the same region. However, it may well be that very old rugs from other regions, particularly from Anatolia, represent Turkoman weaving at earlier times. It is also possible that examples in Western public and private collections, with documented histories going back to the second half of the 19th century may in fact be considerably earlier. For these reasons, many of the dates given for individual pieces in this book should be treated as approximate guides; we can only hope that in time, research will furnish us with firmer evidence.

The first steps towards a scientific basis for establishing age are being taken in laboratories. The last few years have seen striking advances being made in the analysis of materials, particularly in such fields as electromicroscopy, carbon 14 and nitrogen analyses, thin-layer chromatography and so on, explanations of which go far beyond the framework of this book. But we should not forget either here or in the next section on structure, that it is the quality of colour and design which should be considered of primary importance.

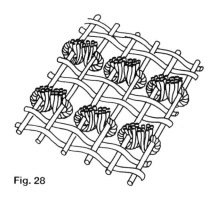

Fig. 28

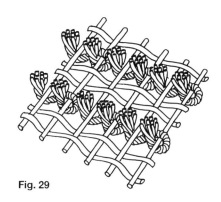

Fig. 29

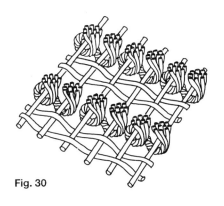

Fig. 30

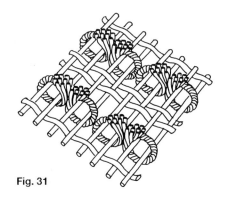

Fig. 31

Fig. 32

Fig. 33

Fig. 34

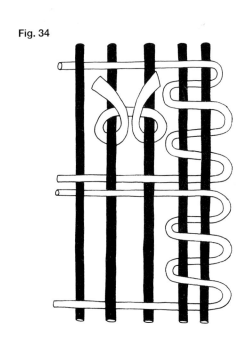

Fig. 35

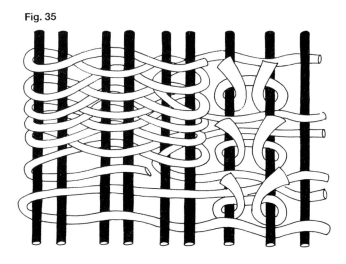

The Structure of Turkoman Carpets

The structure of weavings, how they are made and with what, is considered of far greater significance today than it was by an earlier generation of writers; many of the latter were aware that structure might be able to reveal much information but were incapable of analysing it themselves. Over the last three or four decades, many writers, researchers and collectors have studied the structures of large numbers of weavings and, basing their conclusions on this large body of material, have put forward many new and convincing theories as to origins and dates. Though there is a growing tendency to present analyses in a consistent manner understandable to everyone with some experience, a common terminology has yet to be agreed.

The foundations of pile weavings consist of warps and wefts. The warps are first attached to a warp beam; the Turkoman nomads usually used a horizontal loom (see fig.25), as opposed to a vertical one which is harder to erect. Warp materials can be wool, cotton or goat-hair and sometimes a mixture of wool and goat. Goat-hair was usually used for warps of more finely woven pieces as it can be very finely spun while retaining great strength. Machine-spun yarns began to appear in the second half of the 19th century, although were generally used only for commercial weavings, not for those items made for domestic consumption. Like their counterparts in most tribal societies, Turkoman women were expert spinners of animal fibres and machine-spun yarns were expensive.

The materials used for Turkoman weavings are spun in an anti-clockwise direction, usually designated in technical analyses as 'Z'; when two or more Z-spun yarns are plied, the plying is clockwise, designated as 'S'. The combination of Z-spinning and S-plying is characteristic of almost all Oriental weavings with the exception of the wool found in Egyptian-made rugs, which is spun and plied in the opposite directions (see figs.26-27). In the standard abbreviations now used in technical analyses, the material is given first, followed by the direction of the spinning, the number of yarns which have been plied, followed by the direction of the plying. Thus 'W Z2S' means that the material is wool, the direction of the spinning is anti-clockwise, i.e. 'Z' and that two (2) strands have been plied in a clockwise direction (i.e. 'S'); these same abbreviations are also used when describing the wefts, the structure of which always appears after that of the warps. Measurements are usually given with the length (i.e. the warp) first and the width (i.e. the weft) second; some writers and publications (i.e. the specialist magazine *Hali*) give the width first but they are in a minority. In both cases measurements are normally made along and across the central axes. Most measurements do not include flat-woven ends and fringes.

The pile of a rug consists of what, in strictly technical terms, is a form of discontinuous wefting attached to the warps; it seems rather pedantic to express it as such, however, and 'knotting', although a misnomer, has now been almost universally accepted as a term of convenience. The forms of knotting most usually encountered are described as asymmetric

24

Fig. 36

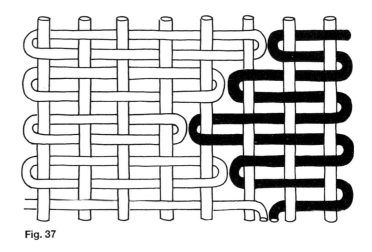

Fig. 37

Fig. 38

Fig. 39

Fig. 40

(abbreviated to As, also 'Persian' or 'Sehna'), which can be 'open' to the left or right (see figs.29-30) and symmetric (abbreviated to Sy, also 'Turkish' or 'Ghiordes', see figs.28 and 31). The easiest way of determining what kind of knot has been used is to bend the rug gently back along the weft, so that one can look down at the base of a knot. In many instances, alternate warps lie at different depths, a phenomenon called warp depression (see figs.32-33).

The materials and the ways in which they are used are of inestimable value in determining the origins of weavings. Also of considerable significance is the fineness of weaving, which in structure analyses is normally measured by the number of knots to the square inch and/or square decimetre (i.e. 10cm. vertical by 10cm. horizontal). Other important aspects of structure are the type and number of colours, the way a weaving feels (the 'handle') and the way it is finished both at the sides (selvedges) and ends; in many instances, of course, the condition of the piece will be such that some of these features will no longer be present or will have been replaced (for selvedge weave techniques see figs. 34-37).

Structural Characteristics of Turkoman Tribal Weavings

The major tribal groupings for Turkoman weavings from Central Asia are Salor, Saryk, Tekke, Yomut, Arabachi, Chodor and Ersari. With the exception of Chodor, their characteristics are tabulated on pages 29-30. There are also many minor groupings. Amongst the Yomut are the Göklan, Jaffarbai, Ogurjali, Imreli, Igdyr, Atabai and Abdal and among the Ersari are the Chob-Bash, Beshir and Kizil Ayak. In addition, some believe that it is possible to distinguish the Tekke weavings from Mary (Merv) and those from Achal.

The problem with such a list is that it implies a greater degree of certainty than is justified at present. There are many problems in attributing weavings to specific tribes, and even more when it comes to sub-tribes or groups. Colours, designs and motifs are not sufficient in themselves, as there were many designs and motifs used by all or some of the major tribes and the borrowing of patterns occurred more often than one realises. This was increasingly the case with the growth of commercial weavings in the second half of the 19th century. There are some Turkoman carpets obviously made in a commercial environment which are of very good quality and bear surprisingly early dates which there is no good reason to challenge; some of these, it is interesting to note, bear woven Armenian inscriptions, proof if it was needed of their manufacture in a commercial workshop or factory.

One can hardly ignore individual tribal attributions, especially as those of the best known and most common types of weaving to specific tribes are not in much doubt. Such attributions assist a learner towards a clearer understanding of Turkoman weaving as a whole, as well as being of value in dating, assigning specific motifs and, of course, in determining rarity and market value.

An excerpt from an essay by the British writer and Turkoman specialist Robert Pinner sums up very well the progress which has been made in Turkoman scholarship and the continuing problems caused by attributions. The essay, entitled 'Work in Progress', appeared in *Hali* (no.42, London, 1988, pp.15-19) and I am grateful to Mr Pinner for his permission to reproduce part of it below:

> 'There are three reasons why Turkoman carpets have been investigated in greater detail than others: the initiative of the Russian authors and collectors of the turn of the century, headed by Dudin, Bogolyubov and Felkerzam; the great collector interest which set root in Europe and America before World War II; and the strong tradition that maintained relatively distinct characteristics of designs, drawing style, structure and colours for the rugs of the different tribes.
>
> Siawosch Azadi's catalogue of his 1970 Hamburg exhibition, itself strongly influenced by the Soviet ethnographer V.G. Moshkova, was the forerunner of post-war Western literature on Turkoman carpets, as was indeed Jon Thompson's publication of the 'S group', later identified as Salor.

Not all the groups of Turkoman weavings identified during the last decade on the basis of uniform characteristics could be attributed to specific tribes. It proved possible for those of the Arabachi and, more speculatively, for the Göklen (who took over the place briefly occupied by the 'Imreli') but is has so far proved impossible, for instance, for the group characterised as 'Fine Brown Yomut' or as 'Eagle Group 2' which shares many designs and design elements with 'Göklen' pieces, but differs in structure and colours.

Indeed, an advance in taxonomy can itself multiply our questions: for instance, we can now identify three distinct groups of weavings which appear to be sub-groups of the Chodor and three or four of the Saryk. We have hardly started to identify individual groups of weavings among the Yomut and Ersari – although some Soviet authors now believe that they can distinguish between pieces woven in the major weaving centres in the Amu Darya valley (the 'Beshir' weaving area).

Compared with our understanding of tribe-related designs and technical features, we have made much less progress in our ability to date Turkoman carpets. It is not difficult to come to believe that we can date most Turkoman rugs with a fair degree of accuracy, when we are really following, and in turn supporting, a dating schema which is conventional rather than one based on evidence. The fact is that we have sufficient evidence to date fairly accurately most – but not all – Turkoman carpets made in the last 100 years. We can make more or less intelligent guesses at the dates of a fair proportion of pieces made 50 years before that but, with rare exceptions, we have no evidence on which to judge the date of rugs made at the beginning of the 19th century or earlier.'

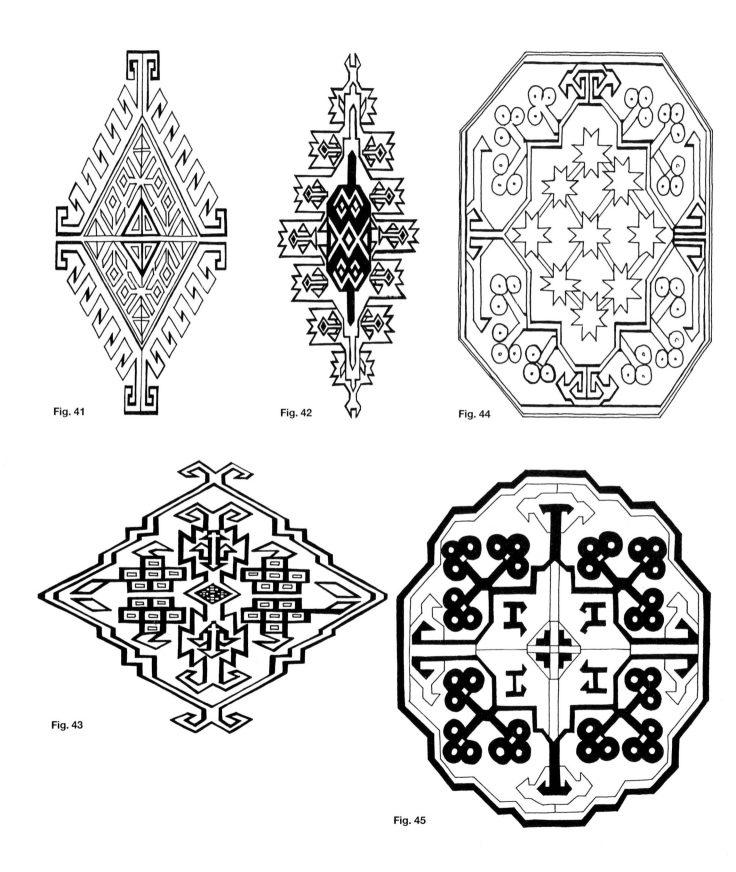

Fig. 41

Fig. 42

Fig. 44

Fig. 43

Fig. 45

TABLE

Horizontal
Warp – weft – type of knot – knot density – height of pile – selvedges – end finishes – specific motifs – names used for sub-tribes or related groups

Vertical
Salor – Saryk – Tekke – Yomut – Arabachi – Ersari

Salor
Warp: W(ool), ivory/brown and/or G(oat-hair), grey/brown
Weft: Mostly natural brown, sometimes dyed red
Knot: Usually As(ymmetric)3
Knot density: Main carpets 2,000-3,500 per dm²
Pile height: 5-8mm.
Selvedges: W, usually dark blue
Ends: Main carpets with broad, flat-woven, ends with stripes in one or more colours; bags with long dark blue fringes added (i.e. not part of the foundations)
Other nomenclature: 'S group'

Saryk
Warp: W or G, ivory/brown
Weft: W, various shades from grey to red-brown
Knot: Sy1/Sy2. Late pieces As
Pile height: 6-8mm.
Selvedges: Frequently two coloured 'chequerboard' pattern
Ends: Main carpets same as Salor; upper end of *ensis*, bags and panels often with a blue border; lower end often with a long blue fringe added as with Salor

Tekke
Warp: W, ivory
Weft: W, brown
Knot: Mostly As2, sometimes As4
Knot density: 4,000-6,000 per dm²; early pieces below 3000 per dm²
Pile height: 4-10mm.
Selvedges: Usually simple and in dark blue wool
Ends: Main carpets sometimes with broad flat-woven ends
Particular design types: 'animal tree' *ensis* and *asmalyks*, 'bird' *asmalyks, ak-chuvals*

Specific designs: Although certainly not used exclusively by the Tekke, the 'curled leaf' border pattern is found on some of the earliest and greatest of their weavings to have survived, including some very rare main carpets
Other nomenclature: Achal-Tekke, Merv-Tekke

Yomut
Warp: W/G or W/C(otton), undyed
Weft: Usually W, undyed; sometimes C
Knot: Sy1, or As with specific sub-groups such as 'Eagle Group' weavings
Knot density: 1,800-3,000 per dm²
Pile height: 3-6mm.
Specific types: Although not exclusive to the Yomut, the majority of the following types of weavings are usually attributed to them: *bokche, okbash, pentagonal asmalyks*
Specific designs: Although not exclusive to the Yomut, the following types of *gul* are most often found on weavings attributed to them or on the weavings of one of the 'sub-groups' now or previously associated with the Yomut: *dyrnak*, 'Eagle' or 'Ogurjali', *kepse*, 'C-gul'. Also *asmalyks* with the *erre* (saw-tooth or tree-like) design are almost always Yomut
Other nomenclature: Imreli (now rejected as a serious attribution by most experts), 'Eagle group' (divided into three groups probably not all made by the same tribe or sub-tribe; this is now the widely accepted nomenclature of weavings previously called Imreli, 'Fine brown' Yomut or Ogurjali; some are attributed to the Göklen but future research may yield more exact and dependable provenances), Igdyr, Jaffabai, Atabai

Arabachi
Warp: W/G, various shades from brown to grey
Weft: W/C, very dark brown/speckled white ('salt and pepper')
Knot: As1/As3
Knot density: 1,500-2,500 per dm²
Pile height: up to 7mm.
Selvedges: G, dark brown, multiple cords

Ersari
Warp: G, usually dark brown
Weft: non-specific
Knot: As1-As4
Knot density: 800-1,500 per dm²
Pile height: up to 10mm.
Selvedges: G, multiple cords, usually dark brown, often very wide
Ends: non-specific
Other nomenclature: Beshir, Ersari-Beshir, Kizil Ayak, Chob-Bash

Aspects and Theories concerning the Origins and Meanings of Turkoman Weaving Designs and Motifs

The weavings of the Turkic peoples show a wealth of designs and motifs, the origins of which may, in some instances, go as far back as the Neolithic (i.e. before 5000 B.C.). There has long been ethnographic and anthropological interest in the peoples and the weavings of Central Asia, but it was not until the early 20th century that field research revealed the names used by the actual weavers for many of the patterns. However, it soon became apparent that the names used by weavers for the various designs and motifs could not shed much light on the latter's origins and the same phenomenon is still experienced by today's field-workers all over the Near and Middle East.

One of the pioneers of research into the Central Asian peoples and their weavings was the Soviet anthropologist V.G. Moshkova (1902-1952), who was a member of six field expeditions into the weaving areas of West Turkestan. From this wealth of practical experience came her book *The Carpets of the Peoples of Central Asia in the 19th and 20th Centuries: Material from Expeditions 1929-1945*, published in Russian in Tashkent in 1970 and published in a German translation by B. Rullköter in Hamburg four years later as *Die Teppiche der Völker Mittelasiens im Späten XIX und XX Jahrhunderts. Materialien der Expedition von 1929-1945* (an English version was published in instalments over many issues of the *Oriental Rug Review*). In this, Moshkova identifies several key factors which must be taken into account when discussing Turkoman designs and motifs: those of botanical origin; those of zoological origin; those with a protective or amuletic function; those which denote cosmological elements; those which are intended as aids – e.g. to fertility in humans, animals and crops, success in warfare, and so on; motifs of an anthropomorphic nature; and heraldic motifs.

Research into the last of these, motifs of an heraldic nature, led to Moshkova's much discussed hypothesis of *guls* as identifying symbols of individual tribes and sub-tribes and thus to the theory of 'live' and 'dead' *guls.*

The Age of Turkoman Rugs as Demonstrated by the Heraldic Nature of their Designs

The *gul* has three principal characteristics: its basically octagonal shape; its internal quartering with one basic pattern repeated four times, which is emphasised by the diagonal colouring of these four individual sections; complete or fractional representations of animals, usually birds, in each quarter, which in some instances have become almost completely abstract in their rendering, similar in some respects to European coats of arms or escutcheons. Similar emblematic motifs with these three characteristics can be found on the weavings of many Turkic peoples from widely differing regions.

According to Moshkova, Turkoman *guls* are tribe-specific, i.e. certain *guls* were originally used only by one tribe. The *gul* shown in fig.38 was, according to Moshkova, originally the tribal emblem of the Salor; the *gul* shown in fig.39, the so-called Saryk *gul* (fig.43), was, as its name implies, used originally only by the Saryk tribe, the *gul* seen in fig.40 was that of the Tekke, the *dyrnak* (fig.41) and *kepse* (fig.42) *guls* were used by two sub-tribes of the Yomut and the *ertman gul* (fig.43) was used only by the Chodor. The *gulli-gul* of the Ersari is also shown here (fig.44), although it is, arguably, an amalgam of the *gul* found on Salor main carpets (fig.45) and the *tauk nuska* ('chicken') *gul* found on the main carpets of several different tribes and sub-tribes, in particular the Yomut (fig.47). Some *guls* may be found in quite different renderings; compare, for example, the differing external shapes and internal decoration of the *kepse guls* on six Yomut main carpets illustrated in nos.98-103.

Depending on the importance with which each of the proud Turkoman tribes viewed their principal heraldic motif, its main use would obviously be as a repeat pattern on the large main carpets. The designs and individual motifs found on less important weavings would usually be drawn from a wealth of patterns not necessarily belonging to one tribe only.

For this reason, the literature on Turkoman weaving sometimes differentiates between the tribe-specific principal motifs of main carpets, which originally had an heraldic function, by calling them *göls* or, in Moshkova's terminology, 'living *göls*'. These motifs used on bags or as minor motifs on main carpets are differentiated by the spelling *gul* (*gül*). These are the 'dead' heraldic motifs of tribes which had lost their autonomy, the motifs themselves becoming less significant as a result. Thus what Moshkova described as the 'Salor *gul*' is not found on any known main carpet by that tribe but on later weavings by the Tekke and on some attributed by Siawosch Azadi and others to the Göklen. It is, in other words, a 'dead *gul*'.

Moshkova explains that before the middle of the 19th century, the great tribe of the Salor was defeated in a series of battles with the Tekke and was absorbed by the latter. They were driven from their ancestral grazing lands by the Tekke and Saryk and with this loss of both sovereignty and, eventually, identity, their tribal emblem ceased to have any heraldic

Fig. 46

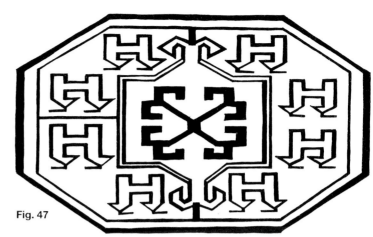

Fig. 47

Fig. 49

Fig. 48

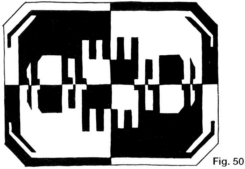

Fig. 50

Fig. 52

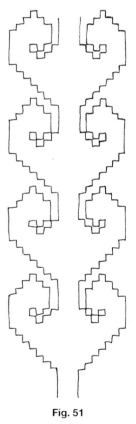

Fig. 51

Fig. 53

significance; it was taken over by their conquerors and was used subsequently both by them and by other tribes and appeared mainly on bags (see the Tekke examples nos.63-65).

In contradiction to Moshkova's hypothesis, however, a different *göl* (we have opted for the more usual and anglicised spelling *gul* throughout the English edition of this book) appears on all the known main carpets attributed to the Salor (see fig.45). Nevertheless, her principal thesis has never been properly discussed or adequately disposed of. It seems strange, not to say improbable, that a victorious tribe should have adopted the main emblem of the tribe it had defeated; indeed, it might seem a more convincing hypothesis were it to be argued that the defeated tribe would have adopted the emblem of its conquerors or, as seems possible with the Baluch tribe, to have been forced to abandon their own emblem altogether, a development which can be seen on the Baluch rugs from East Iran and Afghanistan, many of which have Turkoman *guls*, variants thereof (e.g. fig.46) and other elements borrowed from the repertoire of Turkoman weaving. Furthermore, we have seen at least one typical Salor main carpet which, were it not for its design and colour, would have been dated unhesitatingly by most experts to the second half, perhaps even the last quarter, of the 19th century.

Equally difficult to reconcile with Moshkova's hypothesis is the *tauk nuska gul* (fig.47) which appears in many variant forms on the main carpets and other weavings of several different tribes and sub-tribes, including those of the Yomut, Ersari, Arabachi and Chodor (see nos.108-110, 202-3, 215-6, 235, 237-8, 240).

Dietrich Wegner (*Tribus*, no.29, Linden Museum, Stuttgart, 1980) offers an alternative explanation for the difference between 'göl' and 'gül'. He argues that equating the term *göl* with the Farsi word for flower, *gul*, is hardly logical or sensible. Although motifs similar to Turkoman *guls* appear on tribal and village weavings from Iran, the Caucasus and Anatolia and are called *guls* in these regions, Wegner points out that the old Turkish word *köl* forms part of the names of many rivers and lakes between the southern Altai and West Turkestan; he states that every kinship group had a particular river or lake which it revered because of the part it played in its differing but similar death rites. Thus the *gul* illustrated in fig.38 could be interpreted as a pre-Islamic motif showing a lake surrounded by *yurts* (tents). More recently, the archaeologist, James Mellaart, in *The Goddess from Anatolia* (Milan, 1989), has pointed out that *gul* is Turkish for 'lake' and that this, rather than 'flower' is the origin of its usage in the context of Turkoman motifs.

Another interpretation of the *gul* as an heraldic symbol is the hypothesis that it developed from the *tamgha* or *oneghun*. The 14th century historian Rashid-ad-Oghuz listed twenty-four tribes of the Oghuz, the ancestors of the Turkomans, and said that each was allocated its own brand (*tamgha*) and totem in the form of a bird (*oneghun*). The *tamghas* were simple motifs, that of Salor Khan, founder of the Salor tribe, being a hook-like form (fig.48);

for Mahmud Kashgari in the 11th century, this same *tamgha* had become a slightly more complex arrow-head form with an extra extension (fig.49). The Soviet author Karpov states that the '*tagma*' or '*tavro*' has been used by both Mongolian and Turkic nomads as a sign of ownership since ancient times. But in '*Tagma* – Brands of the Turkomans' (*Turkmenovedenie* nos.8-9, *Turkoman Research*, vol.2), he assigns yet another *tamgha* to the Salor.

It is possible that these originally simple 'brands' were rendered in an increasingly complex manner through the generations until they became the *guls* we know from 19th century Turkoman weavings. If one takes this original theory further, it is possible to argue that at some stage, the *oneghun* or animal totem was also incorporated. In this context, it is interesting to consider the motif (fig.50) seen on a weaving depicted by a 15th century Italian painting attributed to Sassetta, *The Madonna and Child in the Palazzo Cini, Venice* (after Pittenger, 'A Miscellany in Oils', *Hali* 38, 1988, diagram 1). It is interesting that the reciprocated hook forms in the four corners of this motif have been interpreted as residual representations of birds and the motif within the Chodor *ertman gul* (fig.43) certainly seems to have an avian origin.

However, firm evidence for the development of the *gul* from the *tamgha* does not exist because such apparently simple motifs as the latter have become lost in the complexity of the modern *gul*. But it is interesting to speculate that all the tribal *guls* had a common origin and that all the Turkomans were once, long ago, an homogeneous group. Certainly we know that at one time the Salor, Saryk and Tekke had common settlements and were known as the 'Stone Salor'.

The Symbolic and Ritualistic Characteristics of Turkoman Rug Designs

'Religious officials among the Turkomans can be divided into three types: the official Moslem *pastors*, the Sufi teachers of the Ishane sect and the pre-Islamic priests or shamans called *porchanes*. This is why Islam often seems like a shell covering the hidden forms of pre-Islamic belief...'

'In our view, the most common indicators of pre-Islamic beliefs are such "superstitions" as the "evil eye", malevolent ghosts, faith in the powers of various talismans and amulets, faith in the power of prayer to heal, pilgrimages to holy places related to nature cults, obvious remnants of religious fetishism and totemism, beliefs connected to the powers of plants and trees, the Jildiz star and other omens and belief in Piri, the benign rulers of natural forces, livestock and so forth.'

The two important quotations given above (M.B. Durjev and M. Demidov in *Turkoman Research*, op.cit., vol.VIII) represent one significant starting point for research into Turkoman weaving, namely the interpretation of the motifs found on such weavings as iconographic, with mythical and ritual overtones. The Islamisation of Central Asia never succeeded in eradicating completely earlier shamanistic beliefs; even after

Islam was officially adopted in the major centres such as Samarkand and Bukhara, these beliefs still exerted considerable influence, together with the continuance of what might be described as 'Turkmenoglyphs'. The ability to interpret such iconographic motifs was gradually lost, as was knowledge of their origins, even though their talismanic power remained.

As a result, many of the more ubiquitous motifs have been given different meanings depending on the philosophical and religious inclinations of the interpreter:

The Tree. According to common shamanistic belief, heaven and earth are connected by a tree which grows at the earth's centre. This has to be climbed by the shaman spirit on its journey to heaven; on the way, the spirit has to pass through various levels, denoted by the tree's branches. The so-called 'Tree-of-Life' at the centre of the Islamic Paradise is related to this concept as, of course, is 'The Tree of the Knowledge of Good and Evil' which, according to Genesis, grew in the Garden of Eden.

The Bird. This also has a major role in shamanistic belief, a role so rich and varied that it cannot be discussed fully here (see R. Pinner, 'The Animal Tree and the Great Bird in Myth and Folklore' in Robert Pinner and Michael Franses, eds., *Turkoman Studies I*, London, 1980, pp.204-251). The bird symbolises the 'flight' of the human soul and thus stylised trees are often delineated in concert with equally stylised birds, the latter either 'complete' or in part. Eventually, tree and bird 'merge' into one motif (see figs.51-52).

With this in mind, it is possible to offer an interpretation of those *ensis* with the 'cross' (so-called *hachli*) design. This design can be said to reflect the idea of a cosmos with a tree at the centre of the earth, the latter 'represented' by the design found within the lower *elem* panel. The four separate fields created by the cross-shaped composition (see fig.53) represent the cardinal points, the hook-like motifs, reminiscent of candelabra, within them representing the various spiritual levels through which the soul must pass. A more banal, albeit equally possible, theory of this type of *ensi* composition is that it is a stylised representation of a wooden door with cross-beams, *ensis* taking the place of doors in the nomadic *yurt*.

The Ram. Reverence for this animal also has an important role in the shamanistic beliefs of the Turkomans and their ancestors. It is not only a symbol of strength but was also regarded as containing the spirit of dead forebears. It is hardly surprising, therefore, that its horns were used as part of the design repertoire of Turkoman weaving, being known as the *kotshak* motif (see figs.54-56). The pelts of mountain rams were supposed to have served in the ecstatic journey of the soul, a use similar to that accorded to tiger skins in Tibet and China. The ram's skin is also supposed to have been spread as a prayer mat in shamanistic rituals and was subsequently represented, albeit in a highly stylised manner, on felts (see figs.57-58).

There are also Turkoman prayer rugs of comparatively recent date on which pairs of huge horns appear as the principal motifs (see no.246). Carpets from many different weaving cultures and from many different periods have motifs which are either obviously stylised representations of stretched animal skin or pelt or can, and have been, interpreted as such; look, for example, at the motif from a well-known design group of late 19th-early 20th century rugs from the Kazak weaving area of the western Caucasus illustrated in fig.59 (the so-called 'bug motif'). Certainly there seems a logical progression from animal skins being used for warmth underfoot and over the body to their representations in woven textiles, particularly pile rugs, which imitate the fleece of a sheep in a number of obvious respects.

The Talisman or Amulet. Many motifs have a talismanic function. For example, they were used as protection against the 'evil eye', as agents to ensure or to encourage fertility, good health and so on. The *elem* of the Ersari *chuval* illustrated in no.265 bears the so-called *muska* motif, which was also used for silver pendants (fig.95) and as a motif on silk embroideries (it is sometimes rendered as quite a realistic hand and is called the 'Hand of Fatima', although it retains the same or similar talismanic functions). There is also the totemic *aidi gul*, which appears piled on the narrow flat-woven lower end of the Tekke *namazlyk* or prayer rug illustrated in no.51.

For a clearer understanding of the many theories surrounding Turkoman weavings, it is as well to have a simplified table of Central Asian history. Over many millennia, the peoples of this region were subject to many different influences and dominated by many different powers. Urban cultures were never homogeneous but the 'melting pots' of diverse ethnic groups, which were partly assimilated but also brought with them their own customs and beliefs to add to the rich cultural 'stew'. These influences, of course, also spread outwards to touch the lives of the various nomadic and semi-nomadic tribes living 'beyond the pale'.

Influences, Aspects and Historical Analogies

Early Stone Age. Rock paintings at Terme.

5th millennium B.C. Painted pottery.

From the 3rd millennium. The first urban cultures.

1000 B.C. Indo-Aryan immigrations.

550 B.C. Turkestan incorporated into the Achaemenid Empire as a province.

323 B.C. Following the conquest of Turkestan by Alexander the Great and his death, the founding of the Graeco-Bactrian Empire.

140 B.C. Indo-Bactrian Empire founded by the Sakes. Spread of Buddhism. Growing importance of the Silk Road as a link between the Far East and the Roman Empire.

1st century B.C. Appearance of the first equestrian nomads.

200-500 A.D. Division of Turkestan into provinces.

6th century A.D. Turkomans from southern Siberia take power in parts of Turkestan.

568 A.D. Conquest by the Chinese Tang dynasty.

632 A.D. Death of the Prophet Muhammad.

705 A.D. Islamic Conquest.

To 999 A.D. Samanid Empire, with far-reaching trade links; carpets from Bukhara reach Scandinavia.

11th century A.D. The Seljuks, a Sunni branch of the Oghuz, leave their Central Asian grazing lands and move westwards into Anatolia, founding a great empire which, however, became increasingly fragmented; the Sultanate of Rum, the Seljuk opposition to the Eastern Roman Empire, ceased to exercise much power after the first wave of Mongol conquests in the mid-13th century and disappeared at the beginning of the 14th century.

13th century A.D. The Mongols, themselves of Turkic origin, under their leader Chinggis (Gengis) Khan (died 1227), storm through Turkestan, Iran and Anatolia.

Late 13th to late 14th century. Gradual establishment and growth of the Ottoman Empire, the Ottomans or Osmans being another branch of the Oghuz, which reached its peak in the late 15th to 16th centuries.

14th century A.D. Founding of the Timurid Empire, which at its peak stretched from Samarkand to the Mediterranean, including much of Iran and the Near East.

16th century A.D. Uzbek domination.

19th century A.D. Russian conquest.

There are certain 'markers' within this chronology which are of considerable importance to the history of the pile carpet and which will be discussed in more detail later.

14th century B.C. Late Bronze Age graves containing knives for cutting the wool pile of carpets.

5th century B.C. The Pazyryk carpet (symmetrically knotted), together with

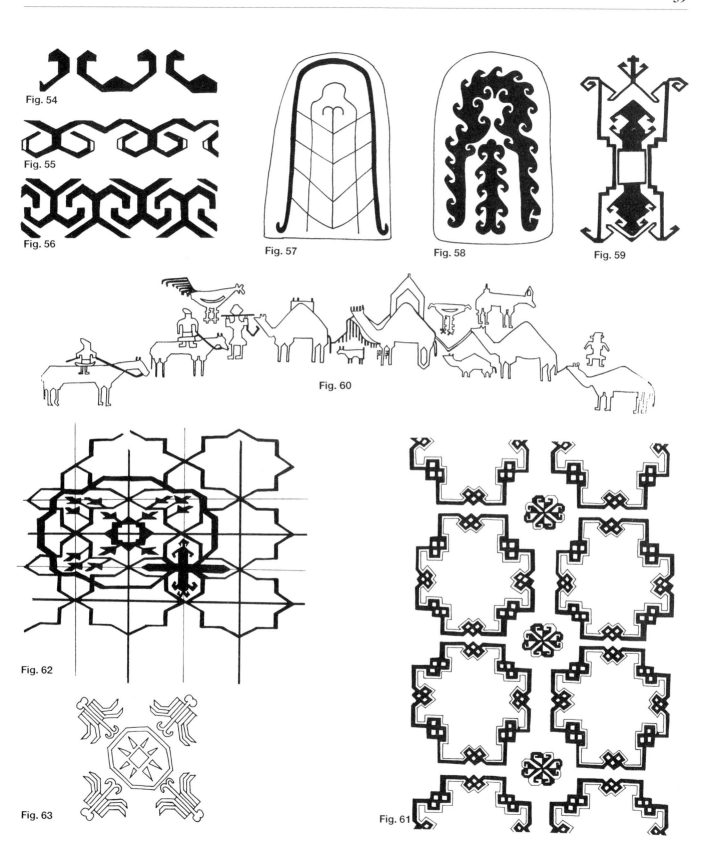

Fig. 54

Fig. 55

Fig. 56

Fig. 57

Fig. 58

Fig. 59

Fig. 60

Fig. 62

Fig. 63

Fig. 61

felts and fragments of asymmetrically piled carpets, interred in Scythian funeral barrows in the Altai Mountains of southern Siberia (discovered in 1947 by the Soviet archaeologist, S.I. Rudenko).

11th-14th centuries. Putative dates of so-called Seljuk carpets made in Anatolia.

15th century or earlier. Surviving Anatolian 'animal' rugs and depictions of such rugs in European paintings.

15th-16th centuries. Egyptian rugs of the so-called 'Mamluk' type. After 1517, when the Ottoman Turks completed their conquest of Egypt, 'Mamluk' rugs were made probably by the same weavers together with rugs of the so-called 'Cairene Ottoman' design type.

15th-16th centuries. Anatolian rugs with so-called 'Holbein' designs. Persian carpets with medallion and flowers designs; also 'hunting' carpets. Earliest Caucasian 'dragon' carpets, probably dating from the end of the 16th century.

16th-17th centuries. Persian 'vase technique' carpets from Kerman and establishment of looms in Esfahan by Shah Abbas in 1601-2.

Caucasian 'blossom' carpets (18th century).

Without doubt, beliefs and ideas which originated in other cultures and which were expressed in symbolic form on weavings, had to some extent influenced the iconography of Turkoman rug designs.

Islam

It would seem obvious to look for Islamic influences on Turkoman carpets but to what extent these exist is debatable. The representation of animals and human figures on Turkoman weavings is not particularly unusual; see fig.60, for example, which shows what is probably a wedding caravan from the *asmalyk* illustrated in no.194. A similar procession of animals is shown in the bottom border and a hunting scene in the field of fig.1. This drawing is of a felt *asmalyk* in the State Museum of Fine Art of the Turkmenian SSR in Ashkabad and is considered by some authorities to date from the 18th century.

It cannot be assumed that Islamic proscriptions against depicting living creatures, particularly human beings, were generally followed. Such proscriptions were certainly ignored by the artists working in the royal ateliers of the great Islamic dynasties of the Ottomans, Safavids and Mughals, who even went so far as to depict the Prophet Muhammad and his followers, though the Prophet's face is often left blank or is veiled. Depictions of human beings on tribal rugs from all the great Islamic weaving countries of the East are also not unusual, especially on weavings made to celebrate or commemorate weddings. However, it could be argued that a certain uneasiness persisted when it came to representing human figures, hence the great emphasis on abstract or semi-abstract ornament in Islamic, as well as in early Christian and Byzantine art.

Thus, when asking how far Islam influenced Turkoman art, one should remember that the question could just as easily be asked the other way round. Mongol influence spread out over the whole of Central Asia, Persia, the Caucasus and Anatolia and was, arguably, the basis of the wealth of patterns available to all Turkic peoples; it is the most important ingredient in the melting pot of influences from many different cultures. If we bear such antecedents in mind, design comparisons can often be most revealing.

Fundamental to the field designs of Turkoman carpets is the concept of the infinite repeat. Anatolian rugs of the 15th-16th centuries (and in some cases perhaps earlier) with so-called 'Holbein' designs are sometimes strongly reminiscent of Turkoman rug designs. fig.61 shows a detail of the repeat pattern on a rug in the Vakiflar Museum, Istanbul, which is dated to the 15th century by Belkis Balpinar and Udo Hirsch, whose monograph on the pile rugs in that museum appeared in 1988 (see no.3). The plaited-like effect of the design of this and other Anatolian carpets of roughly the same period can still be found in the *guls* of 19th century Turkoman weavings. The *gul* shown in fig.38 is particularly striking in this context, but the use of star-like motifs is found not only on 15th and 16th century Anatolian carpets but also in the work of most areas in which Turkic peoples had some influence. In Ayyubid and Mamluk Egypt, such designs had already reached a high degree of sophistication by the 13th century and the rich variations on this theme seem endless. An example of a quite simple 'star and cross' repeat can be seen in the detail of the so-called *kejebe* design from a Charshango Ersari carpet in fig.85. The field designs of Tekke main carpets have a similar derivation (see fig.62).

The relationship between Anatolian and Turkoman design can also be seen in the field pattern of another carpet in the Vakiflar Museum. The principal motif of this rug is one large 'star' medallion which is flanked by four small star-filled octagons, each of which is flanked by four semi-abstract motifs (see fig.63). That this is intended as an infinite repeat is shown by the fact that the border 'cuts into' the overall field design; the relationship between the secondary motifs and, for example, the minor *guls* on an Arabachi *chuval* (fig.64, no.209) can hardly be disputed.

There is also an obvious relationship between some Turkoman *guls* and the stylised floral palmettes found on 18th century Caucasian 'blossom' carpets, a detail of one such rug being shown in fig.65. A well-known large fragment of a main carpet in the Metropolitan Museum, New York (see fig.66), despite its 'eagle group' type design, does not have the structural features considered to differentiate the three 'eagle groups' both from Yomut weavings and from each other. Its structure bears some similarity to Caucasian rugs and its field motifs are clearly related to those of some Caucasian 'blossom' carpets, especially the motifs with 'serrated' edges, as they are to the Yomut *kepse gul* (fig.42). Many more such analogies could be made as one looks at the weavings illustrated on the following pages and they show that Turkoman weavings share certain designs and motifs with Anatolian rugs which date back until at least the Seljuk period.

Similar analogies can also be found for border patterns. The so-called 'curled leaf' border seen on Tekke *asmalyks* (see nos.94-96), Salor and Tekke *kapunuks* (see no.93) and on a very small number of early Tekke main carpets (see fig.68), can also be found in very similar form on 18th century 'shield' carpets from the Caucasus (see fig. 67 and detail no.285a).

The so-called *kotchanak* border (figs.69-70) seems, at first glance, to be a series of rectangles with double-hook projections at top and bottom alternating with highly stylised palmettes. However, comparisons with the borders of early rugs from Anatolia which have border patterns generally accepted as being based on Kufic script (see figs.71-73) suggest that this is its origin.

The use of script as ornament is an extremely important characteristic of Islamic art, deriving from the extraordinary calligraphic artistry which developed because of the Koran and other sacred and secular literature. Thus it is possible to find other potential sources for carpet patterns in both Persian and Turkish manuscripts. A miniature from a manuscript of Nizami's Khamseh, painted in the late 15th century in Herat, then the capital of Iran's easternmost province, Khorasan, shows the ruler of Samarkand seated on a carpet; this carpet's field has a repeat pattern related to the 'plaited star' or 'star and cross' design mentioned earlier (see fig.74).

From the late 19th century onwards, it becomes easier to identify influences from neighbouring Islamic regions; this is particularly true of the field designs of many Ersari 'Beshir' carpets, which often have patterns associated with 19th century Persian rugs, for example the 'Herati' pattern (no.281) and the *mina-khani* pattern (no.279). Lastly, rugs with more or less realistic depictions of mosques are all probably no earlier than the last quarter of the 19th century and were made by Turkoman peoples in Afghanistan; it is questionable, however, whether such rugs can be considered the 'genuine' products of Turkoman weaving culture.

Other historical and cultural entanglements provide bases for the interpretation of designs and motifs. Rather less obvious than either Persian or Anatolian influences are those traceable to China, although one would expect to find strong East Asian influence given the conquest of Turkmenistan by the T'ang dynasty rulers in the 6th century B.C. In Mackie and Thompson's *Turkmen* (op. cit., fig.34), Turkoman *guls* are interpreted as being Chinese 'cloud-collar' medallions (see fig.75), taken from Chinese Ming porcelain. According to this theory, the Turkoman *gul* evolved from variations of this round medallion-like form, as on the early east Anatolian rug illustrated by Balpinar and Hirsch (op.cit.,no.62) drawn in fig.66. Remembering the Tekke *gul* in fig.43, the resemblance is clear. It is supposed that from such early motifs, there developed the four principal *gul* forms:

1. 'Lobed *guls*', like those of the Tekke and Salor (see figs.40 and 45).
2. 'Archetypal' *guls,* such as that of the Saryk (fig.39).
3. Octagonal *guls*, like the *gulli-gul* (fig.44).
4. Rhomboidal *guls,* such as those in figs.76 and 77, which have affinities to 'lobed' *guls* (as does the internal ornamentation of the *gulli-gul*) and

can be traced to the main carpets of the Saryk and Ersari. Because of many of its features, it appears to be a link between the 'lobed' *gul* of the Salor (fig.45), the 'archetypal' *gul* of the Saryk (fig.39) and the octagonal *gulli-gul* (fig.44).

The 'dragon and phoenix' is considered one of the principal motifs on carpets to have East Asian origins. A typical Chinese version (fig.78) and an Anatolian version such as that on a rug in the Vakiflar Museum (fig.79; Balpinar and Hirsch, op.cit., Pl. 7) make good starting points for tracing the motif's influence. When considered as a section of a larger repeat design, as in fig.80, the motif is seen to form a larger octagon; it also begins to resemble the interior quartering of a *gul* (fig.81) attributed by Moshkova to the Uzbeks (Moshkova, op.cit., Pl.10/5). Comparisons with the *tauk nuska gul* (fig.47) are also relevant, as is the possibility of a connection with the 'animal tree' motif found just above the *elems* of a rare and keenly collected group of Tekke *ensis* (nos. 57-58). Robert Pinner has discussed this motif at length in his essay 'The Animal Tree and the Great Bird in Myth and Folklore' (*Turkoman Studies*, op.cit., pp.204 ff.), tracing it back to at least the 4th millennium B.C. in various cultures. For the purposes of further comparison, we also show the 'dragon and phoenix' motif from the famous 15th century rug in the Islamic Museum, Berlin, which, significantly, was known to an earlier generation of scholars as the 'Ming' rug (fig.82). More or less stylised 'dragons' appear on a number of later carpets, including, of course, the 17th century Caucasian 'dragon' rugs (fig.83) and on a type of Caucasian flatweave called *verneh* (erroneously called *sileh* in Western literature), although on only one extant example does the motif bear much resemblance to a stylised 'dragon' (fig.84, the McMullan example now in the Metropolitan Museum, New York). At least one other exists which suggests that the majority of so-called 'dragon *silehs*' are, in fact, stylised representations of a camel train and almost all surviving examples can be dated no earlier than the 19th century. Another East Asian connection is provided by the design of a Chinese painted scroll (fig.96), which is discussed in greater detail below.

One should exercise caution, however, in making what would appear to be obvious design comparisons and drawing conclusions as to the evolution of design history from them. A recent example is Volkmar Gantzhorn's *The Christian Carpet* (German, French and English eds., Cologne, 1990), a full-blown version of the author's doctoral thesis at Tübingen University in 1987. In this, the author seeks, without much evidence or success, to prove that the art of pile carpet-making had a Christian, specifically Armenian, origin, with the iconography traceable back to Hittite art of 2nd millennium B.C. Anatolia, Phrygian and early Attic art of the early 1st millennium B.C. and so on. Any stylistic comparisons that can be made between Christian Armenian art (fig.86) and the designs of eastern weavings, indeed anything vaguely cruciform on the latter such as the *kejebe* pattern (fig.85), the minor motif on Yomut *chuvals* (fig.87) and so on are all used to prop up this thesis. The earliest known pile-knotted textiles date from 15th century B.C. Egypt

44

Fig. 64

Fig. 65

Fig. 66

and are made of flax; the earliest wool pile carpet, the Pazyryk (detail fig.89) was found in the 5th century B.C. tomb of a Scythian prince in the Altai Mountains of Siberia; most authorities, including Hubel, Schürmann and most recently the archaeologist David Stronach, have considered it a work of the Persian Armenian Empire, although exactly where in this large region is a matter of debate.

This is not to say that Armenians have not always played an important role in the production of carpets; we know that they have in modern times and they might well have in ancient ones. But playing a role is one thing – writing the play quite another.

The Turkoman Way of Life
There are fewer problems when considering the influences of the Turkoman lifestyle on their weaving patterns. This includes nomadism and semi-nomadism, settled dwelling, customs and beliefs, some of the latter obviously having an ancient myth and cult character. Identifying such traces among representational images, such as the depictions of *yurts*, animal trains and wedding caravans, hunting scenes and so on, is easy. We can see them on tentbands (no.137), *asmalyks* (nos.192-4) and from *ensis* by the Salor, Arabachi and Chodor (no.222). Human figures are often clearly recognisable, although they are also encountered as highly stylised anthropomorphic forms, as at the top and bottom of the Saryk *chuval* illustrated in no.24 (see also the top of the *chuval* in no.25). Even simple rhomboidal motifs are sometimes considered to have an anthropomorphic origin.

The Turkoman Wedding
The Turkoman wedding ceremony had considerable influence on its cultural artefacts. A white ground seems to have been reserved specifically for objects woven for wedding ceremonies. Particular designs or motifs are often considered to pertain specifically to weddings; the *kejebe* motif, for example (fig.91), is said by many authors to represent a bride's litter on the wedding camel.

Felt
Further points to consider when discussing the origins of Turkoman pile-knotted carpet designs may lie in other areas of Central Asian arts and crafts which have left their mark on weaving patterns. Stylistic evidence may be found, for example, in one traditional nomadic craft, felting, from which it is often presumed that many carpet designs derived. Felt represents an important aspect of Central Asian culture and was often decorated in appliqué, so that both positive and negative patterns appeared. This reciprocal effect is one of the key elements of Turkoman design (as it is of early Anatolian weavings, both piled and flat-woven) and might well have its origins in felt work (see figs.1, 57-8 and 92).

Kilim Designs

The same applies to patterns which have obviously been transposed from the slit-tapestry (kilim) technique to pile-knotting. Kilim patterns are characterised by stepped outlines since rounded colour divisions are extremely difficult to accomplish in this technique. Accordingly, some patterns associated primarily with kilims keep their characteristics even when transferred to a medium such as pile knotting where they are no longer necessary (compare figs.93-4 with nos.55-6, 73).

Ikat and Suzani Patterns

Different types of textiles such as *suzanis* (Farsi for needle) and *ikats* (tie-dyed silks and velvets) seem to belong principally to urban cultures, although some rug patterns owe their origins to textiles in these techniques. Even if nomads led a virtually independent and isolated existence, there must still have been some cultural contact with towns and cities; indeed, pile weavings of a semi-nomadic origin are known with designs derived from *suzanis* and *ikats*; see no.255 for an *ikat*-design piled saddle-cover. *Ikat* patterns, because of the technique used for the original models, have solid areas of colour flowing into each other (see no.244). Silk embroidered Tekke *asmalyks*, similar in technique to *suzanis*, are known (see the pair illustrated in no.97) and the style of drawing of the floral meanders on the Ersari Beshir prayer rug illustrated in no.298 may also owe something to *suzani* design.

Turkoman Jewellery and Other Influences

Similar parallels can be drawn between the weavings of the Turkomans and the design and iconography of their silver jewellery (see the Yomut *asmalyks* nos.193-4), although the jewellery itself may have been made in urban workshops. Fig.95 shows a so-called *tumar*, consisting of a cylindrical amulet contained within a triangular head-piece.

The decorative elements of mosque and other early Muslim architecture – especially the richly detailed panels of ceramic tiles – have also been a fruitful source of inspiration for rug designers..

Archetypes

Another area which has given rise to much debate in the last few years is the connection, if any, between certain Turkoman weaving motifs and designs and those ornaments and apparent iconographic motifs which are known from ancient history and prehistoric times. The word 'archetype' seems appropriate in this context, primarily because of the similarities which exist between certain prevalent motifs in many different cultures. One of the best known of these is the hooked cross or swastika, usually identified as a sun symbol, which is found on many different types of artefact from many different periods of ancient and modern art in Central Asia and elsewhere (including China and the pre-Columbian Americas). The motif itself is sometimes connected with others, giving a zoomorphic effect not unlike a backbone; perhaps it is not unconnected to the 'animal tree' motif discussed above.

Other important archetypes are the 'hooked diamond' (see A.K. Ambroz, 'A Cult Symbol of Early Peasants', in *Turkoman Research*, op.cit., vol.7) and what H. Wifling describes as the 'hooked cross-arm motif' (see H. Wifling, *Teppich-Motive der Türkvölker*, Vienna, 1985). The hooked rhombus or diamond, which can be described as a cross within a diamond, has always been interpreted as a fertility symbol and appears in endless varieties, although it probably has a consistent 'mother earth' connotation. A highly emblematic variant can be seen on the Uzbek felt in fig.92 and appears in similar form on the Chinese scroll painting of the Lady Wen-Chi of around 440 A.D. (fig.96). A series of linked hooked diamonds are sometimes used to create a highly stylised 'tree of life'.

Wifling's discussion of the 'hooked cross-arm' motif is an interesting attempt to demonstrate that it is an archetypal form from which much of the Turkoman design vocabulary was derived. His starting point is the argument that the almost infinite varieties, both complex and simple, negative and positive, to which the form lends itself make it the basic building block of many other motifs; he believes that even such complex motifs as the *dyrnak gul* (fig.41) have this origin.

Such attempts to explain the history of motifs are significant pointers to the wealth and richness of Turkic design. It is a vocabulary of design which creates its own microcosm and obeys its own laws of logic. As the individual, and subjective, weaver handles these basic building blocks of design, she is subject to these laws and, with certain exceptions, must stay within their bounds; thus the microcosm of design can become an iconographic or allegorical representation of the real cosmos. In the context of design history, there are certain patterns in which one can identify clusters of motifs by their outlines and other shared features; in such patterns, the individual characteristics of motifs are blended into a whole, the parts of which, whether positive or negative, simple or complex, can nevertheless still be recognised (see no.32).

However, this very subjective and hypothetical approach to design analysis should not distract us from the well-documented research into prehistoric motifs. Many recent writers on Anatolian and Turkoman weaving (see, for example, Jack Cassin and Peter Hoffmeister, *Tent Band — Tent Bag*, 1988) have presented comparisons with ancient designs from the Bronze Age and earlier which could be useful to future researchers into the history of weaving and carpet designs. Archaeological research into the ancient cultures of southwest Turkestan has provided its own interesting comparative material; compare, for instance, the design on a Central Asian pottery vessel of about 3000 B.C. (fig. 97) to that on the Yomut weaving illustrated in fig.98 and in no.182.

Collecting

Collecting works of art, for whatever reason, has a very long history and is probably as old as handmade carpets themselves. Such early collections may have consisted of unusual, decorative and precious objects intended to show the owner's status in society; the buyers or acquirers of such objects had no particular aim other than this. Even the kings and princes of the European Renaissance who acquired large numbers of Oriental carpets at a time when purchasing and commissioning works of art had become fashionable, were not attempting to create what would now be called a 'structured' collection. But it is certainly evidence that the Oriental carpet was a greatly desired and highly valued commodity at that time.

By the Age of Enlightenment, people had already begun to discuss the meaning and purpose of collecting; it was considered a suitable subject for intellectual argument of a high order, as was shown by Goethe and others. As a result, a very idealistic concept of collecting developed, in which ownership and the competition of the marketplace were considered of minor significance; the acquisition of knowledge and the preservation of art for future generations became central issues. Within such an intellectual framework, it was possible for a collector to range widely over the whole field of art.

Many of the greatest collections of tribal weavings, now mostly in museums, were formed at a time when such activities were considered exotic or merely eccentric. Even by the 1930s, the number of collectors was small, so that those active at that time, such as the American, Joseph McMullan, could afford to take their pick, using, as their principal criteria, beauty and age.

We do not have the same licence today and anyone who does not enjoy almost limitless financial resources must think carefully about what the collection is trying to achieve; it will only approach 'completeness' when the chosen area or areas of specialisation have been fully covered. With this in mind, it would be impossible today to make Turkoman weaving in its entirety a viable possibility.

It can, of course, be immensely pleasurable to acquire individual Turkoman weavings simply for their beauty and quality. Such a type of collecting has its own merits but has a different purpose and value to intense specialist collecting.

It is important for the first-time buyer to seek advice from experts and experienced collectors, although he or she should not be too discouraged by the inevitable, and sometimes costly, mistakes which all collectors make at the beginning of their careers. After buying power, knowledge is the collector's greatest asset and there is an enormous number of publications on Turkoman weavings available today which should give anyone at least a theoretical knowledge of the subject. However, there is no substitute for 'hands-on' experience and until that is gained, it is advisable to consult knowledgeable friends, dealers and auction-house experts.

Making contact with like-minded collectors is made easier by the large number of carpet societies which have sprung up in many major cities throughout the world in recent years; these are usually open to anyone with sufficient enthusiasm. Regular meetings and, in some cases, excellent programmes of lectures and discussions about interesting and unusual rugs, plus the added bonuses of being able to meet and talk to well-known scholars in various fields and to visit great museum collections with expert guides together constitute an entertaining way of getting to know one's subject.

Many collections all over the world, both private and public, offer programmes of study aided by catalogues and other published material. The literature of Turkoman weaving is both given in the bibliography to this book as well as being cited in the captions to the plates. One should also keep an eye on such specialist publications as the carpet and textile magazine *Hali*, which appears six times a year in London and is available on subscription only, as well as on general arts and antiques magazines which frequently carry articles on weaving.

Various auction houses publish regular catalogues either devoted entirely to carpets and textiles or containing a significant number of them within the framework of more general groupings of works of art. Again, it is advisable to discuss potential purchases with experienced collectors or with the relevant expert at the auction house itself, although in the latter case one should satisfy oneself as to which firms are reliable and have good reputations in the carpet and textile fields. In some instances, the quality of cataloguing is extremely high, making the catalogues themselves important works of reference; in some cases, the publication of pre-sale estimates followed by lists of actual prices received can both show one the reliability of the auction house and give one a good idea about values and trends.

Fig. 67

Fig. 68

Fig. 71

Fig. 72

Fig. 73

Fig. 69   Fig. 70

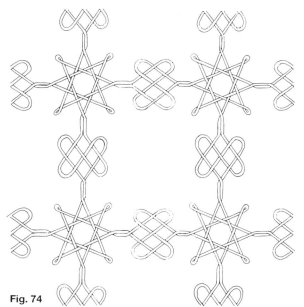

Fig. 74

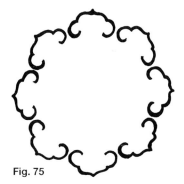

Fig. 75

Fig. 76

Fig. 77

Carpet Prices and Trends

The word 'value', when used in the context of works of art, can have many layers of meaning and is a complex term which needs clarification. Basically, the value of a work of art — and this may be especially true of carpets — is only concrete when it makes a price, i.e. when it is sold. Even then, the sum paid for it is dependent on many conditions.

Thus the value of a work of art is only 'measurable' in terms of hard currency to a limited extent and this value must be interpreted according to various circumstances: why and where is it being sold? Is the valuation placed upon it considered to be an average value or is it for insurance purposes? Is the value 'fictional' or notional, as in the case of museum pieces being valued for exhibitions? To what extent is the value based upon extraneous matters such as, for example, anthropological importance or the object's rarity value for certain collectors? All these things have to be taken into consideration when faced with the problem of deciding what an object is worth.

When watching out for market developments and price trends, the sums given at auction may be especially helpful. Naturally these are not 'absolute', as they can be influenced by the history of the piece in question, whether or not it is well-known, how many prospective buyers there are when it comes on to the market and so on. There are also many types of carpet, as of other works of art, which rarely appear at auction but which regularly change hands privately for unpublished and unknown prices.

Apart from those market-dependent factors which affect the values of so-called 'collectors' carpets, each individual piece has its own characteristics which also have an important bearing on its monetary value. These include age, rarity, condition, aesthetic merit, the materials used and size. If a piece has a well-known and distinguished provenance and/or if it has been published, these factors can also make it worth considerably more than if it appears out of nowhere and is previously unknown to writers and scholars. Very similar pieces published in the literature can also affect the value of an unknown example but it is also true that previously unpublished pieces can be valued very highly because of their rarity and because of their 'freshness' on the market.

When all these things are considered, it can only be concluded that every weaving is unique unto itself with its own set of inbuilt characteristics influencing its value. Thus it would be unwise to give prices in a book such as this in the same way as one would, for example, see the prices for objects of whatever kind in a mail-order catalogue; such sums would only be misleading for the most part and would, of course, very rapidly become outdated.

Today, hardly any great Turkoman weavings can be expected to emerge from their place of origin, although we cannot at this moment evaluate what effect the 'opening up' of the former Soviet republics in the south may have on supply. Certainly many previously unknown types of Caucasian weavings have appeared on the market in the last few years, as a direct

Fig. 78

Fig. 79

Fig. 80

Fig. 81

Fig. 82

Fig. 83

Fig. 84

Fig. 85

result of new political freedom, but there has, as yet, been no obvious effect on the Turkoman market nor on the supply of rare pieces. It is also true that twenty years of concentrated collecting in the West has greatly altered our opinion of the relative merits of many Turkoman weavings and what were often thought to be important objects before this period are now no longer taken very seriously by experienced collectors, and some things which were formerly thought to be very rare are now known not to be so. There has been a much needed 'sorting out' period, with some groups of weavings sinking on the general price scale and others rising enormously. The coming of stability to the market in old and antique collectors' carpets is the basis for suggesting that in the future, Turkoman weavings of a generally accepted importance and quality will prove to be really worthwhile investments.

Selected Structure Analyses

For abbreviations, see pp.23-25, **The Structure of Turkoman Carpets.**

No. 1

(Analysis by the owner). Warp: Z2S, animal hair, natural fawn to light grey-brown. Weft: W, medium to dark brown, second shoot wavy. Pile: W/S, As3, about 3,500 knots per dm². Sides: 2 pairs of warps bound with brick red wool. Colours include cochineal red and steel blue silk.

No. 5

(Analysis by the owner). Warp: W, Z2S, natural fawn. Weft: W, dark to medium brown. Pile: W/S, As3, about 4,800 knots per dm². Sides: simple, W, red-brown. Upper end: dark blue added fringe. Lower end: natural ivory kilim turned under. Colours include W, red, orange, blue; S, cochineal red.

No. 8

(Analysis after Tzareva). Warp: W, S2Z, ivory. Weft: 2 shoots W, S2Z, brown. Pile: W/S, As3, 3,675 per dm². Upper end: red and white striped kilim turned under, red wool plaited cord sewn on. Lower end: red kilim (incomplete). Colours: 12.

No. 34

Warp: W/G, S2Z. Weft: W, dark brown. Pile: W/C/S, Sy2, about 2,000 per dm². Sides: 2 x 6 warp bundles wrapped in G. Upper end: Dark blue kilim turned under and stitched in red. Lower end: kilim with weft-faced patterned strip. Colours: 8.

No 45

Warp: W, S2Z, ivory. Weft: 2 shoots, W, S2Z ivory/fawn. Pile: W, As2, about 2,400 knots per dm². Sides: W, plain, blue. Upper and Lower ends: not original. Colours: 7.

No 54

Warp: W, Z2S, ivory. Weft: 1 shoot, W, ivory or brown. Pile: W, As4, about 4,800 knots per dm². Sides: Not original. Upper and lower ends: narrow ivory kilim striped. Colours: 5.

No. 64

Warp: G, Z2S, ivory. Weft: 2 shoots, W, grey-brown. Pile: W/S, As4, about 4,500 knots per dm², ht. 3mm. Sides (selvedges) and ends: not original. Colours: 8.

No. 82

Warp: W, Z2S, ivory. Weft: 2 shoots, W, red-brown. Pile: W, As2, about 6,500 knots per dm², 4 rows of Sy edging knots each side, ht. 3-4mm. Sides: plain red. Upper end: kilim, sewn under. Colours: 7. Handle: soft, silky.

No. 85
(Analysis by the owner). Warp: W, Z2S, natural. Weft: 2 shoots, W, Z2S, natural. Pile: W/S, As, about 5,000 knots per dm².

No. 88
Warp: W, Z2S. Weft: 1 shoot, W, Z2S, dark brown. Pile: W, As2, about 5,200 knots per dm². Sides and ends: not original. Colours: 6. Handle: soft, floppy.

No. 89
Warp: W, Z2S, ivory. Weft: 2 shoots, W, Z2S, dark brown. Pile: W, about 2,400 knots per dm². Sides: W, plain, dark brown. Colours: 6.

No. 90
Warp: W, S2Z, ivory. Weft: 2 shoots, W, dark brown. Pile: W/C/S, As2, about 6,200 knots per dm². Sides: not original. Upper end: red kilim, sewn under. Colours: 9. Handle: soft, fine ribbing on back.

No. 93
Warp: W, Z2S, ivory to light brown. Weft: 2 shoots, W, light brown. Pile: W, As2, about 6,000 knots per dm². Sides: W, plain, blue. Upper end: striped red kilim, sewn under, edge stitching in blue partly preserved. Colours: 8. Handle: Velvety, fine ribbing on back.

No 95
(Analysis after Tzareva). Warp: W, S2Z, ivory. Weft: 2 shoots, camel. Pile: W, As2, 2,236 knots per dm², ht. 3mm. Sides: W, plain, red. Upper end: strip red kilim, sewn undcr. On three sides an added patterned wool band. Colours: 6.

No. 99
Warp: G, S2Z, grey-brown/ivory. Weft: 2 shoots, W, brown. Pile: W, As2, about 2,400 knots per dm². Sides: W, 2 bundles of 4 warps bound in red and green in chequerboard pattern. Upper end: cordlike kilim strip in red and white, two-coloured decorative additions. Lower end: stitched. Colours: 7.

No. 100
Warp: W, Z2S, ivory/grey-brown. Weft: 2 shoots, W, brown. Pile: W, Sy1, about 1,400 knots per dm². Sides: W, cord of 5 warps bound in red and green. Upper end: kilim strip, white, remains of cordlike two-coloured decorative additions. Colour: 7.

No. 108
Warp: W, S2Z, fawn-grey. Weft: 2 shoots, W, brown. Pile: W, about 1,800 knots per dm². Sides: not original. Ends: mostly not original. Colours: 7.

No. 113
(Analysis by the owner). Warp: W, natural grey. Weft: W/C, brown. Pile: W, As, open left, about 2,500 per dm². Sides: W, blue and red, double, alternately off-set, outer edge, W, brown-black, partly original.

No. 118
(Analysis after the catalogue of the Danker Collection). Warp: W, Z2S. Weft: 2 shoots, W, brown. Pile: W, Sy3, about 2,500 knots per dm². Sides: W, 2 x 4 warps bound in red and blue chequerboard pattern. Upper end: kilim strip, white. Colour: 7.

No. 126
(Analysis after Troost). Warp: W/G, S2Z, ivory. Weft: W, ivory. Pile: W, As2, about 2,000 per dm², ht. 2-3 mm. Colours: 8

No. 127
Warp: W, S2Z, ivory. Weft: 2 shoots, W, ivory. Pile: W, Sy2, about 4,300 knots per dm². Sides: W, plain, red, white, blue. Ends: kilim strip, ivory. Handle: velvety.

No. 153
(Analysis after Troost). Warp: W/G, S2Z, natural colours. Weft: W, brown. Pile: W, Sy1, about 2,600 knots per dm². Sides: W, plain, red-brown. Upper end: kilim strip sewn under. Colours: 9.

No. 181
Warp: W, S2Z, ivory. Weft: W, dark brown. Pile: W, As2, about 2,500 knots per dm², rows of Sy edging knots at sides. Sides: W, blue, red-brown. Colours: 8.

No. 182
Warp: W/G, S2Z, ivory/light brown., Weft: 2 shoots, W, dark brown. Pile: W, As2, about 2,100 knots per dm². Opening side: kilim, undyed, turned under, red and blue stitches. Upper end: 4 pairs of warps, bound in red and blue, hanging two-coloured wool plaits, six-coloured wool tassels. Colours: 6

No. 196
Warp: G, S2Z, grey-brown. Weft: 2 shoots, W, grey-brown. Pile: W, Sy1, about 2,800 knots per dm². Upper end: red kilim strip, sewn under.

No. 201
(Analysis by the owner). Warp: S2Z, undyed. Weft: 2 shoots, W. Pile: W, Sy, about 2,400 knots per dm². Upper end: kilim strip, brown.

No. 203
Warp: W, medium grey. Weft: 2 shoots, W/C, ivory, dark brown. Pile: W, As3, about 1,400 knots per dm². Sides: W, several colours, chequerboard pattern. Ends: narrow kilim strips. Colours: 8. Handle: ribbed, firm.

No. 222
Warp: G, S2Zm grey-brown. Weft: W/C, fawn. Pile: W, As2, about 1,800 knots per dm². Sides: 2 warps bound in two-coloured wool in chequerboard pattern.

No. 246
Warp: W, S2Z, ivory. Weft: 2 shoots, W, pale red. Pile: W, As2, about 1,500 knots per dm², Sy edging knots. Sides and ends: not original. Colours: 7.

No. 261
Warp: W/G, undyed. Weft: 2 shoots, W, light brown. Pile: W, As2, about 1,500 knots per dm², ht. 4-5mm. Upper end: W, kilim, turned under. Colours: 7.

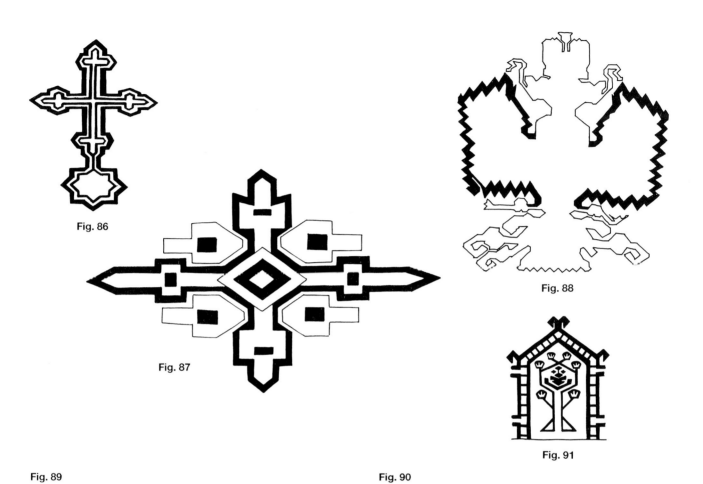

Fig. 86

Fig. 87

Fig. 88

Fig. 91

Fig. 89

Fig. 90

59

Fig. 92

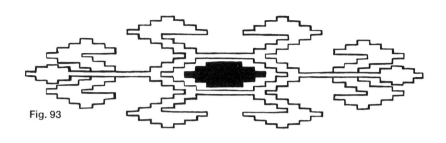

Fig. 93

Fig. 94

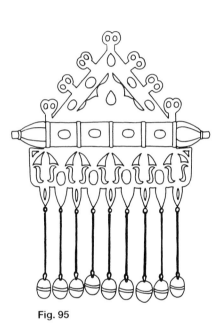

Fig. 95

Fig. 96

Fig. 97

Fig. 98

Fig. 99

BIBLIOGRAPHY

Alte Teppiche aus dem Orient, exhibition catalogue, Gewerbemuseum Basel, 1980

Andrews, P. and M., *The Turkoman of Iran*, exhibition catalogue, Abbot Hall Art Gallery, Kendal, 1971

Antique Oriental Carpets from Austrian Collections, Gesellschaft zur Förderung der Textil-Kunst-Forschung, Vienna, 1986

Aschenbrenner, E., *Battenberg Antiquitäten-Kataloge-Orientteppiche – Bd.2: Persische Teppiche*, Battenberg Verlag, Munich, 1981

Azadi, S.U., *Asmalyk - Eine entdeckte Gattung*, in Pinner/Franses, chapter 16, p.172, Oguz Press, London, 1980; *Turkoman Carpets and the Ethnographic Significance of their Elements*, Crosby Press, Fishguard, 1975; *The Goklen Turkmen and their Carpets* in: Pinner and Denny (eds.) *Oriental Carpet and Textile Studies*, Vol.3 part 2, London 1990.

Azadi, S.U., A.&V. Rautenstengel, and H.C. Sienknecht, *Wie Blumen in der Wüste. Die Kultur der turkmenischen Nomadenstämme Zentralasiens.* Paul Hartung, Hamburg, 1993

Balpinar, B./Hirsch U., *Flatweaves in the Vakiflar Museum, Istanbul,* Verlag Uta Hülsey, Wesel 1982

Ibid., *Carpets in the Vakiflar Museum, Istanbul,* Verlag Uta Hülsey, Wesel 1988

Bausback Ltd., exhibition catalogues 1969-1988

Ibid., *Antike Orientteppiche*, Klinkhardt & Biermann, Brunswick 1978

Bernadout, R., *Turkoman Weavings*, Bernadout, London 1974

Bennett, I. (ed.), *The Country Life Book of Rugs and Carpets of the World*, Hamlyn, London, 1973. Reissued as *Rugs and Carpets of the World* by Quarto of London in 1977, and by New Burlington, also of London, in 1985

Beresneva, L., *The Decorative and Applied Art of Turkmenia*, Aurora Art Publishers, Leningrad 1976

Bernheimer, *Alte und antike Knüpfarbeiten der Turkmenen*, Munich 1977

Bernheimer Fine Arts Ltd., *Oriental Carpets and Textiles*, exhibition catalogue, London 1987

Bogolyúbov, A.A., *Carpets of Central Asia*, The Crosby Press, Hampshire 1973

Brüggemann, W./Böhmer, H., *Rugs of the Peasants and Nomads of Anatolia* (English edition), Verlag Kunst und Antiquitäten, Munich, 1982

Camman, Schuyler, V.R., *Ancient Symbols in Modern Afghanistan*, Michigan, 1957

Ibid., *Symbolic Meanings in Oriental Rug Patterns, The Textile Museum Journal III, 3.*, Washington D.C. 1972

Cassin/Hoffmeister, *Tent Band - Tent Bag - Classic Turkmen Weaving*, Magna Mater Verlag, Coburg/Esbach, 1988

Christie's East, New York, auction catalogues until April 1989

Clark, Major Hartley, *Bokhara, Turkoman and Afghan Rugs*, Bodley Head, London, 1922

Danker Collection, *Meisterstücke orientalischer Knüpfkunst*, exhibition catalogue, Städtisches Museum, Nassauischer Kunstverein e.V., Wiesbaden 1966

Day, Susan, *Un Singulier tapis Turkmène dans les collections du Musée des Arts Décoratifs* in: La Revue du Louvre, Paris 1981

Der Manuelian, L. Eiland, M.L., *Weavers, Merchants and Kings - The Inscribed Rugs of Armenia*, exhibition catalogue Kimbell Art Museum, Fort Worth, 1984

Dovodov N./Chodzamuchammedov, *Teppiche und Teppichprodukte Turkmenistans* (from the collection of the Turkoman State Museum of the Visual Arts and the Turkoman Rug Society), Reinhold Schletzer Verlag, Hamburg, 1987

Dupaigne, B., *Le grand art décoratif des Turkménes* in: Objets et Mondes, Paris 1978

Eder, D., *Battenberg, Antiquitäten Kataloge - Orientteppiche - Bd. 1: Kaukasische Teppiche*, Battenberg Verlag, Munich, 1979

Eiland, E./Shockley, M., *Tent Bands of the Steppes*, exhibition catalogue, Berkeley/California, 1976

Eiland, Dr. Murray Lee, *Oriental Rugs from Western Collections, featuring a comprehensive display of Turkoman Rugs*, Univ. of California Art Museum, Berkeley (CA/USA), 1973; *The Origins of Turkoman Guls* in: Oriental Rug Review, Meredith (NH/USA), II/4, July 1982; *Moshkova and the Turkoman Rug* in: Oriental Rug Review, Meredith (NH, USA), II/9, December 1982

Elmby, H., *Antikke Turkmenske Tæpper/Antique Turkmen Carpets,* Elmby, Copenhagen, 1990; *Antikke Turkmenske Tæpper II/Antique Turkmen Carpets II,* Elmby, Copenhagen, 1994

Enay, M./Azadi S., *Einhundert Jahre Orientteppich-Literatur -1877 bis 1977,* Verlag Kunst und Antiquitäten, Hanover 1977

Erdmann, K., *Oriental Carpets, an Account of their History,* Zwemmer, London, 1955

Ibid., *Europa und der Orientteppich,* Verlag Kupferberg, Mainz, 1962

Ibid., *Seven Hundred Years of Oriental Carpets,* Faber & Faber, London, 1970

Ettinghausen, R., *Prayer Rugs,* exhibition catalogue, Textile Museum, Washington D.C., 1974

Firouz, I.A., *Silver Ornaments of the Turkoman,* Hamdani Foundation, Tehran, 1978

Francke, W., *Hauptteppiche der Gruppe der Jomudturkmenen, Weltkunst,* issue 8, p. 872ff., Munich, 15th April 1978

Franses, J., *Tribal Rugs from Afghanistan and Turkestan,* London, 1973

Gans-Reudin, E., *Modern Oriental Carpets,* Thames & Hudson, London, 1971.

Ibid., *Iranian Carpets, Art and History,* Thames & Hudson, London, 1978

Ganzhorn, V., *Der christlich orientalische Teppich, dissertation,* Tübingen, 1987

Ibid., *The Christian Oriental Carpet,* Cologne, 1991

'GHEREH', Turin, from 1993, bi-monthly

Grote-Hasenbalg, W., *Masterpieces of Oriental Rugs,* Batsford, London, 1925

Ibid., *Der Orientteppich - Seine Geschichte und seine Kultur,* vols. I-III, Scarabäus-Verlag, Berlin, 1922

Gombos, K., *Old Turkmenian Rugs,* exhibition catalogue, Museum of Applied Art, Budapest, 1975

Ibid., *Alte zentral asiatische Teppiche,* Kataloge der Museen des Komitats 63, Nadasdy Ferenc Museum, Sarvar, 1979

HALI, The International Magazine of Antique Carpet and Textile Art, London (quarterly since 1978; six times annually since 1989)

Hadji Baba Exhibitions, *Weavings of the Tribes of Afghanistan,* Washington, 1972

Ibid., *Tribal Rugs from Turkmenistan,* Washington, 1973

Herrmann, E., Exhibition catalogues, Munich, 1978 onwards

Hodjamukhamedov, N and N. Dovadov, *Carpets and Carpet Products from Turkmenistan,* Turkmenistan, Ashkabad, 1983

Hoffmeister, P., *Turkoman Carpets in Franconia,* The Crosby Press, Edinburgh, 1980

Housego, J., *Tribal Rugs,* Scorpion Publications Ltd., London, 1978

Hubel, R.G., *The Book of Carpets,* Barrie & Jenkins, London, 1970

Iten-Maritz, J., *Enzyklopädie des Orientteppichs,* 3rd edition, Bussesche Verlagshandlung, Herford, 1984

Kalter, J., *The Arts and Crafts of Turkmestan,* Thames & Hudson, London, 1984

Kendrick A. F./Tattersall, *Handwoven Carpets, Oriental & European,* Benn, London, 1922

King, D, R. Pinner and M. Franses, *Turkoman Rugs in the Victoria and Albert Museum,* Hali, London, 1980

König, H., *Ersari Rugs in Mackie/Thompson,* p. 190, Washington D.C., 1980

Ibid., *Ersari Rugs - Names and Attributions,* in *Hali* 4/2, p. 135, London, 1981

Lefevre & Partners, *Central Asian Carpets,* exhibition catalogue, London, 1976

Lindahl, D./Knorr, T., *Uzbek,* exhibition catalogue, Basel, 1975

Loges, W., *Turkoman Tribal Rugs,* Munich, 1978

Ibid., *Tent Doors of the Chodor,* in *Hali* 26, p. 30ff., London, 1985

Lorentz H.J., *Chinesische Teppiche,* Callwey Verlag, Munich, 1975

Mackie, L.W./Thompson, J., *Turkmen - Tribal Carpets and Traditions,* Textile Museum, Washington D.C., 1980

Mangisch, auction house, Zurich, catalogues since Nov. 1987

Martin, H.E.R., *Orientteppiche,* W. Heyne-Verlag, Munich 1983

Ibid. *Orientteppiche - Erkennen - Kaufen - Erhalten,* Gondrom-Verlag, Bayreuth 1984

McCoy Jones, H./Boucher, J.W., *The Ersari and their Weavings,* exhibition catalogue, International Hadji Baba Society, Washington D.C., 1975

Ibid. *Rugs of the Yomud Tribes,* exhibition catalogue, International Hadji Baba Society, Washington D.C., 1976

McMullan J.V., Collection, *Islamic Carpets,* Arts Council of Great Britain, London, 1972

Milhofer, S.A., *Die Teppiche Zentralasiens,* Fackelträger Verlag, Hanover, 1968

Moschkova, *Die Teppiche der Völker Mittelasiens,* FAN Publications, Tashkent, 1970

Moshkova, V.G., *Carpets of the Peoples of Central Asia,* Meredith, (NH, USA.); *Gols auf turkmenischen Teppichen*, Archiv für Völkerkunde, Vienna, 1948

Nagel, Auktionshaus Dr. Fritz Nagel, art and collector carpet auction catalogues and specialist carpet catalogues (until incl. 327th auction, 1989)

Neff, I./Maggs, C., *Dictionary of Oriental Rugs,* Ad. Donker Ltd., London 1977

O'Bannon, G.W., *The Turkoman Carpet,* Duckworth, London, 1974

O'Bannon, G.W., et al. *Vanishing Jewels: Central Asian Tribal Weavings,* Rochester Museum and Science Center, Rochester (NY, USA), 1990

ORIENTAL RUG REVIEW, Meredith (NH,USA), From 1981, monthly at first, then bi-monthly

Ostler, H./Geisselmann, Ä., *Die Teppichkunst des Orients und die Kunst der Moderne,* Galerie Ostler, Munich, 1980

Pakzad, M., *Persische Knüpfkunst,* Kleeblatt-Verlag, Fr. Grimsehl, Hanover, 1978

Pietsch, G.U., *Vom Zauber alter Teppiche,* Bibliothek Rombach, Freiburg im Breisgau, 1981

Pinner R./Franses, M. (Publishers), *Turkoman Studies I,* Oguz Press, London, 1980

Pinner, R., *The Beshir Carpets of the Buchara Emirate, Hali 3/4,* p. 294ff., London, 1981; *The Rickmers Collection: Turkoman Rugs in the Ethnographic Museum, Berlin,* Museum für Völkerkunde, Berlin, 1993

Ibid., *Work in Progress,* in *Hali 42,* p. 15ff., London, 1988

Pinner, R./Denny, W. (editors), *Oriental Carpet and Textile Studies,* vols. I and II, *Hali* OCTS, London 1985

Rautenstengel, A. & V., and S.U. Azadi, *Studien zur Teppich-Kultur der Turkmen,* Rautenstengel, Hilden, 1990

Reed, C.D., *Turkoman Rugs,* Fogg Art Museum, Cambridge/Mass. 1966

Rheinisch, *Saddle Bags,* Verlag für Sammler, Graz 1985

Rippon Boswell, carpet auction catalogue nos. 10-29, Frankfurt/Wiesbaden, 1980 to 1989

Rosetti, B., *Die Turkmenen und ihre Teppiche. Eine ethnologische Studie,* Reimer Verlag, Berlin, 1992

Rostkowski, J. and M. Ciprut, *Les Turkmen 'Hommes du vent' OU l'Iran des Steppes,* Maisonneuve, Paris, 1979

Rudenko, S.I., *The World's Most Ancient Carpets and Fabrics from the Ice Covered Kurgan Mountains of the Altai*, Moscow, 1968

Schurmann, U., *Caucasian Rugs,* Cologne, 1964

Ibid., *Central Asian Rugs* (English edition), *Osterrieth,* Frankfurt, 1969

Smith Collection, exhibition catalogue *The Smith Collection,* Smith Art Museum, Springfield, 1970

Sotheby's, carpet auction catalogues, New York

Spuhler, F., *Oriental Carpets in the Museum of Islamic Art, Berlin,* Faber & Faber, London, 1987

Straka Collection, *The Oriental Rug Collection of Jerome and Mary Jane Straka,* published by J.A. Straka and L.W. Mackie, Textile Museum, Washington, 1978

Thatcher, A.B., *Turcoman Rugs,* The Holland Press, London, 1977

Thompson, J., *Carpets from the Tents, Cottages and Workshops of Asia* (new edition of *Carpet Magic* 1983), Barrie & Jenkins, London, 1988

Thompson, Dr. J., *Turkmen and Antique Carpets from the Collection of Dr. & Mrs. Jon Thompson,* Sotheby's, New York, 1993 (Note: Sotheby's wisely allowed this renowned Turkoman expert to write his own catalogue)

Troost, *Die Yomut,* exhibition catalogue Galerie Schreiber, Düsseldorf, 1984

Turkmenenforschung, vols. 1 to 13, Reinhold Schletzer Verlag, Hamburg, 1979-1987

Tzareva, E., *Saryk Tent Bags in the State Museum of Ethnography of the Peoples of the USSR,* in *Hali 1/3,* p. 277ff., London, 1978; *Tappeti dei nomadi dell 'Asia Centrale della collezione del Museo Russo di Etnografia, San Pietroburgo',* S.A.G.E.P., Genoa, 1993

Ibid., *Salor Carpets, Hali 6/2,* p. 126ff., London, 1984

Ibid., *Teppiche aus Mittelasien und Kasachstan,* Aurora Art Publications, Leningrad, 1984

Whiting, M.C., *Tent Bags and Simple Statistics,* Pinner/ Franses, chapter 12, p. 90, Oguz Press, London, 1980

Wilfling, H., *Teppich-Motive der Türkvölker. Das hakenbesetzte Kreuzarm-motiv und seine Varianten,* Braumüller, Vienna, 1985

Yetkin, S., *Early Caucasian Rugs in Turkey,* vols. I and II, Oguz Press, London, 1978

Zipper, K./Fritzsche, C., *Oriental Rugs, Volume 4: Turkish,* Antique Collectors' Club, Woodbridge

PICTURE SOURCES

J.Lister Arditti, 88 Bargates, Christchurch, Dorset, BH23 1QP, England, tel. 01202 48 54 14

Bausback GmbH, Teppichantiquitäten, N3, 9 (Kunststrasse), 68161 Mannheim 1, Germany, tel. 0621/25800, fax 0621/105957

Christie's East, Manson & Woods International, Inc., 219 East 67th Street, New York, NY 10021, USA, tel. 212/606 0400, fax 212/737 6076

Galerie Dani Ghigo, Corso San Maurizio 52, 10124 Torino, Italy, tel. 011/831636

HALI Publications Ltd., Kingsgate House, Kingsgate Place London NW6 4TA, England, tel. 0171/328 93 41, fax 0171/372 5924

Galerie Kibitka, Thomas Knorr and Undine Berczuk, Turmstrasse 22, 79539 Lörrach, Germany, tel. 07621/43673, fax 07621/43663

Auktionshaus Rudolf Mangisch, Mühle Tiefenbrunnen, Seefeldstr. 227, 8008 Zurich, Switzerland, tel. 01/55 50 33, fax 01/55 36 41

Kunst- und Sammlerteppich/Auktionshaus Dr. Fritz Nagel, P.O. Box 10 35 54 , 70030 Stuttgart, Adlerstrasse 31-33, Germany, tel. 0711/64969-0, fax 0711/64969-69

Galerie Ostler, Thomas Wimmer Ring 3, 80539 Munich, Germany, tel. 089/2289264, fax 089/220377

Galerie Freydoun Pakzad, Königstrasse 18, 30175 Hanover, Germany, tel. 0511/342043, fax 0511/319603

Rippon Boswell & Co., 65185 Wiesbaden, Friedrichstrasse 45, Germany, tel. 0611/372062, fax 0611/307369

Robert W. Skinner Inc., Auctioneers & Appraisers, Route 117, Bolton, Mass. 071742, USA, tel. 617/779 5528

Galerie Sailer, 5020 Salzburg, Wiener Philharmoniker-Gasse 3, Austria, tel. 0662/846483, fax 0662/8425609

Orient-Teppich-Haus Wedel, H. Eitzenberger, Rosengarten 6a, 22559 Wedel/Hamburg, Germany, tel. 04103/89689, fax 04103/97734

CATALOGUE OF COLOUR PLATES

SALOR PILE WEAVINGS

In the history of Salor pile weaving three events are of particular interest. According to Elena Tzareva, in her article 'Salor Carpets' in *Hali* 6/2, a number of the Salor tribe migrated from Turkmenistan to Khorasan, to Iraq and to the south Persian province of Fars in the 11th century. During the Seljuk period some of them returned to Turkmenistan. In the 17th century, as a result of a catastrophic drought, they reputedly migrated again and settled in the Khiva and Bukhara regions. In the early 19th century, they were defeated by the Persians and finally were forced to surrender to the Saryk and Tekke. The ensuing loss of sovereignty also put an end to a particular 'Salor weaving period', the rare products of which have been called 'S group' pile weavings. The surviving pieces of this tribal group are generally dated to the late 18th or early 19th centuries, but theoretically they could have been made much earlier.

In comparison with Tekke weavings, 'authentic' Salor pieces tend to be characterised by their loose weave, asymmetric knots open to the left and strongly depressed warps. But there are, nevertheless, 'borderline cases' which are less easily identified (no. 63). Even symmetrically knotted pieces are sometimes attributed to the Salor, but these tend to be comparatively late weavings, which appear to have been made by weavers of Salor descent.

Early Saryk pile weavings can show great similarities with Salor products, but the former are woven in the symmetric knot. It is also highly unusual to find areas piled in cotton in Salor pieces, although cotton piling is sometimes used almost to excess in later Saryk weavings.

The rarity of some Salor pile weavings makes it difficult to estimate prices, as they can achieve very surprising sale results either in the trade or at auction.

1. Salor - Main Carpet. 18th-19th century

Size: 320 x 272 cm.

The owner dates this classic main 'wedding' carpet to the 18th century. It has six rows of twelve 'Salor guls' and the obligatory rhombus-shaped secondary gul. Traditional colours include red field and details of the design in apricot silk. Clear drawing with almost round primary guls. Narrow border, as is usual, with quartered main border ornament and finely decorated secondary borders. Bausback, Mannheim.
Literature: McMullan, 1972, pl. 45; Mackie and Thompson, fig. 4; Tzareva,1983, figs. 1-3; Loges, pl. 17

1

2

3

**2. Salor - Decorative Panel.
18th-19th century**

Size: 85 x 220 cm.

The owner dates this piece to the 18th
century. The inner field shows a section of the
kejebe gul repeat (see fig. 85). Examples are
known with one, two or three central
medallions. As as is usual, the field is framed
on three sides with *chamtos* border, here cut
on left, the original purpose of which is not
clear. The narrow sides in the centre have
remnants of an added blue fringe. The
direction of the pile on these panels is in the
oposite direction to the design. The inner
decoration of the medallions, partly worked
in silk, is worth comparing to the medallions
found on carpets with so-called 'Holbein'
designs (see fig. 61).
Sailer, Salzburg
*Literature: Mackie & Thompson, pl. 14;
Schürmann, pl. 7*

3. Salor - Decorative panel. 19th century

Size: 61 x 188 cm.

When offered at auction, this carried a high
estimate of SFR 56,000 because of its good
condition. The panel has one medallion and,
as is usual, is piled in wool with silk
highlights. A panel with two medallions
fetched $67,100 at Sotheby's New York in
1986 and $148,500 at the same auction house
four years later, making an auction record for
a Turkoman weaving on each occasion; this is
the example published by Ulrich Schürmann
in *Central Asian Rugs*, plate 6 and is
generally considered the best of its type.
Mangisch, Zurich
*Literature: Schürmann, pl. 6; Tzareva, 1984,
pl. 16; Thompson, no. 3*

4

5

4. Salor - Decorative panel. About 1800

Size: 58 x 135 cm.

In contrast to the two pieces just illustrated, this has only one *kejebe* medallion on the inner field. Unlike the other examples, this inner field is not surrounded by a border with the *kochanak* pattern but contains simple geometric ornaments. The typical three-sided 'framing' shows, on the narrow sides, a variant of the *chamtos* pattern (Compare Moshkova, pl. 39/15). On the lower edge and sides are rows of linked hooked rhombs, typical on this type of Salor weaving. In an American auction in May 1987, this panel fetched $37,400.
Skinner
Literature: Tzareva, 1984, no. 10; HALI, vol. 6, no. 2, fig. 15.

5. Salor - *Torba*. 18th-19th century

Size: 50 x 124 cm.

The owner dates this piece to the 18th century. The *kejebe* pattern is used here without the usual round medallions. Instead, there is a series of rhomboidal motifs flanked above and below by the so-called *kejebe* motifs. The outlines of the rhomboidal medallions still show clearly the character of plaited bands. Weavings with this simple variant of the *kejebe* pattern were made by all the tribes discussed in this book. As is usual on decorative panels and *torbas*, the lower side as an extra border containing the *chamtos* pattern. A rare and early piece with a wonderful array of colours.
Bausback, Mannheim
Literature: Tzareva, 1983, pl. 14; Mackie and Thompson, pl. 10; Cassin and Hoffmeister, pl. 4

6

6. Salor - *Chuval*. 18th-19th century

Size: 84 x 135 cm.

One of the earliest and best preserved
examples of this type. The owner dates it to
the 18th century. In the inner field are three
large guls in a single row, with the so-called
charch-Palak secondary motifs with inner
gelin-barmak motifs (Moshkova pl. 34/2).
Cochineal-dyed silk is used to highlight both
the main and secondary guls, as well as in the
rosettes of the so-called *kochanak* main
border. Three-branched tree motifs are
arranged diagonally on the cut lower panel,
this panel being called an *elem*. Salor *chuvals*
of this quality, beauty and in this condition
are rare.
Kibitka, Lörrach
*Literature: Cassin and Hoffmeister, pl.5;
HALI vol 4, no. 2, fig. 93 (Victoria and Albert
Museum, London, acquired in 1880)*

7

7. Salor - *Chuval.* **18th-19th century**

Size:

To add depth to this section on Salor weaving is this piece from the Russian Museum, St. Petersburg; the chances of acquiring an example of this type and quality today are minimal. Another example of these little-known Salor bags was published by Werner Loges, *Turkoman Tribal Rugs*, pl. 19. The primary gul is also found as a secondary motif on Salor main carpets and *chuvals* - see, for instance, nos. 8 and 10, and as a primary motif on some Tekke weavings, no. 85. Loges dated the example he illustrated, which has many characteristics typical of the so-called 'S-group', to "circa 1800 or earlier".
Courtesy *HALI,* London

8

8. Salor - *Chuval*. 18th-19th century

Size: 85 x 132 cm.

This large bag, in the Museum of Ethnography, St. Petersburg, is dated by Tzareva in *Rugs & Carpets from Central Asia*, no. 6, to the late 18th century. The inner field contains four rows of four so-called *chuval* guls. The grounds of their rhomboidal centres are piled with rose-coloured silk and are derived from the so-called *kejebe* pattern (see nos. 2-6). The octagonal gul, here used as a secondary ornament, appears as the main motif on no. 7. The *kochanak* main border is flanked by fine lines made up of linked 'S' motifs (called by Moshkova, pl. 65/20, the *chamak* pattern). On the apron are diagonally arranged (both actually and chromatically) floral motifs.
Courtesy *HALI*, London
Literature: Hoffmeister, no. 58; Beresneva, pl. 15; Mackie and Thompson, fig. 6

9

10

9. Salor - *Torba*. 18th-19th century

Size: fragmented

This is a very rare example and is, unfortunately, fragmented. The main motif is a stepped rhombus with hooked outlines and an interior eight-pointed star, the so-called 'Memling' gul which is named after the Flemish painter Hans Memling, who depicted carpets so decorated in a number of his paintings towards the end of the 15th century. It is one of the most important motifs on weavings by Turkic peoples. As a principal motif on *torbas,* it is also found on examples woven by the Saryk, Yomut and certain Ersari groups. It is accompanied here by an interesting secondary motif with Gothic-like 'plaited' outlines; this appears as an interior motif of guls on main carpets by the Saryk and Ersari (see no. 232). Peter Hoffmeister, *Turkoman Carpets in Franconia,* no. 57, illustrates a splendidly preserved torba with Memling guls by the Saryk, which he dates to the 18th century.
Courtesy *HALI,* London
Literature: Hoffmeister, no. 50 (Saryk), 57; Thompson, no. 5

10. Salor - *Chuval*. First half of the 19th century

Size: 90 x 144 cm.

Condition: edges much damaged, clear signs of age.
The vertically elongated form of the guls is a particularly archaic feature. Instead of rhombus-shaped central motif within the main guls, the centre here is quartered diagonally by colour and within each segment there is a St. Andrews cross motif (see Moshkova, pl. 40/5, the 'Saryk gul'); this gul-centre motif is analogous to the design in the main border and in the outer guard. The tree motifs in the *elem* change colour alternately.
Nagel, Stuttgart
Literature: Cassin and Hoffmeister, pl. 2; Mackie and Thompson, no. 7; Tzareva, fig. 8

11

11. Salor - *Torba*. Second half of the 19th century

Size: 38 x 122 cm.

Condition: signs of wear.
As can somtimes be seen on textiles illustrated in Timurid miniatures, the field of this *torba* is divided into a rectangular lattice containing eight-pointed stars (sometimes called the 'Medean' star); piled weavings with a similar composition can be found among the work of other Turkoman tribes (see nos. 52-3). In contrast to another example illustrated in Mackie and Thompson's *Turkmen*, pl. 13 (first half of the 19th century), no silk has been used in the pile. In all other respects this is a typical Salor weaving, with asymmetric knots open to the left, strongly depressed warps, a *chamtos* design at the base and a dark blue added fringe.
Nagel, Stuttgart
Literature: Thompson, no. 90

12. Salor - *Torba*. 18th-19th century

Size: 45 x 112 cm.

The *chemle-gul* is a pattern common to the work of several Turkoman weaving tribes; it was obviously very popular as decoration for bag-faces and is here knotted in wool and silk. It is rarer on main carpets (see Loges, pl. 115). In the past, the individual motif which, when repeated, makes up this pattern, was interpreted as a mosque lamp. Less speculative are the comparisons with early Anatolian carpet patterns, for example the lattice-like patterns of a few 13th century fragments from Fostat (see Erdmann, 1977, figs. 1, 3, 5 and pl. 99). Even more obvious is a comparison with the palmette motifs found over hundreds of years on both Persian and Anatolian carpets (see no. 283). The appearance of Saryk *chemle-gul torbas* can be very close to that of Salor examples; the former, however, are always executed in symmetric knotting.
Courtesy *HALI* Publications
Literature: Tzareva, plates 13-14; Mackie & Thompson, no. 11; Loges, pl. 21

12

13

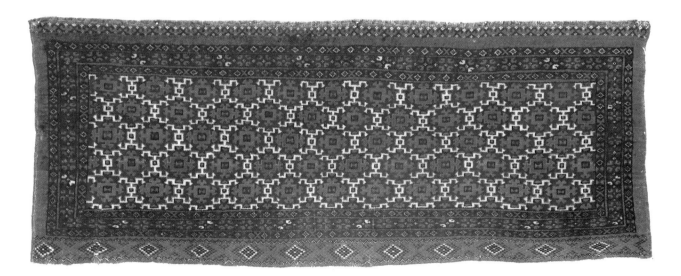

14

13. Salor - *Torba*. 18th-19th century

Size: 41 x 129 cm.

The fiery-red honeycomb of the *chemle-gul* pattern (see no. 12) covers the inner field; there is a large amount of cochineal and silvery-white dyed silk, which over time has corroded to give a relief-like effect. There is also a lavish use of silk in the border. Typical As3 knotting.
Nagel, Stuttgart

14. Salor - decoative panel. Second half of the 19th century

Size: 52 x 139 cm.

Condition; shiny. velvety wool, pile excellent. The origin of the *ak-su* field pattern is controversial (see also nos. 32, 78, 172). Parallels can be found in early Chinese carpets. If the field pattern is seen as a repeat of complex and tightly drawn motifs arranged in diagonal rows on a white ground, then the red oblong motifs with their four extensions are laid on midnight-blue polygons. Both these forms are found on both Persian and Caucasian carpets (see Bennett, plates 117 and 175). Harmonious and majestic in colour, with fine nuances in the red tones which, in the field, are arranged diagonally.
Nagel, Stuttgart

SARYK PILE WEAVINGS

According to Tsareva (*Hali* 1/3, p. 280), historical sources inform us about the presence of the Saryk in the region from the Caspian Sea to the Amu Darya. In the 19th century, Saryk groups migrated to Murgab and Merv, whence they were driven out by the Tekke in 1857. These groups finally settled in the Pendeh region after the Russian conquest.

It is rarely difficult to distinguish between Saryk weavings and those of other Turkoman groups; the only possible problems might occur with Ersari weavings. But the use of symmetric knots tends to distinguish Saryk work from Ersari group weavings, usually attributed to the Beshir, which are asymmetrically knotted. There are very few early Saryk pieces and these may be very similar to Salor products, which, however, are woven with asymmetric knots open to the left. The Saryk not only have numerous carpet designs but also specific weaving formats in common with the related Salor tribe. We also know of Saryk variants of the *kejebe* design.

Despite the common use of symmetric knots by the Saryk and some Yomut tribes, it is generally easy to distinguish between these two types of weavings. Saryk pieces of the second half of the 19th century, in particular, are usually easily identified as such. This is especially true of those woven from the last quarter of the 19th century onwards. The increasingly darker palette and the occasionally excessive use of silk and white cotton in the pile are very characteristic. We also know of some asymmetrically knotted weavings dating from the end of the 19th century and later, but they have the characteristic palette mentioned above.

Elena Tzareva's article 'Saryk Tent Bags' (*Hali* 1/3, p. 277) is one of the few contributions dealing specifically with Saryk Turkoman pile weavings. Tsareva draws the following conclusions from structural analyses of 24 Saryk chuvals and torbas: symmetric pile; undyed, occasionally bleached, woollen warps; extremely fine wefts of natural brown wool or red dyed camel hair (!), usually two shoots. The majority of bag fronts are piled in a mixture of wool, silk and cotton. Elsewhere she refers to the changing proportions of the field to the borders in later pieces: the borders and additional design panels progressively take up more space.

15. Saryk - Main Carpet. Mid 19th century

Size; 273 x 230 cm.

Condition; very good condition, a little worn in places, some restorations.

Very few other published examples can be compared to the arrangement of colours on this main carpet; it has warm red-brown, a soft mandarin orange, deep blue and vivid white. In contrast to later large Saryk carpets, the colours here are lighter and are dominated by the warm red-brown ground. This demonstrates its origin in the pre-synthetic period, before about 1880. Typically for carpets of this group, the clarity and vividness of the white areas are achieved by the use of bleached cotton in the pile. Cyclamen-coloured silk is used sparingly, mainly in the border. The almost square format is also an indication of an early date; the pile is symmetrically knotted in velvety wool on finely spun natural white wool warps and brown wool wefts. There is a typical blue and red-brown chequerboard pattern selvedge. Both in the quality of weave and aesthetically, this is a masterpiece.

Nagel, Stuttgart

Literature: Schürmann, pl. 10; Grote-Hasenbalg, 1922, pl. 85; Thatcher, pl. 6

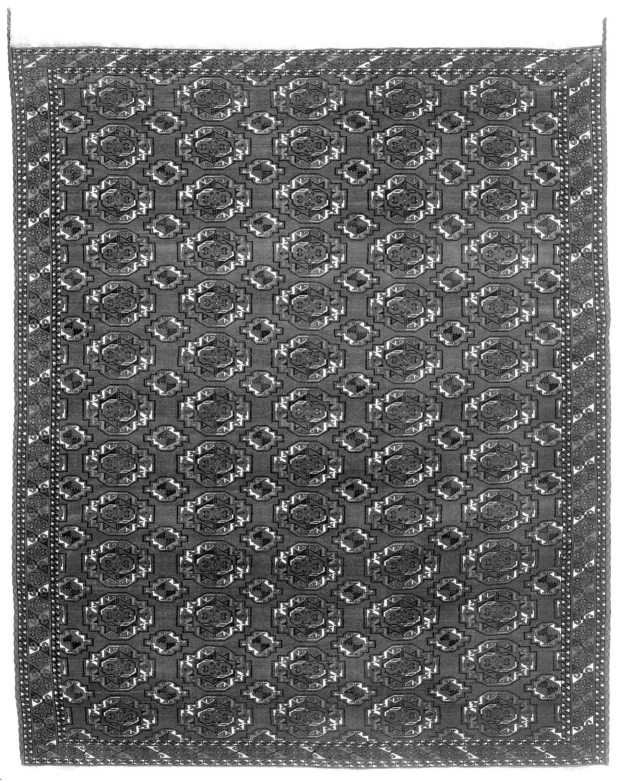

15

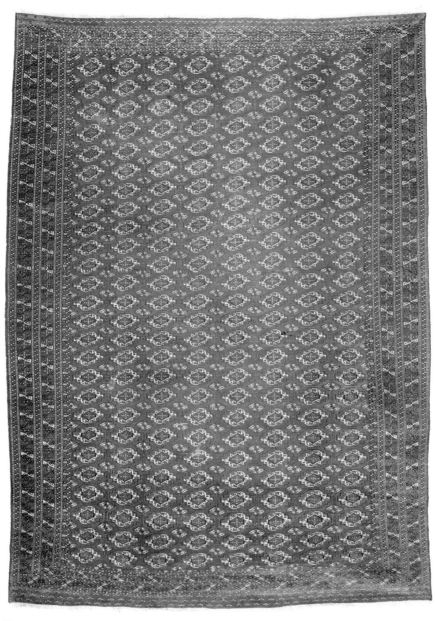

16

16. Saryk - Main carpet. End of the 19th century

Size: 363 x 268 cm.

Condition: worn.
An unusual feature for carpets of this type is that the pile of this example is woven almost entirely of silk. This is, in fact, an unusual phenomenon on any Turkoman weaving of good age; silk carpets with Turkoman motifs do occasionally appear on the market but they are almost always post 1945 in date. It is interesting to compare this example with the earlier Saryk main carpet just illustrated (no. 15). The main field here has more tightly composed rows of guls and the result is more crowded and less spacious. Also the main borders, consisting of two rows of the same pattern, show the same density of motifs. The octagonal minor gul in the field is interesting (see nos. 1 and 39). An unusual feature is the addition of single stripes of pattern down the long inner sides of the field, made up of triple-headed flower motifs.
Nagel, Stuttgart

17. Saryk - Main Carpet. End of the 19th century

185 (225 inc. kelims) x 145 cm.

Condition: excellent.
This piece was exhibited in 1970 in the exhibition *Nomadenteppiche aus Turkmenistan* at the Hamburg Museum für Völkerkunde and was published in Siawosch Azadi's catalogue as plate 2. It is worth noting that the publication of carpets and other weavings can have the effect of pushing up their prices. The relatively dark palette is typical of Saryk work from the late 19th century; ruby-red silk and bleached white cotton have been used for highlights.
Nagel, Stuttgart
Literature: Loges, no. 25

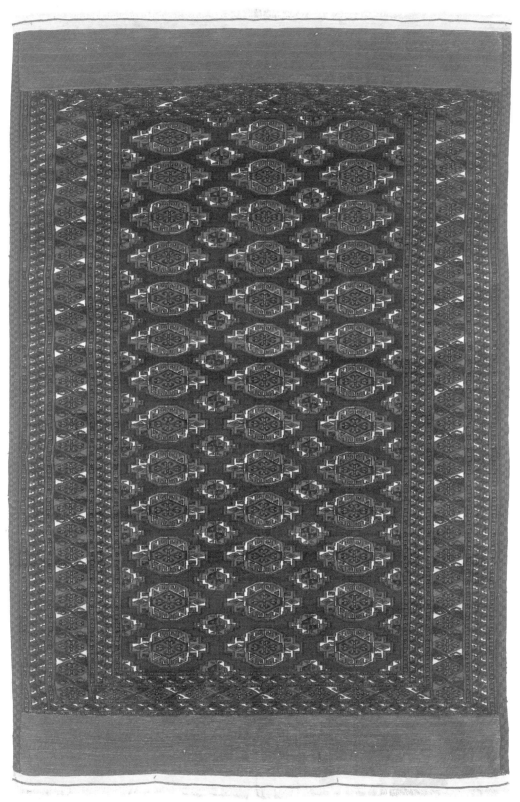

17

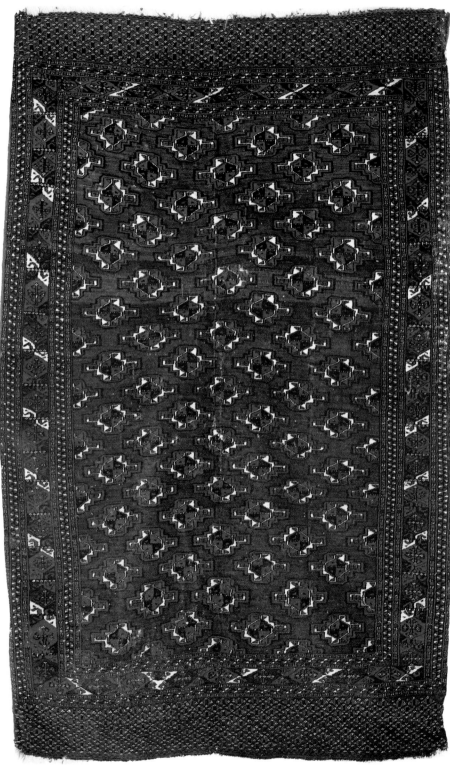

18. Saryk - Main Carpet. First half of the 20th century

Size: 174 x 114 cm.

Condition: long tear, now repaired.
The so-called 'Saryk gul' is not present in this piece which, from a collector's point of view, would be considered relatively late. Instead, diagonal rows of what is usually the minor gul cover the violet-brown field and there is no minor gul to complement this main motif. The colours are rather dark and sombre. The coarseness of knotting sems to contradict the fine design in the main border and the *elem*.
Nagel, Stuttgart

19. Saryk (?) - Main Carpet

Size: 140 x 103 cm.

Condition: signs of wear, patched in places, moth damage.
A very distinctive carpet, the almost square guls covering the field arranged in very harmonious balance. Their hooked extensions at the axes are drawn with unusual clarity. The design in the main border is unusual; in place of the usual hooked cruciform motif (*naldag*), there is an eight-pointed star. There is a relatively coarse flatweave at either end and the selvedges are of brown undyed goat's hair; these features point to an Ersari origin, probably from the Pendeh Oasis. The relationship between Saryk and Ersari weaving makes this carpet an interesting item for collectors.
Nagel, Stuttgart
Literature: Mackie and Thompson, fig. 18

18

19

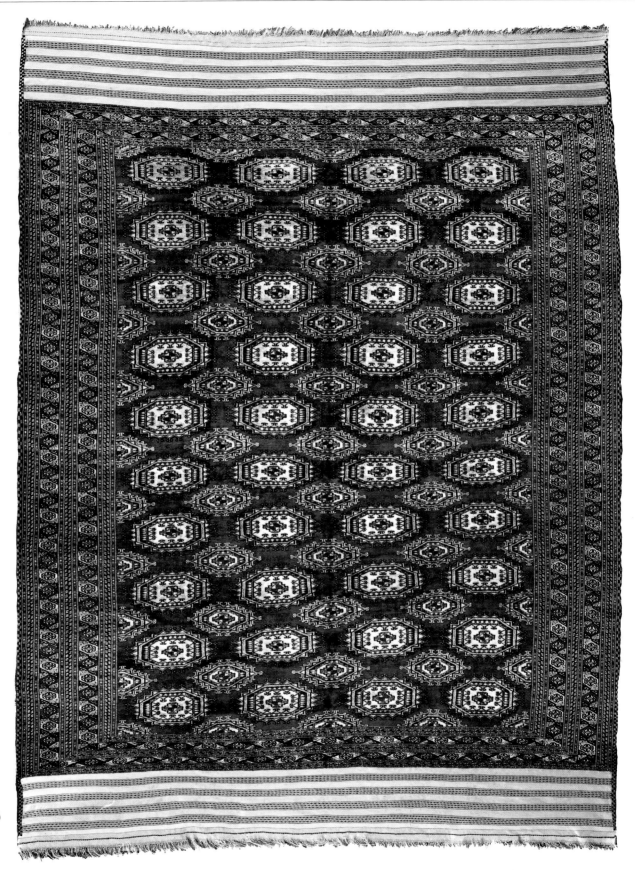

20. Saryk - Main Carpet. Beginning of the 20th century

Size: 296 x 278 cm.

Condition: silk areas a little corroded, otherwise very good.
The fine, exact, knotting and the use of shiny wool and pale pink silk give this carpet a very precious and luxurious appearance. The main and secondary guls in the field are quite similar, the major difference being one of size. For a long time, the major gul seen here was called the 'Salor gul', in spite of the fact that it does not appear on Salor main carpets but only on Salor *chuvals*. The end and side finishes are both excellently done; the sides have typical chequerboard selvedges. The ends have bands of ivory-coloured flatweave alternating with embroidered bands in two colours.
Nagel, Stuttgart
Literature: Moshkova, pl. 54; Franses, fig. 9; Iten-Maritz, fig. 242

21

21. Saryk - *Ensi*. About 1880

Size: 162 x 148 cm.

Condition: small hole, patched and repaired.
Early Saryk *ensis* from the pre-synthetic period are very rare. Commercial production of such pieces is believed to have increased after the Saryk settled around the oasis of Pendeh, and to have been on a scale still largely under-estimated. The horizontal central bar of Saryk *ensi* are almost always filled with the *Gas-Ajak* motif on a silk ground (red wool on early examples) or a very regular rhomboidal lattice. They often have three panels at the base, of which the third may be kelim (missing from this piece). Typical for their period is the dark and restrained overall palette, which contrasts with the lavish use of silk and white cotton.
Nagel, Stuttgart
Literature: Ettinghausen, pl. 35; Thatcher, pl. 9

22

22. Saryk- *Ensi*. End of the 19th century

Size: 199 x 145 cm.

The field colour of this rug can be presumed to have been uniform when it was woven but has not faded evenly so that it now has a rather startling light-coloured *abrash*. Such unexpected colour variations occur when wool from different dye batches was used, something which never bothered peasant or nomad weavers, who did not consider this to have a negative effect on the overall aesthetic appeal. A typically Saryk feature is the blue and red chequerboard across the top. A typically Saryk feature is the blue and red chequerboard across the top.

Nagel, Stuttgart

Literature: Schürmann. pl. 37; Bogolyubov, no. 4

23. Saryk - *Ensi*. Second half of the 19th century

Size: 170 x 130 cm.

Condition: very thin.

A very individualistic design, especially when compared with no. 21. The classic *ensi* design has been extended by two fields. The various vertical and horizontal bars contain oblong 'boxes', which also appear in the outer border. White cotton has been used for the *sainak* motifs, which typically appear only on three sides (not across the lower end); on the long side, it is used in the centre of the main border. Another distinctive feature is the inscription in the upper right corner (see 23a), which possibly contains the haegira date 1289 (1872 AD). An unusual piece with rather atypical loose knotting.

Nagel, Stuttgart

Detail 23a

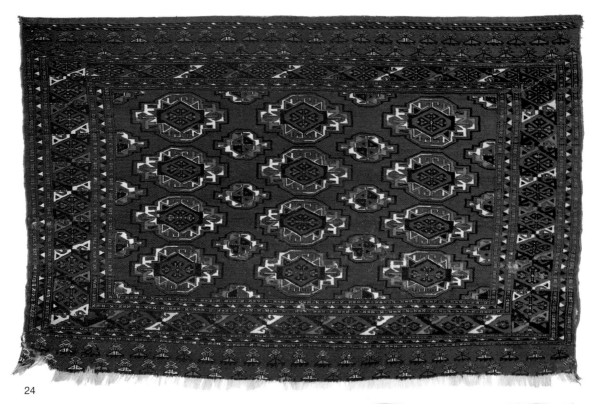

24

25

26

24. Saryk - *Chuval*. First half of the 19th century

Size; 83 x 134 cm.

Condition: edges damaged.

This large tent- or carrying-bag has similar motifs to no. 15; the palette both of field and borders is also similar and both pieces probably come from the same region and were made around the same time. Characteristic features of Saryk *chuvals* include the quite wide extra panel above the upper border with a seam decorated with diagonal stripes along the opening edge. The piece has a velvety pile and the white areas are piled in cotton.

Nagel, Stuttgart

Literature: Loges, no. 32; Bogolyubov, no. 1

25. Saryk - *Chuval*. End of the 19th century

Size: 85 x 145 cm.

Condition: very good.

Easily recognisable as a late weaving, despite the similarity of its design to earlier examples. Both the design and the colours are dull, particularly the liver-brown ground. Contrast is provided by the lavish use of rose-coloured silk and glowing white cotton. As on the previous piece, it has diagonally arranged motifs in the lower *elem* and above the *kotshak* strip at the top. Moshkova (pl. 42/8 - 11) described these as highly abstracted anthropomorphic forms; in fact, they resemble pre-historic female figures with exaggerated torso and with arms akimbo on hips. The upper edge is finished with a dark blue strip in soumak technique and at the bottom there is a white flatwoven strip.

Nagel, Stuttgart

26. Saryk - *Torba*. Second half of the 19th century

Size: 37 x 125 cm.

Condition: some damage and repairs.

A larger Saryk bag of similar design in the Ethnographical Museum, St. Petersburg, is illustrated by Tzareva as no. 21, where it is dated to the first half of the 19th century. In contrast to the previous piece, this has the *chemche* gul as its secondary motif, which is part of the design repertoire of many Turkoman weaving groups. All the white areas are piled in white cotton. The centres of both the major and minor guls, as well as the motifs in the borders are piled partly in cochineal and green-blue silk. An unusually fine weave for a Saryk rug.

Nagel. Stuttgart

Literature: Hoffmeister, pl. 48

27

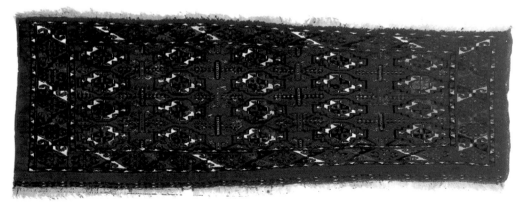

28

29

27. Saryk - *Chuval*. End of the 19th century

Size: 97 x 152 cm.

Condition: some wear at lower edge.
The combination of ornaments on this bag are reminscent of those on the main carpet illustrated as no. 20. The main border pattern is typical, as is the addition of an extra patterned 'frieze' at the top and the design of the *elem*. A characteristic example for its date, with a lavish use of silk and white cotton.
Nagel, Stuttgart
Literature: Loges, pl. 33; Tzareva, fig. 24; Bennett (1972), p. 110

28. Saryk (?) - Decorative Panel. Mid 19th century

Size: 37 x 152 cm.

Condition: worn, some slight repairs.
The use of the 'Saryk gul' is unusual on *torbas* and decorative panels. Note the relationship to a small Turkoman rug illustrated by Schürmann (1969, no. 4), which may also have originated in the Merv Oasis. The Saryks were driven from there by the Tekkes in 1857. Like the small rug referred to, this piece is not symmetrically knotted but has asymmetric knots open to the right and warps of white goat-hair (see no. 19). Moshkova also reports the appearance of the 'Saryk gul' on weavings from Merv; the *muska*-like motifs (see no. 265) on the left edge are remarkable. The piece has its original end finishes and the remains of an added fringe in two alternating colours.
Nagel, Stuttgart
Literature: Bogolyubov, no. 1

29. Saryk - *Torba*. End of the 19th century

Size: 33 x 127 cm.

Condition: remarkably good.
As in the Salor example with this design (see no. 5), the gabled motifs 'grow' out of the surrounding field area towards each other. Their interior motif has been interpreted as either the panniers used on camels or perhaps the ornate chair or howdah used by a bride and which would have been mounted on a camel's back (see no 91); it has also been associated with ancient cult altars which would have been surmounted by animal heads. Two delicate shades of red have been used in the borders as well as light-blue silk in the so-called 'S' pattern guards. Symmetrically knotted and with its original plaited bands and blue added fringe.
Nagel, Stuttgart
Literature: Tzareva, no. 15; Loges, pl. 28; Thompson, no. 15

30

31

30. Saryk - *Torba*. **End of the 19th century**

Size: 34 x 117 cm.

In the use of border motifs, this tent bag shows great similarity to the Salor *torba* illustrated as no. 13, which has the traditional *chemle*-gul field pattern. The ground colour used here is different, being a typical violet-brown. It has an extensive use of white cotton and rose-coloured silk as well as wool in the pile. The colours of the field design are arranged diagonally. Its Saryk atribution is confirmed by its symmetric knotting and a typical Saryk feature is the dark blue strip at the upper edge.
Nagel, Stuttgart
Literature: Loges, pl. 31

31. Saryk - *Torba*. **End of the 19th century**

Size: 37 x 132 cm.

Condition: very good.
In contrast to the *ak-su* pattern on the Salor *torba*, no. 14, here the two colours - oxblood red wool and rose silk - are arranged diagonally. The silk pile is unusually long as is the white cotton, suggesting a date towards the end of the 19th century. It has symmetric knots and strong warp depression resulting in a ribbed back and stiff, boardlike handle. The blue flat-woven strip at the top and the added blue fringe are also both typical Saryk features.
Nagel, Stuttgart
Literature: Bogolyubov, no. 9; Thacher, fig. 8; Milhofer, no. 71

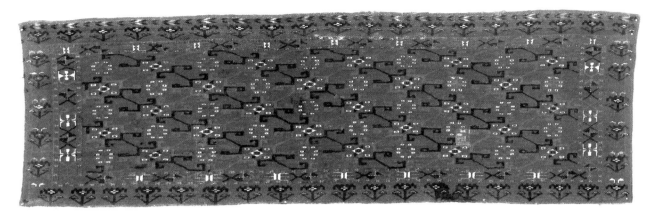

32

33

32. Saryk - *Torba*. First half of the 19th century

Size: 36 x 122 cm.

Of the few *torbas* known with this field pattern, this beautiful example must be one of the earliest. Its lattice design seems related to the *ak-su* pattern and is similarly composed of double 'T' shapes (see no. 14). However, here they are arranged diagonally both graphically and by colour. There are small white dice-like forms, flower-heads, and hooked rectangular motifs enclosing eight-pointed stars in the octagonally-shaped negative spaces (see no. 33). It has a dense and velvety symmetrically knotted pile.

Nagel, Stuttgart
Literature: Moshkova, pl. 40/15; Tzareva, fig. 58 (described as Tekke); Troost, pl. 11 (described as Yomut)

33. Saryk - *Torba*. Second half of the 19th century

Size: 40 x 124 cm.

Condition: minimal repairs.
Saryk bags with a compartment field composition usually have the *sekme*-gul (see no. 34); here, however, the motif used is the *aina-kochak* and is closer to the design repertoire of the Tekke (see no. 67). A constituent of both patterns is an eight-pointed star. In no. 32, the *aina-kochak* is made up of double 'T' forms in a lattice arrangement; here, however, it appears in white in each compartment, which is divided diagonally into four sections by colour; in each corner is a small dice-like flower. Symmetric knotting and velvety wool.
Nagel, Stuttgart

34

35

34. Saryk - *Germech*(?). First half of the 20th century

Size: 20 (33 inc. kilim) x 96 cm.

Research into the differing characteristics of weavings used for the base of the tent entrance as opposed to those of other woven panels might provide us with more information (see Thomas Cooper, 'An Ersari Germech', in *HALI*, vol. 4, no. 2, p. 151). Pointers to identifying panels as being specifically *germeche* might be: the format, the *ensi*-like outer border and the broad lower panel with weft-float brocade (see no. 87). Symmetrically knotted with a wool, silk and cotton pile.
Nagel, Stuttgart

35. Saryk - *Kapunuk* (*Kaplyk*). Mid 19th century

Size: 94 x 133 cm.

Condition: wear, repiled areas, tears and sides repaired.
The *ashik* pattern, seen here, with an interior meander, is the most common design found on all Turkoman weavings of this type. Apart from this, Saryk *kapunuks* with the *ak-su* pattern are also found. This is one of the weavings used to decorate the tent entrance and this example has a large amount of ruby-coloured silk used in the pile and the outer guard is entirely piled in silk in the obligatory symmetric knot.
Nagel, Stuttgart
Literature: Azadi, 'Der turkmenische Kaplyk' (1966); Beresneva, fig. 41

36

36. Saryk - *Khorjin*. End of the 19th century

Condition: complete.
Saryk double saddle-bags with several different patterns are known, including the *chemle, aineh* and *kejebe* designs. The type of *khorjin* shown here is quite striking since its front panels, in common with *ak-* and *kizil-chuvals* (see nos. 80-81) have a mixture of pile and uncoloured flat-woven strips. The Kurds from the Veramin area of northwest Iran made *khorjins* which are similar both technically and in design. The striped pattern seen here is similar to that found on some Anatolian carpets of the Seljuk period and is reminiscent of Kufic calligraphy (see nos. 71-3). Fine symmetric knotting. The central brocaded area which joins the two bags is worked in silk.
Nagel, Stuttgart
Literature: Reed, no. 8; Bogolyubov, no. 43

TEKKE PILE WEAVINGS

At one point it was not uncommon to subdivide Tekke pile weavings into several sub-groups and attribute them to tribal groups such as Tekke, or regions such as Merv and Achal. But it quickly became obvious that the identification of certain types of pile weaving with tribal groups which themselves have historically been difficult to differentiate, is nothing more than speculative.

But lovers and collectors of Turkoman weavings will at least be able to make comparisons between the design, palette and structure of particular types of pile weaving. Most of the surviving examples of Turkoman pile weavings can be described as 'Tekke'. In the 19th century, Tekke groups were settled in many areas of Turkmenistan; they were also the largest and most powerful of all the tribes. Carpets with the trade description of 'Bukhara' and 'Tekke gul' became ubiquitous. Sometimes the name of the market town of 'Bukhara' was even adopted for the weavings of other tribes as a kind of quality seal.

37. Tekke - Main Carpet. First half of the 19th century

Size: 260 x 186 cm.

Condition: very good, some expert repairs.
A main carpet with four rows of ten guls on a red-brown ground; next to the *chemche,* the *kurbaka* minor gul seen here is most often found on Tekke main carpets. In contrast to Tekke main carpets made around 1900, earlier examples such as this important collectors' piece are very rare. The large and rounded main Tekke guls and the archaic-looking secondary motifs are arranged with a characteristic spaciousness on the field, surrounded, as is usual, by one main border. A particular feature of examples made in the first half of the 19th century is the design of the upper and lower borders. The individual octagons in the borders, with their cruciform star interiors, are free-standing, although a compartment-like effect is achieved by the dividing ornaments. First class wool and colour.
Rippon Boswell
Literature: Loges, no. 1; Hoffmeister, pl. 3; Gombos, fig. 7

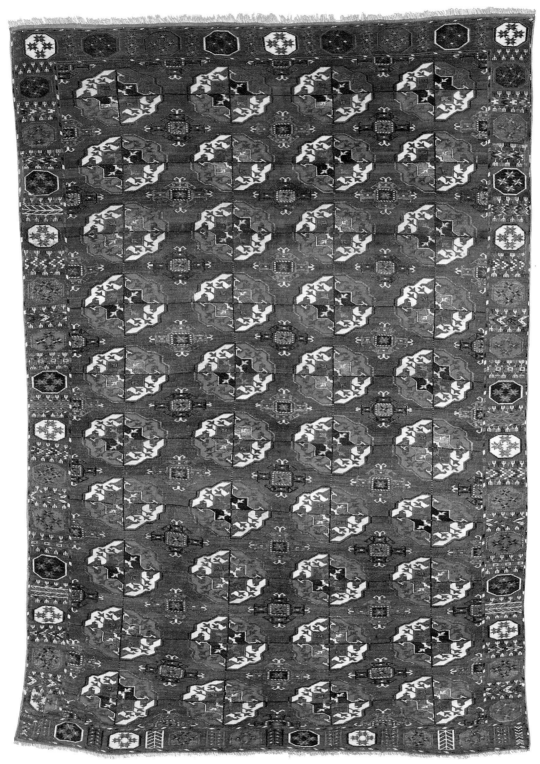

37

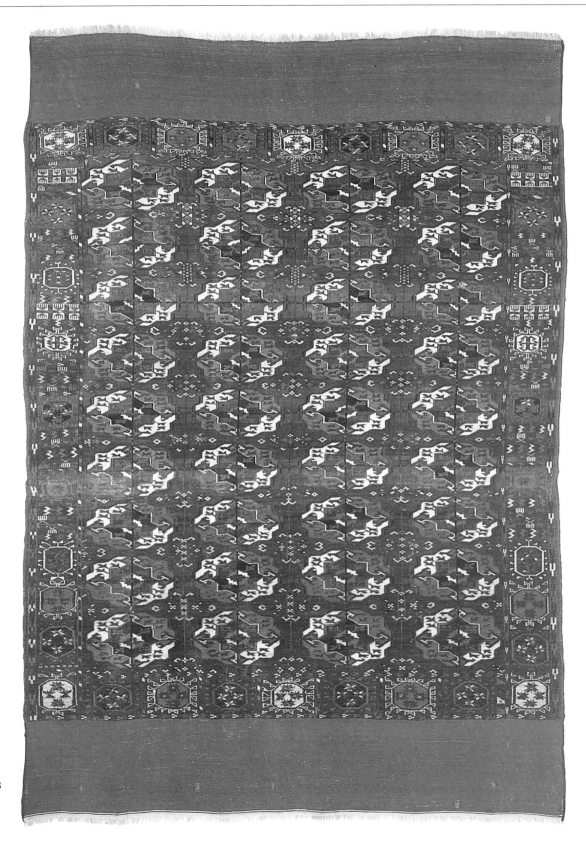

38

38. Tekke - Main Carpet. Mid 19th Century

Size: 196 (250 inc. flatwoven ends) x 182 cm.

Condition: minimal repairs.
Almost square in format, this main carpet has
only nine guls in each of its four rows; this is
regarded by some authors as the earliest lay-
out of the characteristic Tekke field.
However, the comparatively greater density
of motifs overall suggests that this may be a
later example than the one just illustrated.
The powerful and boldly-drawn guls are
quartered diagonally in their centres into blue
and blue-green areas. The *chemche* secondary
motifs are joined vertically by fine lines. Four
of the octagons with 'rayed' outlines in the
main border (called *shelpe* by Moshkova, pl.
47/7-15) contain a *kochanak* motif instead of
the usual four stars. This carpet still has its
finely striped woven ends, which is somewhat
of a rarity in pieces of this age. A beautiful
collectors' piece.
Nagel, Stuttgart
Literature: Azadi, pl. 3; Gombos, fig. 2;
Gewerbemuseum, Basel (1980), no. 119

**39. Tekke - Main Carpet. Second half of the
19th century**

Size: 292 x 195 cm.

Condition: worn in places, some areas of
repair.
An unusual feature of this example is the
secondary gul, which also appears on some
main carpets of the Salor (see no. 1); and on
some smaller weavings by the Tekke and
other tribes as either the secondary or as the
main motif (see nos. 7, 85-6). The delicate
rectangular lattice which runs through the
main guls is typical. The minor guls are also
connected by fine lines and there are two
small rhombs between each minor gul on the
vertical axis. The *shelpe* octagons of the main
border are here arranged quite close together
and there is a compartment arrangement in
the upper and lower borders. Flanking the
main borders are narrow *kochak*-patterned
guards with diagonally striped outlines. Very
fine knotting.
Nagel, Stuttgart
Literature: Mackie/Thompson, fig. 28

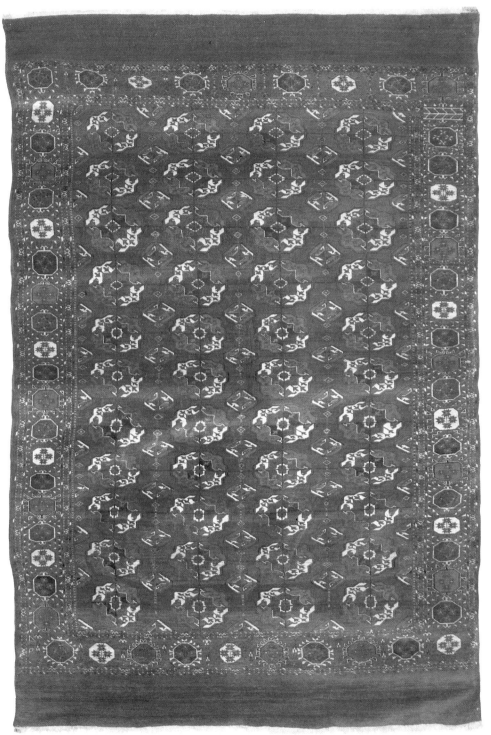

39

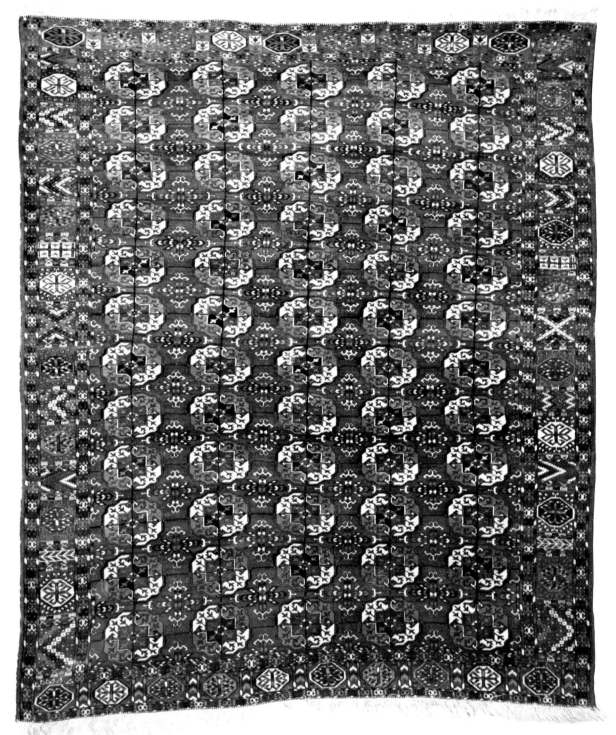

40

40. Tekke - Main Carpet. Second half of the 19th century

Size: 238 x 206 cm.

Condition: good.
The composition of this example, with its five rows of twelve guls, is clearly more crowded than the previous examples; together with the secondary *chemche* guls, they form a tile-like field pattern. However, despite the density of ornamentation, the drawing is quite clear and it has excellent colour. The pattern of the main border is also well-balanced and effective. On the long sides, the *shelpe* octagon compartments alternate with compartments containing a variety of different motifs, almost like the presentation of a repertoire of ornaments. In overall colour, a very appealing carpet.
Nagel, Stuttgart
Literature: Azadi, pl. 5

41. Tekke - Main Carpet. Second half of the 19th century

Size: 290 x 205 cm.

Condition: velvety pile perfectly preserved.
Again a piece with five rows of octagons and a dense overall composition, probably from the late 19th century. The ground colour is a warm tomato-red, which is also found on early Tekke carpets. The quartered ground colours of the main guls vary attractively in many areas of the field. The octagons of the main border have hooked, cross-armed, outlines. Of especial interest is the design in the *elem* panels at either end. In contrast to the Saryk version of this pattern (see no. 32), with its enclosed eight-pointed stars, the pattern in each rectangular area is similar to the *sekme*-gul (no. 34).
Nagel, Stuttgart

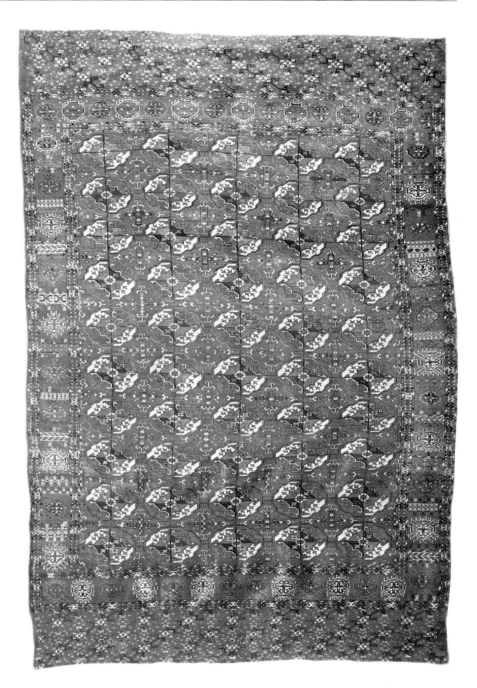

41

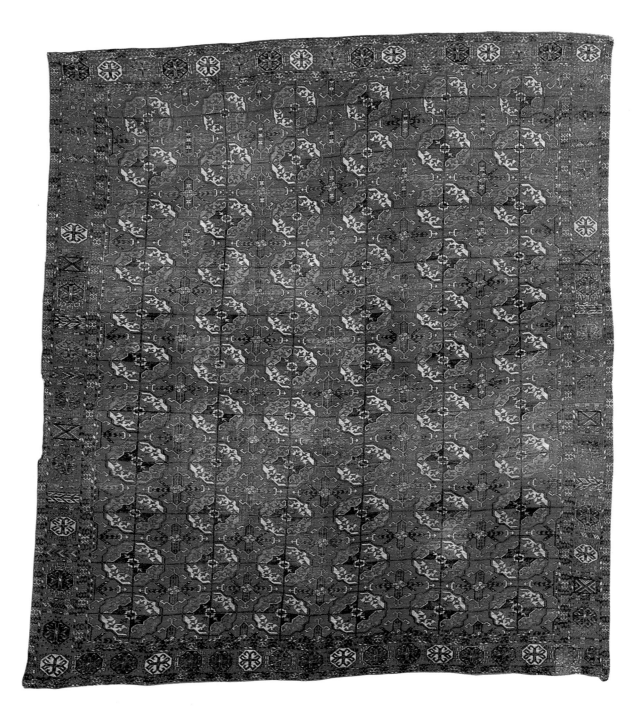

42

42. Tekke - Main Carpet. Mid 19th century

Size: 238 x 221 cm.

Condition: signs of wear, restoration, sides slightly cut.

The main field lay-out of six rows of guls is unusual for a Tekke main carpet. Its colour, variety of motifs and structure suggest a connection with a group of brilliant Tekke weavings, predominantly represented by *torbas* with 2 x 3 guls, the origins of which are presumed to go back to the first half of the 19th century (nos. 83-4). The *torbas* of this group have large secondary *chemche* motifs comparable to those seen on this carpet; similar also is the quality of the tightly clipped velvety wool pile.

Nagel, Stuttgart

43. Tekke - Small Rug. About 1900

Size: 161 x 120 cm.

Condition: very good.

Many carpets made by various Turkoman groups have cords attached to their upper corners for hanging on walls; they are even found on carpets of large size and are often beautifully plaited and well-preserved. The guls on this rug are rectangular and sharp-edged, which suggests a late date. Characteristic of rugs of this date is the overall patterning of the *elems* and the fact that it is the same at both ends; the white ground edging line is also quite commonly seen. However, an unusual feature of this example is the use of silk in the pile, which is used for the dark red gul centres. The rug has rich colouring, with several shades of red, blue-black, steel blue, blue-green, ivory and, sparsely used, yellow.

Nagel, Stuttgart

Literature: Loges, no. 3; Grote-Hasenbalg (1921), folder II, pl. 38 (81)

43

44

44. Tekke - Small Rug. Dated 1933

Size: 100 x 86 cm.

Only two details are shown here of this small Tekke rug, which has Tekke main guls and *kurbaka* secondary guls (see no. 37); in structure it is similar to the previous example. Although relatively late, this piece is interesting because of the fact that it is dated twice with a Christian date and has an inscription in Cyrillic, possibly a signature, in its *shelpe*-pattern main border. Turkoman carpets are rarely dated and even more rarely signed and when they are, the date is usually in the Islamic calendar. Normally European dating only appears on 20th century weavings made in the Soviet Union. However, earlier examples sometimes have Armenian inscriptions and dates in the Gregorian Calendar (see no. 48).

Nagel, Stuttgart
Literature: HALI 35, pp. 11 ff. (huge carpet with an Armenian inscription made in Merv and dated 1889)

45. Tekke - Small Rug. End of the 19th century

Size: 115 x 112 cm.

Condition: fully preserved pile.
This example was probably made at the same time and in the same place as no. 43. The primary motif is a combination of the so-called *chuval*-gul of no. 46 and the main motif of no. 43.

Nagel, Stuttgart

45

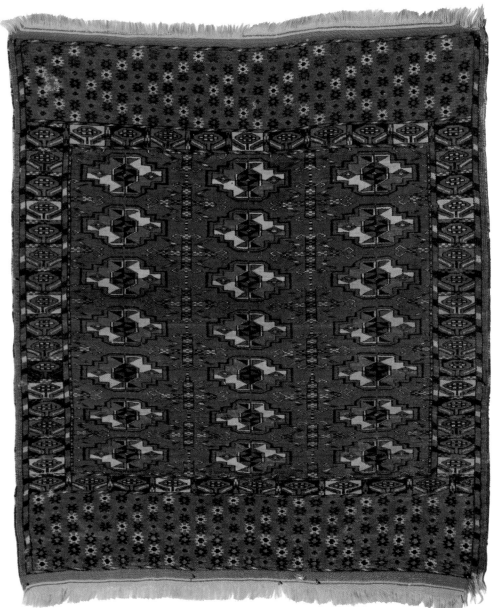

47. Tekke - Main Carpet. End of the 19th century

Size: 270 x 200 cm.

Condition: good.
In the centre of these compartment fields is an eight-petalled rosette, a detail often appearing on Tekke weavings. The design in each *elem* is different, although these repeat patterns belong to a design theme which has many variations; variants most often appear in the *elems* of Tekke weavings dating from the late 19th and 20th centuries.
Nagel, Stuttgart
Literature: Martin, 1984, pl. 30 (in the small rug format)

46

46. Tekke - Small Rug. Second half of the 19th century

Size: 94 x 87 cm.

Condition: worn, slight damage to the sides.
A small rug with an almost square format to the field. It has the so-called *chuval*-gul in three rows in the field; this gul, as well as the compartment-like ornament of the main border, are better known from bags (no. 72). The stylised shrubs seen in the main border all grow upwards, something also found on bags (called by Moshkova, pl. 53/10 the *sakar gishik* ornament). A rare piece.
Nagel, Stuttgart
Literature: Straka Collection, cat. no. 27

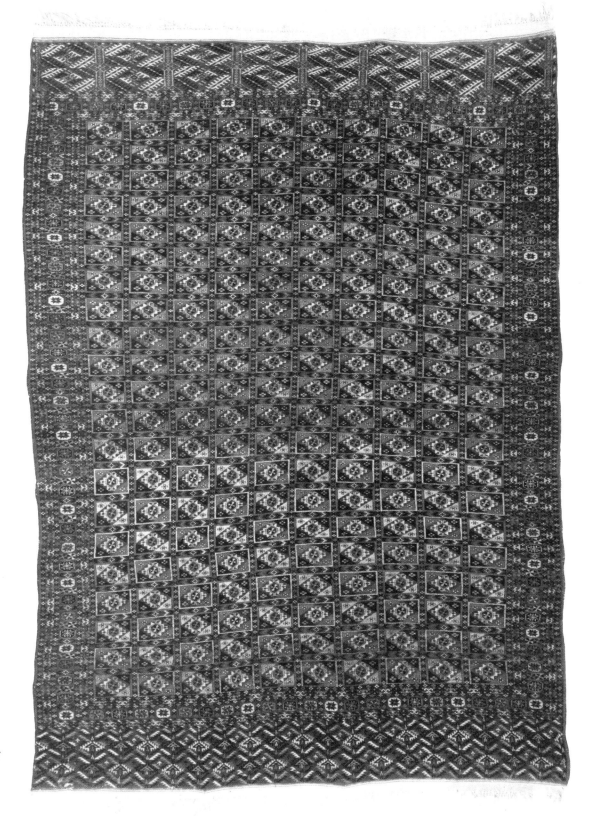

48

48. Tekke(?) - Rug. End of the 19th century

Size: 180 x 117 cm.

Condition: signs of wear, repiled areas, edges
damaged.
Carpets of this design group, with octagonal
'Salor' guls and so-called *chuval*-guls as
secondary motifs, have in the past been
attributed to the Salor. Moshkova called the
main motif a 'Salor' gul but called the minor
motif seen here the 'Saryk' gul (Moshkova,
pl. 40/5). The problem of classification is
made more difficult by the fact that some
carpets of this design type have asymmetric
knots open to the left and others open to the
right. In contrast to early Salor carpets, with
their rounded guls, rugs of this design type
are much thinner, have less warp depression
and a short clipped pile. It is interesting to
note that a similar rug illustrated in Der
Manuelian and Eiland, 1984, fig. 20, has an
Armenian inscription and is dated 1886.
Nagel, Stuttgart
*Literature: Azadi, pl. 1; Straka Collection,
cat.no. 13*

49. Tekke (?) - Rug. Second half of the 19th century

Size: 164 x 115 cm.

Condition: slight signs of wear, but generally
good.
As with the previous piece, the origin of this
rug is not clear. Structurally it is Tekke, but
looking at no. 201, there seems to be a
relationship with Yomut weaving. The
dominant ivory ground is a very special
feature, particularly on an old example; so,
too, are the designs used in the borders.
Nagel, Stuttgart
*Literature: Reed, no. 7 (as Salor); O'Bannon,
p. 66, pl. 6 (Kizil-Ayak torba with similar field
design)*

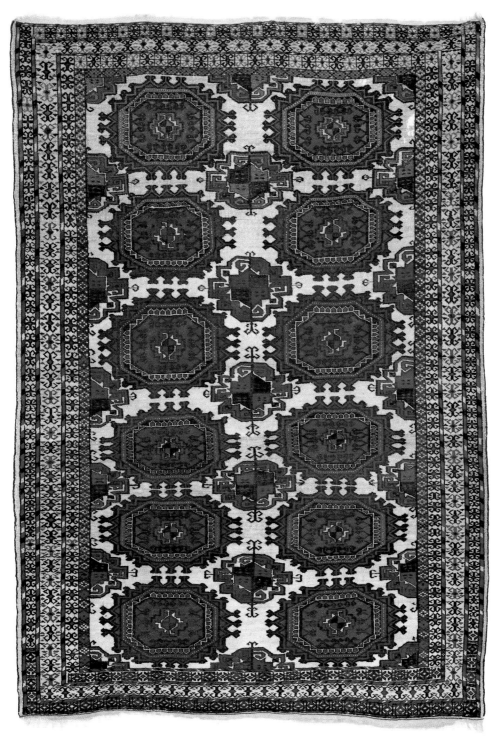

49

50

50. Tekke - Rug. End of the 19th century

Size: 109 x 94 cm.

This has the same ordered compartment field as no. 47. In the centre of each compartment is an *aina-kochak* gul, a hooked stepped polygon with an eight point star in its interior (see no. 33). In a more formal and simplified version it is repeated in the main border as a hooked cross-arm motif. Also like no. 47, each *elem* has a different pattern; the diamond lattice containing a three-stemmed shrub motif in the lower one is often found on Saryk weavings. In the outer guards on the long sides is the so-called *gul-aidi* pattern; here, in contrast to the next example illustrated, it is flat-woven in what is often called the 'border technique'. The structure is typically Tekke: the warp and weft are of finely plied ivory wool, the knotting is asymmetric open to the right with symmetric edging knots; it is very finely knotted with about 4,200 knots per dm^2.

Nagel, Stuttgart

51. Tekke - *Namazlik*. Second half of the 19th century

Size: 125 x 103 cm.

51

As on the previous piece, the principal motif is the *aina-kochak* gul. The lay-out of the field, however, reminds one of so-called safs with rows of *mihrabs* (prayer niches). These *mihrabs* are outlined by white-ground gabled bands containing typical double-hooked elements. A very similar piece was in the Turkoman exhibition at the Musée de l'Homme, Paris, 1979, no, 6 and is supposed to have been made about 1860 in Ashkabad. The white-ground *gul-aidi* pattern strip at the lower end is piled (see no. 50). This rug has about 3,600 knots per dm^2.

Bausback, Mannheim

Literature: Art Populaire de turkménie, Musée de l'Homme, Paris, 1979, pl. 6; Tzareva, no. 47 (horse blanket)

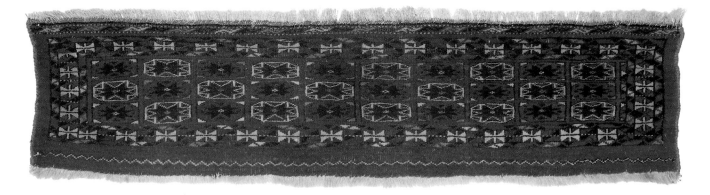

52

53

Yomut. The shimmering grid-like effect of the buff areas of the field are created by the use of natural camel's wool. Remnants of the original selvedges are, unusually, woven in a chequerboard pattern of red and blue; this is a common feature of Saryk weavings. This rug is very finely knotted on a foundation of ivory goat's hair
Nagel, Stuttgart
Literature: Loges, no. 10; Schürmann, pl. 31

54. Tekke - *Namazlyk*. Mid 19th century

Size: 106 x 90 cm.

Condition: some wear, edges damaged, areas of repiling.
Tekke prayer rugs are highly desirable collectors' pieces, especially when, as here, what is already a rare rug is rendered more so by the use of a white ground with a 'star' pattern and is also an early weaving. The layout is similar to that of no. 51 but here there are only three mihrabs. The design relationship to the Yomut *salachak* (no. 131) is striking. With this prayer rug, the art of Tekke weaving reaches a very high level.
Nagel, Stuttgart

52. Tekke - *Torba*. Second half of the 19th century

Size: 31 x 117 cm.

The division of the field into squares each containing a star is a pattern also found on Salor bags (see no. 11) as well as on those of the Saryk and Ersari. This bag has the characteristic colour of Tekke weavings from the last quarter of the 19th century; white and yellow are used to particularly good effect in the border. However, in contrast to many Tekke weavings from this period, it does not have multiple borders. Knotted in wool on an all wool foundation, it has about 1,600 knots per dm².
Bausback, Mannheim

53. Tekke - Small Rug. Second half of the 19th century

Size: 107 x 116 cm.

Condition: wear and restorations.
Judging by its structure, this Tekke small rug with 'star' pattern should be attributed to the Tekke. However, as with Tekke weavings with white grounds (see no. 49), there is a problem with this attribution. Rugs in a similar format and with similar designs, but using the symmetric knot, are made by the Yomut. However, rugs attributed in the past to them can have either symmetric or asymmetric knotting, although those of the latter type are now considered to represent a weaving culture distinct from that of the

54

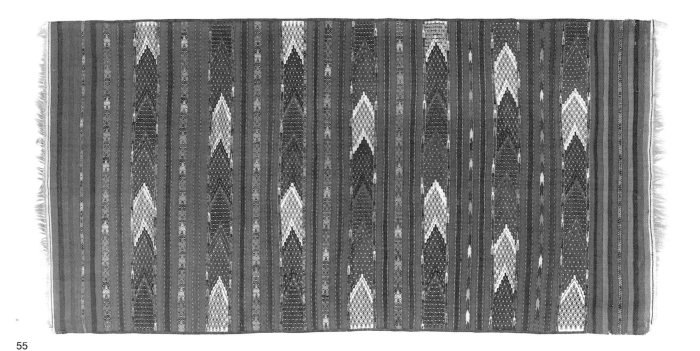

55

55. Flatweave. End of the 19th century

Size: 302 x 149 cm.

Condition: traces of wear around the edges.
Flatweaves of this type are often attributed to
the Yomut, but some very finely woven and
early examples have also been ascribed to the
Tekke. It seems likely that weavings of this
type were actually produced by several tribal
groups. The basic structure is slit-tapestry
(kilim) technique, although there is also a
considerable amount of brocading. Rugs of
this design are sometimes compared to
Anatolian *safs* (multiple mihrab prayer rugs)
and have actually been described as such by
some writers (see no. 217).
Nagel, Stuttgart
*Literature: McMullan (1969), pl. 75;
Gombos, fig. 15; Lefevre, pl. 27.*

56. Tekke - Main Carpet. pre-1890

Size: 211 x 145 cm.

When previously published, this rug was
attributed to the 18th century. The striped
field pattern seems to be a clear case of a
flatweave design being transferred to pile rug
(see also no. 73). As we noted in the previous
caption, flatweaves of this design have been
attributed to both the Tekke and the Yomut.
Another pile carpet of this design was
formerly in the Straka Collection (cat. no. 3)
in the United States and is now in the Textile
Museum, Washington; this latter rug is
usually attributed to the Yomut but is
structurally different from the rug shown
here, being woven on an all-wool foundation
with asymmeric knots open to the right in
about half the density of our rug. In addition
to wool, this piece has camel wool, cotton and
silk in its structure and has a knot density of
about 3,600 per dm^2.
Bausback, Mannheim

56

57

57. Tekke - *Ensi*. 19th century

Size: 141 x 127 cm.

In general composition, very similar to the following *ensi*, which also has the 'animal tree' motif, the latter being one of thirteen examples listed some years ago (see Pinner and Franses, pl. 322). The upper edge of the present piece is finished with a flatwoven end, an unusual feature for a Tekke *ensi*; a fine zig-zag pattern is formed by two differently coloured threads being used as a form of extra wefting. Such is their rarity that it is difficult to place a value on Tekke *ensis* with this highly regarded design variant.
Nagel, Stuttgart

58. Tekke - *Ensi*. 19th century

Size unknown

This *ensi* is another of the few examples known with the distinctive 'animal-tree' motif repeated immediately above the *elem* at the lower end of the rug. Pinner and Franses knew of only 13 examples when they wrote their essay 'The Animal Tree Ensi' in 1980. They concluded that they may have been made for specific occasions since there seems to be no homogeneity of either structure or age - some examples are clearly later than others.
Courtesy *Hali*
Lit: *Pinner and Franses, pp. 134 ff.; Hoffmeister, no. 20*

59

60. Tekke - *Ensi*. Second half of the 19th century

Size: 132 x 108 cm.

Condition: very good.
From no other tribe but the Tekke have so many *ensis* with this distinctive cross-like field survived. However, as was discussed in connection with nos. 57 and 58, examples with distinctive design variations seem for the most part to be early; they are certainly rare and seldom appear on the market. The rarity of this *ensi* is to be found in the use of the large blue motifs in the long borders and, in a variant form and size, in the top border; this tree-like ornament echoes those used in the four central panels, the *inskuch* motif. As on a comparable rug illustrated in Loges and dated to the first half of the 19th century, these latter motifs are arranged in pairs within each 'bar'. The *elem* at the base has the typical pattern of 'figure of eight' rosettes.
Nagel, Stuttgart
Literature: Loges, no. 4

59. Tekke - *Ensi*. End of the 19th century

Size: 147 x 133 cm.

Condition: minimal traces of wear.
This is a typical example of a Tekke *ensi* from this period. The inner square is divided into four separate field areas, decorated with the *insikush* pattern. The horizontal cross-beam is divided into three stripes, with diagonally arranged hooked motifs. In the top and bottom borders are typical *gapyrga* trees with *dogdan* heads; in the long borders, there is what can be read as one tree with many upward-pointing branches. The outer guard border, which appears on only three sides in an arch-like fashion, contains the almost obligatory *sainak* compartment pattern accompanied by various minor ornaments and motifs which include, on the right, highly stylised animal and human figures. The dark brown ground of the lower *elem* panel is also typical, with a tightly arranged repeated pattern of 'figure-of-eight' rosettes, with a single white brocaded line at the base.
Nagel, Stuttgart
Literature: Danker Collection, cat. pl. 106; Azadi, pl. 18

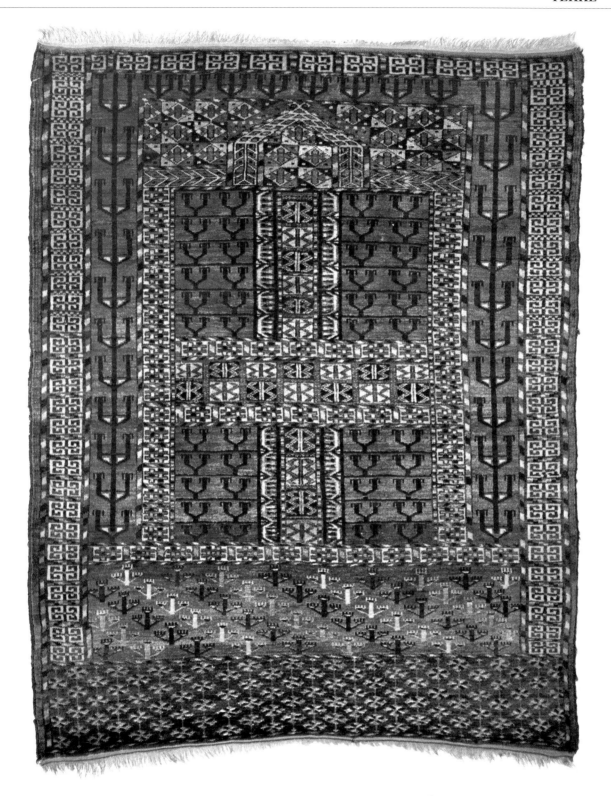

60

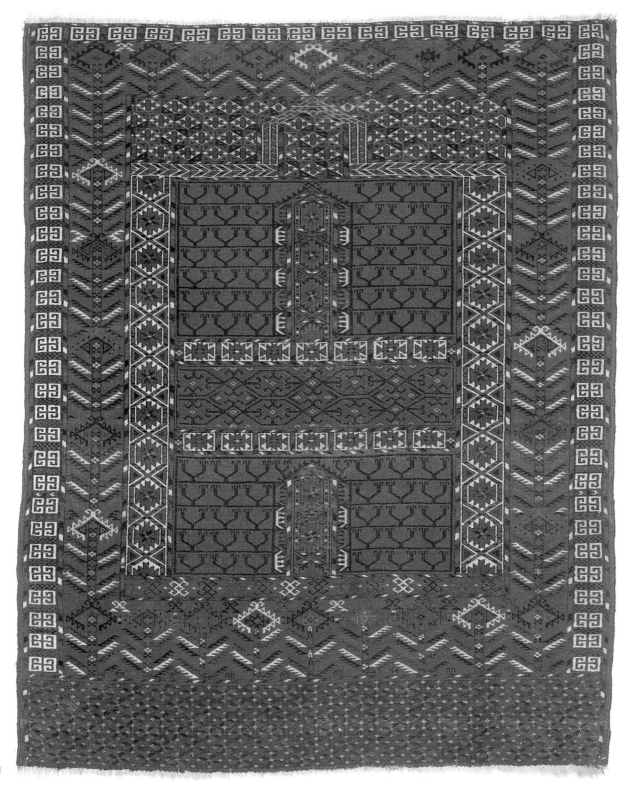

61

61. Tekke - *Ensi*. About 1900

Size: 148 x 119 cm.

Condition: worn thin in places.
A very stiffly drawn piece, with the overall design composed in almost too exact a manner. One interesting design feature, is the blue open red trellis-like pattern in the central and widest of the three horizontal bars in the middle of the field; this is flanked by narrow bars containing the *ashik* compartment pattern, which unusually, do not have designs which correspond to that usually found in the inner minor borders. The latter contains a continuous series, on the long sides, of saw-edged motifs in a stylised white 'vine'; the saw-edged motifs are echoed more closely, although in slightly variant form, in the two mihrab-like vertical bars in the centre of the field. This rug is very finely knotted.
Nagel, Stuttgart
Literature: Ettinghausen, no. 36; Tzareva, fig. 34

62

62. Tekke - *Ensi*. End of the 19th century

Size: 161 x 127 cm.

Condition: Worn thin in places.
What look like spontaneous and deliberate deviations from the usual arrangement of motifs on Tekke *ensis* appear again and again. This variation forms a group as distinctive as those rarer design variants such as the 'animal-tree' *ensis* or those with three small arches at the top of the field. In this particular design variant, of which a small number are known, the usual four central fields are further subdivided into a total of eight, each of which usually contains the *insikuch* motif and which alternate with bars containing the *dogdan* motif.
Nagel, Stuttgart
Literature: Hubel, col. pl. 23

63

63. Tekke - *Chuval*. First half of the 19th century

Size: 78 x 120 cm.

This represents one of the four main design groups of Tekke *chuvals* (see "Some Aspects of the Tekke Chuval" in Mackie and Thompson, pp. 203 ff.); this design type has a repeated pattern of large turreted motifs known as the 'Salor gul'. For a long time, all early examples with this motif were regarded as Salor work. However, there is a great aesthetic, as well as technical, difference between the genuine Salor examples (see no. 6) and those made by the Tekke. Examples by the latter in this design are usually very finely knotted, and have a velvety pile and a pleasingly restrained palette. The much higher knot density along the warps than along the wefts gives the guls their flattened look. The design in the *elem* panel at the base is unusual.

Bausback, Mannheim
Literature: Azadi, pl. 19; Loges, no. 9

64. Tekke - *Chuval*. Mid 19th century

Size: 61 x 112 cm.
Condition: worn thin in places; sides partly cut.
As with the previous example, the field of this *chuval* has six 'Salor guls' with *shararch-palak* minor guls (see detail no. 64a). The centres of both the major and minor guls are piled in cochineal-dyed silk, which is also used sparingly in the inner minor guard. This insect-dyed silk has corroded with age, something which actually adds to the charm of this piece.
Nagel, Stuttgart
Literature: Mackie and Thompson, nos. 31 and 32; Thatcher, pl. 5; Straka Collection, cat. no. 12 (in the latter two cases described as Salor)

65. Tekke - *Chuval*. Around 1900

Size: 69 x 130 cm.

Condition: good, although an area of reknotting in the upper border.
Unlike the two previously illustrated, and earlier, examples, this chuval has a 3 x 3 arrangement of guls in its field; it has the *shararch-palak* minor gul which usually has the *gelin-barmak* motif in its interior; here, however, the four complete minor guls have a motif in their interior called the *aina-kochak*. This is a characteristic example of its period, with a large number of border stripes containing complex patterns. Another pointer to its late date is the crowding of the *ashik* pattern in the *elem*.
Nagel, Stuttgart
Literature: Turkmenenforschung, Vol. XII, no. 77 ('Ashkabad Region').

64

Detail 64a

65

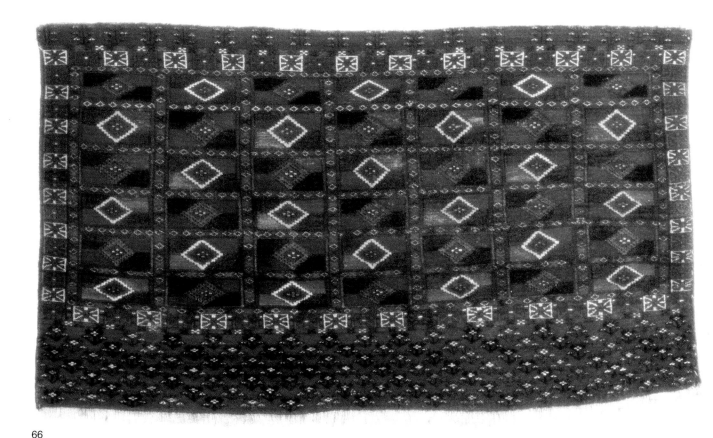

66

66. Tekke - *Chuval*. Mid 19th century

Size: 66 x 108 cm.

Condition: the areas piled in silk have partly corroded.

This example introduces the second major design type of Tekke *chuvals*. The inner field is divided into small rectangular compartments each of which contains a single motif; the latter are usually the *aina gul*, the *aina-kochak* or, as here, the *sekme* gul. Chuvals woven towards the end of the 19th century tend to have a great number of guls in the field, and this applies also to the compartment design group; however, the increasing number of guls cannot be directly related to any chronological progression. The *chaikelbaigi* motif is the one most often found in the main border of early pieces, flanked by rows of hooked cross-arm motifs or the *kochanak* pattern; however, such motifs can also be found on quite late pieces. The quartering of the central compartments into two coloured fields set on the diagonal is quite usual; here, one of the two red areas is piled in chochineal-dyed silk and is placed in opposition to the other red area which is piled in dark red wool.

Nagel, Stuttgart

Literature: Hoffmeister, pl. 23; Mackie and Thompson, no. 41.

67

67. Tekke - *Mafrash*. 19th century

Size: 30 x 71 cm.

An early collectors' piece, comparable to no. 66; this weaving is in the small format of Turkoman bags called *mafrash* and has the *aina-kochak* gul in its field compartments. This is another early Tekke weaving with strong Salor features. It has a very high knot count, about 4,500 per dm^2; the foundations are mainly wool with areas of silk. Its owner believes it to be from the first half of the 19th century.
Bausback, Mannheim
Literature: Benardout, no. 29; Tzareva, no. 56

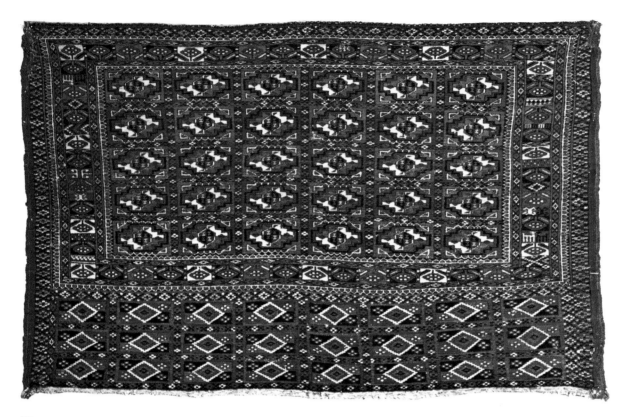

68

68. Tekke - *Chuval*. End of the 19th century

Size: 78 x 123 cm.

Condition: Usual areas of repair, patches on corners where the original hanging cords have been removed.

The field pattern here seems like an intermediate type between *chuvals* with 'compartment guls' and those with the *'chuval'* guls (see nos. 69 and 72). Unlike the large *'chuval'* guls with clearly defined hooked extensions on their axis (see no. 70), this is an example of a *chuval* with small guls. These are not placed diagonally on a quartered ground divided by colour, as on no. 69, nor are they free-standing. In two areas of the main border, there are opposed pairs of highly stylised animals.

Nagel, Stuttgart

Literature: Pinner and Franses, nos. 93 and 148

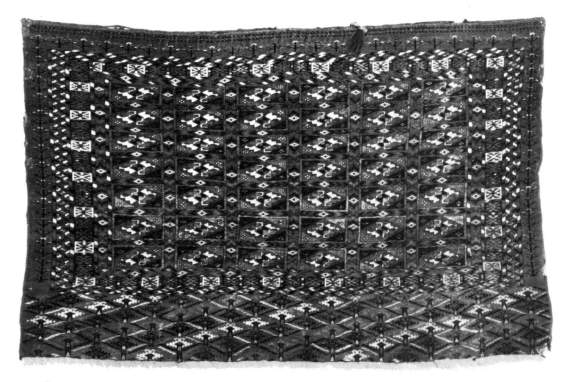

69

69. Tekke - *Chuval*. Second half of the 19th century

Size: 75 x 118 cm.

Condition: very good, the pile fully preserved, edge damage.
As on no. 68, the main field of this *chuval* has been arranged into compartments in the so-called *chamtos* pattern. These compartments contain the *aina-gul* in a 6 x 6 arrangement and cochineal-dyed silk has been used in the quartering. Instead of the 'figure-of-eight' rosette seen on no. 71 or the mosaic-like centre of no. 72, here the gul centres appear in simple quartered form. The small three-branch motifs in the upper outer border relate to the tree-like ornaments used down each narrow side guard. As is usual, the *ashik* forms in the *elem* panel at the base are arranged diagonally.
Nagel, Stuttgart
Literature: Thatcher, pl. 14

70

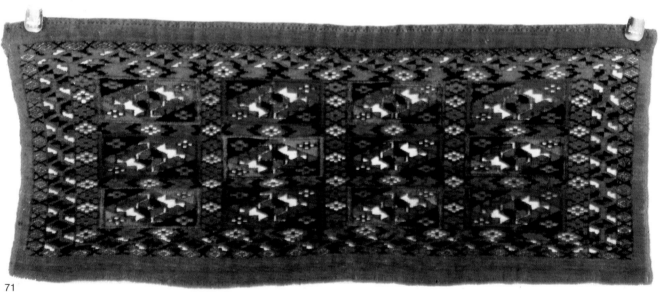

71

70. Tekke - *Mafrash*. Second half of the 19th century

Size: 30 x 71 cm.

Condition: slight wear, some repiling.
This small Tekke bag is reminiscent, in its principal ornament, of an early group of *torbas* with the large *chuval* gul (see nos. 81-3). There also the principal ornament is often used with the *chemche* minor gul and framed by a border containing the *kochanak* motif. On this piece the latter motif is slightly stylised. Each main gul has an eight-pointed star in its centre. An unusual feature is the *elem* at the base with its differently coloured trees. As well as wool, silk and white cotton have also been used in the pile as highlights; this combination of pile materials in Tekke bags is usually an indication of an origin in the second half of the 19th century.
Courtesy Christie's

71. Tekke - *Mafrash*. Second half of the 19th century

Size: 30 x 71 cm.

Condition: good for its age, but some areas have slightly rotted, possibly due to damp. Compared to no. 67, the colours here are somewhat darker. The principal ornament, also arranged in compartments, is the *aina-gul*. Silk and glowing white cotton has been used in some areas to highlight the design.
Courtesy Christie's, New York
Literature: Mackie and Thompson, no. 40; Thatcher, pl. 14; Hoffmeister, no. 52

72

Detail 72a

72. Tekke - *Chuval*. End of the 19th century

Size: 75 x 135 cm.

Condition: signs of wear, edges repaired.
One of the four main design groups of Tekke *chuvals* has the small variant of the *chuval* gul as a free-standing motif in the inner field. It is often accompanied by *chemche* minor guls, which are here linked together. The gul centres are arranged in twelve small triangular areas, an indication of a late weaving (see detail no. 72a). As on no. 68, the main border contains stylised shrubs called *sakar-gishik*. They reappear in the *elem* panel at the base pushing upwards and are shown from three sides in an axial variant. An unusual feature worth mentioning are the small stylised human figures which appear at the outer edge of the field (see no. 72a) as well as in the outer guard on the right. Very finely knotted.
Nagel, Stuttgart
Literature: Azadi, pl. 22a; Straka Collection, cat. no. 24

73

74

75

Detail 75a

73. Tekke - *Chuval* (?). Second half of the 19th century

Size: 77 x 129 cm.

Tekke *chuvals* with flatweave patterns are very unusual and rare (see nos. 55-56). Here we find it in combination with the *aina-kochak* pattern arranged in alternating rows. Although this might appear to be a *chuval*, given its format and construction, the end finish of the warps seems to indicate that this piece never had a flatwoven back. If viewed vertically, it could be interpreted as a small prayer rug. Very finely woven and soft to the touch. A rarity.
Nagel, Stuttgart
Literature: Reed, no. 17; Loges, no. 11

74. Tekke - *Chuval*. End of the 19th century

Size: 77 x 132 cm.

Condition: very slight wear and damage.
A very unusual design feature is the use in several rows of the *kejebe* repeat pattern. On *torbas* it is more often used in a single row (see no. 77). It can also be found on rare double bags of small format (no. 79) and, in even rarer cases, as the field pattern of Tekke main carpets. The piece has several shades of red, deep blue, an unusual amount of white and a little yellow used as highlights.
Nagel, Stuttgart
Literature: Milhofer, no. 40; Turkmenen-forschung, vol. XII, no. 76 ('Ashkabad Region')

75. Tekke - *Chuval*. End of the 19th century

Size: 68 x 119 cm.

Condition: damage caused by use at edges.
A compartment-like effect is achieved on the main field by the vertical linkage of the *chemche* secondary guls. The so-called '*chuval*' gul containing hooked cross motifs seems here like a simplification of the main motif on Saryk main carpets (see no. 17). An unusual variant of the *kochanak* pattern appears in the main borders at the sides. An attractive feature of this bag is the continuous animal frieze in the upper outer guard (see detail no. 75a). Complete with its original flatwoven back.
Nagel, Stuttgart
Literature: Hoffmeister, no. 24; Tzareva, no. 50

76

77. Tekke - *Torba*. Around 1900

Size: 32 x 80 cm.

Condition: good.
An example whose design is characteristic for its date. The small field within its section of *kejebe* pattern is surrounded by many borders containing tiny ornaments. There is an added *elem*-like strip along the bottom with *dogdan* motifs. The piece retains its original flatweave back but the alternately coloured fringes have been added. A unusual amount of white and yellow enlivens the look of the piece.
Nagel, Stuttgart
Literature: Pinner and Franses, no. 150

78. Tekke - *Torba*. End of the 19th century

Size: 28 x 99 cm.

Condition: good.
As can also be seen on no. 77, there is a tendency as the 19th century wears on for weavers to sacrifice the spaciousness of the field to multiple border stripes. This can get to the point where the field itself seems like a small stripe itself. There are Tekke *torbas* where the field consists of 2 or 3 compartment guls or, as here, the *ak-su* field repeat in a single strip (see nos. 14, 31 and 172). The pattern in the main border is one often used by the Saryk (see nos. 15-18). An added row of motifs along the lower edge (here the *kochanak* motif) is typical of Tekke *torbas* of this type; the piece retains its added fringes, side cords and two-coloured top cords for hanging.
Nagel, Stuttgart
Literature: Azadi, pl. 23d

76. Tekke - *Khorjin*. About 1900

Size: 72 x 39 cm.

Condition: typical damage to corners through use.
Only one *aina-kochak* compartment forms the field of each bag-face. In technique, it is the same as no. 79. There is an addititional guard at the base of the lower face containing an animal frieze, similar to the *chuval* no. 75. *Gul-aidi* brocaded amulets are used to ornament the natural white flatwoven ends.
Nagel, Stuttgart
Literature: Reinisch, no. 63 (with an inwoven date of either 1901 or 1921)

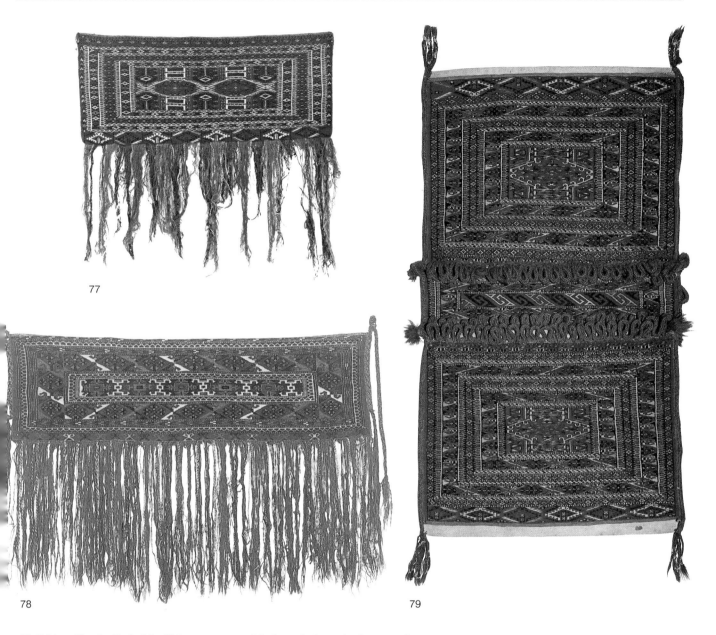

77

78   79

79. Tekke - *Khorjin*. End of the 19th century

Size: 86 x 46 cm.

Condition: excellent.
This Tekke double bag with piled faces and
middle section, was made in one piece. To
close the bags, cords could be run through
closing loops on the upper edge of the fronts
on either side of the central section. Within
the small fields of each bag-face, there is one
medallion from the *kejebe* repeat surrounded
by several narrow borders with different
patterns. The lower finishing panel (see no.

76) is typical, as is the use of
yellow for highlights. Tekke double bags - or
ones attributed to the Tekke - are also known
with 'Salor', '*chuval*', *aina* and *sekme-guls*.
These appear quite often on the market
although they rarely have pleasing colours.
Bausback, Mannheim
Literature: Reinisch,   no.   66;
Turkmenenforschung, vol. XII, no. 65

80

80. Tekke - *Chuval*. Second half of the 19th century

Size: 72 x 104 cm.

Condition: two small areas of repair; some edge damage.
Special types of Tekke *chuval* are those with a combination of flatweaving and piling. The flatwoven stripes, in either red or white, alternate with piled bands of different widths. Large format bags like this are called *ak* (white) *chuvals* if they have a piled white-ground *elem*. These base panels are usually patterned with *ashik* trees or with very stylised versions of these. Occasionally these *chuvals* have a very high knot count, sometimes exceeding 5,000 per dm^2.
Nagel, Stuttgart
Literature: Tzareva, no. 53; Moshkova, no. 58

81

81. Tekke - *Chuval*. Third quarter of the 19th century

Size: 77 x 120 cm.

Condition: some wear, damage to edges.
Like no. 80 in its combination of techniques, this example has only red flatwoven bands alternating with very finely knotted piled bands. As the lower panel has been left red, this type is called a *kizil* (red) *chuval*. Remarkably, these appear to be rarer than the *ak chuvals*. Both types have been attributed to the Yomut in previous publications. The top and side cord finishes are typical for both *ak* and *kizil chuvals*. Compare this with the all-flatwoven *chuvals* of the Yomut (detail no. 162a).
Nagel, Stuttgart
Literature: Housego, no. 132; Mackie and Thompson, no. 34 (entirely in pile) and pp. 211-214.

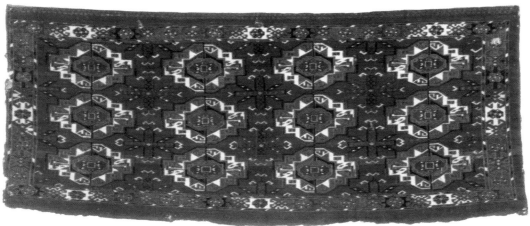

82

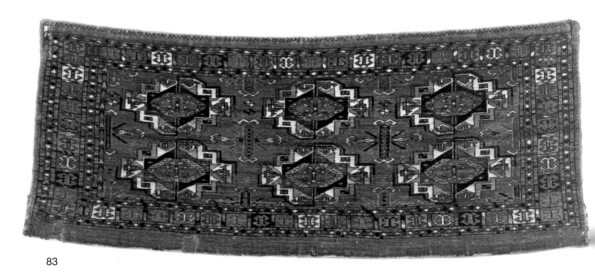

83

82. Tekke - *Torba*. Mid 19th century

Size: 47 x 116 cm.

Condition: worn.

A particular design group of Tekke *torbas* has the large *chuval* gul. Most of them seem to have been made in the second third of the 19th century. This piece, in contrast to the more 'classical' 3 x 3 lay out, has 3 x 4 guls. Because of its very fine knotting, the smallest details of the design are drawn with great precision; notice in particular the interesting design in the centre of the guls and the 'rosettes' of the typical *kochanak* main border. The piece has remarkably beautiful colour.

Nagel, Stuttgart

Literature: Azadi, pl. 20a (Collection of the Museum für kunst und gewerbe, Hamburg); Bernheimer, pl. 36

83. Tekke - *Torba*. Mid 19th century

Size: 46 x 119 cm.

Condition: traces of wear, repiling to the edges.

Like the following piece, this has a 3 x 2 arrangement of guls in the field. This is an excellent example of Tekke weaving art with all the distinguishing characteristics one looks for in this particular design group. The motifs are clearly drawn in a well-balanced composition, the piece has fine, silky, wool and very regular knotting. Compared to those

on the following example, the *chemche* minor guls are reduced in size. As is often found on early examples, the motif in the centre of the guls - here a *kochanak* variant - also appears also in the main border, the latter surrounded by a guard with repeated hexagons.

Nagel, Stuttgart

Literature: Lefevre, no. 5

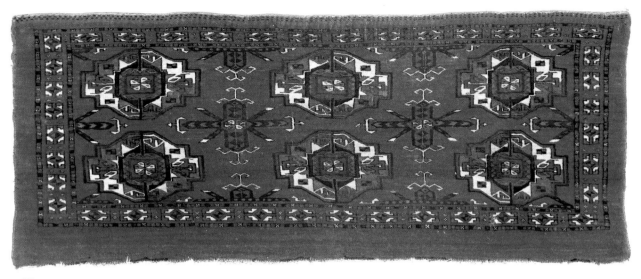

84

84. Tekke - *Torba.* **First half of the 19th century**

Size: 45 x 114 cm.

Condition: excellent.
Another typical example of this early group of Tekke bags; like the previous piece it has the classic 3 x 2 arrangement of guls in its field and has large *chemche* minor guls. Both the main border design here, and the *kochanak* variants seen on the previous two pieces, represent the most admired border designs of this group. Such bags are not only remarkable for their strong, clear and generously drawn motifs but also because of their texture, with thick, silky wool of great lustre. Compared to some of the Tekke bags shown earlier, their pile is quite long and therefore these pieces are very soft to the touch. It is rare for them to retain their added fringes in their entirety; their remains can be seen on this piece in alternating colours.
Nagel, Stuttgart
Literature: Mackie and Thompson, no. 35; Gombos, no. 37

85

86

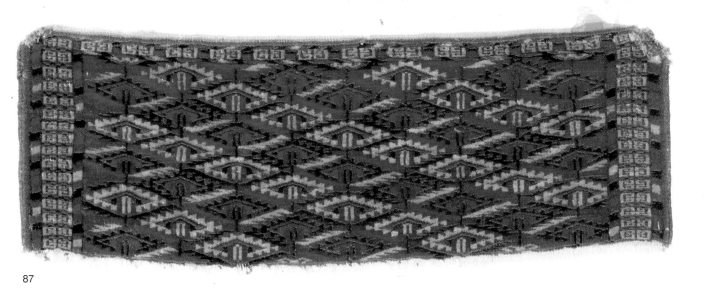

87

85. Tekke - *Mafrash*. 19th century

Size: 31 x 66 cm.

A comparison with the Salor *chuval* from the Russian Museum, St. Petersburg (no. 7) shows the close design relationship between early Tekke work and that of the Salor. Therefore, the dating by the owner of this example to the first half of the 19th century seems justified. An octagonal gul is placed in the field in a 4 x 3 arrangement, accompanied by a minor gul which is a variant of the cross-arm motif with a rhombus centre. The narrow main border with its finely decorated flanking guards is characteristic of early Tekke weaving (see no. 84). There is a partial use of silk in the pile, an unusual feature in early pieces.

Bausback, Mannheim

86. Tekke - *Mafrash*. End of the 19th century

Size: 29 x 76 cm.

Condition: good.
Although later, this piece, like the last, has rare octagonal guls. Here they have X-shapes in their centres which are placed on grounds quartered diagonally by colour (see Moshkova, pl. 57/6). In contrast to earlier but related pieces, the guls are crowded together on the small field, the latter surrounded by many narrow guards with a multiplicity of motifs. Tekke *chuvals* with similar patterns are known. The decorated *elem*-like panel at the base is typical as are the added fringes.
Nagel, Stuttgart
Literature: Turkmenenforschung, vol. XII, no. 75

87. Tekke - Bag Face (?)

Size: 30 x 84 cm.

Condition: typical corner damage, newly fringed-out at base.
It is not clear if this small Tekke pile weaving is a bag-face or not (see caption to no. 34). According to T. Cooper, the *ensi* which covered the tent entrance and the *germesh* which went above it form a distinct unit. This would explain why *ensis* often have areas of flat pattern in their centre panels and why this weaving, for example, has the *sainak* design in its side and top borders, the design typically found in the borders of Tekke *ensis*. The field of this weaving, however, does not have a typical *ensi* pattern, although it is one found typically in the *elem* panels of Tekke *chuvals* (see no. 75).
Nagel, Stuttgart
Literature: Azadi, pl. 23c

88

89

88. Tekke - *Mafrash*. Mid 19th century

Size: 23 x 60 cm.

Condition: Edges damaged, some holes and repiling.
With its white-ground rectangular fields, this *mafrash* represents a remarkable design type. Both *mafrashes* and *torbas* are found in this rare design, sometimes with 2, or as here, with 3 fields. The clearly drawn motif within them has been interpreted as a highly stylised 'animal-tree'. Similar weavings by the Yomut are known (see Tzareva, no. 61) and there is also evidence for the existence of a few white-ground *kapunuks* with 'animal-tree'

designs (see Pinner and Franses, pl. 406, by the Tekke; and *Hali* 37, p. 40, attributed to the Ersari). The main border design seen here seems to be standard on weavings with this field pattern. This is a piece of considerable interest in the history of Turkoman weaving.
Nagel, Stuttgart
Literature: Tzareva, no. 60; Hoffmeister, nos. 44-6; Azadi, pl. 27d

89. Tekke - *Mafrash*. 3rd quarter of the 19th century

Size: 33 x 84 cm.

Condition: minimal moth damage.
This *mafrash* has staggered rows of 'shrubs' in its field, a pattern often found on *kapunuks* or Tekke *khalyks* (see no. 90). A comparable weaving in the Victoria and Albert Museum, London is much more densely knotted. Again, the border pattern seems always to have been used on *mafrashes* with this field design. Another important documentary piece.
Nagel, Stuttgart
Literature: Tzareva, no. 60; Hoffmeister, nos. 44-6; Azadi, pl. 27d

90

90. Tekke - *Khalyk*. Mid 19th century

Size: 59 x 66 cm.

Condition: signs of age; signs of slight cutting on the pointed sides.
Khalyks were probably used to decorate the breast of the bride's camel in a bridal procession or possibly the elaborate sedan-chair in which she sat. Pinner and Franses, in their article 'The Turkoman Khalyk', discuss five design types which can be definitely attributed to the Tekke. A remarkable feature of this example are the small areas of pink silk and white cotton in the pile.
Nagel, Stuttgart
Literature: Pinner and Franses, pp. 192 ff.

91

92

93

91. Tekke - *Khalyk*. About 1870

Size: 54 x 38 cm.

Condition: areas of repair, splits.
Khalyks with *kotchanak* crosses in their fields are a known design group attributed to the Tekke; a rare exception is an example attributable to the Ersari (no. 276). This *kochanak* motif is also found in the central 'beams' of Tekke *ensis* as is this standard border design (see no. 59). The added fringe has been partly preserved.
Nagel, Stuttgart
Literature: Pinner and Franses, nos. 395-8; Loges, no. 12

92. Tekke - *Khalyk*. 19th century

Size: 84 x 31 cm.

Condition: repairs and repiling, but in full pile with remains of original fringe.
Of the three *khalyks* illustrated here, this is the rarest. The motif in the red ground field is the *kochanak,* although it is drawn in a different manner to that on the previous example. The border pattern is also similar; this pattern and also the more mosaic-like version seen in the triangular panel were also used by the Ersari. An important collectors' piece which some experts might date to the first half of the 19th century.
Courtesy Rippon Boswell
Literature: Pinner and Franses, no. 404 (Collection of the Völkerkünde Museum, Lübeck)

93. Tekke - *Kapunuk*. Mid 19th century or earlier

Size: 79 x 111 cm.

Condition: very good, tears to the triangular ends restored in good colour, minimal repiling.
The design of this typical *ashik* pattern Tekke *kapunuk* is very similar to that one the Saryk example (no. 35), although here it is less simplified and there is a richer use of colour. Remains of added fringe in several colours.
Nagel, Stuttgart
Literature: Azadi, 1986, no. 9; Pinner and Franses, no. 410

94

94. Tekke - *Asmalyk.* **Early 19th century**

Size: 61 x 122 cm.

Two distinct design types of Tekke *asmalyks* are known as 'bird' and 'animal-tree' because of particular motifs they bear in their fields; this is an example of the former group, of which only a very small number have appeared on the market since the late 1970s. In their article 'The Bird and Animal-Tree Asmalyks', Pinner and Franses demonstrate that all the examples with these designs can be attributed to the Tekke, principally because of their use of the asymmetric knot open to the right; they also suggest that they could be 18th century in date. The example shown here fetched $71,500 at auction in December, 1988.
Courtesy Christie's, New York
Literature: Pinner and Franses, pp. 114 ff.

95

95. Tekke - *Asmalyk*. 18th century

Size: 88 x 151 cm.

S.M. Dudin (1863-1926), one of the most
important collectors of Turkomans and one of
the pioneers of research into this culture, left
a collection of more than 200 pieces from
Central Asia, among them two pairs of 'bird'
asmalyks. The example shown here, like the
rest of the Dudin Collection, is now in the
Ethnographic Museum, St. Petersburg; the
noted Russian expert Elena Tzareva agrees
with a dating to the 18th century.
Courtesy *Hali*
Published: Tzareva, no. 44

96

96. Tekke - *Asmalyk*. About 1800

Size: 87 x 150 cm.

Condition: some restoration, upper and lower edges a little cut.

The 'animal-tree' motif may be one of the archetypes of weaving designs (see nos. 57-8). Pinner and Franses discussed this group as well as some rare Tekke *chuvals* and main carpets which have the 'animal-tree' motif. There are remarkable similarities between the 'curled leaf' design found in the main white-ground border and that found on a rare group of Caucasian carpets with the so-called 'shield' design. At auction in Germany in May, 1988, this extremely important piece fetched DM 69,600.

Courtesy Rippon Boswell

Literature: Pinner and Franses, nos. 231-5

97. Tekke - Pair of embroidered Asmalyks. Second half of the 19th century

Size: about 60 (70) x 130 (150) cm.

Condition: black areas partly corroded.

Several silk embroidered Tekke *asmayks* are known, although it is unusual to find them still in pairs. In their essay 'Embroidered Asmalyks', Pinner and Franses indicate that all *asmalyks* were originally made in pairs and the majority of surviving examples are by the Tekke. Like the piled 'bird' *asmalyk* (no. 95), these pieces have an attached brocaded band round three sides.

Nagel, Stuttgart

Literature: Pinner and Franses, nos. 352 and 362-4

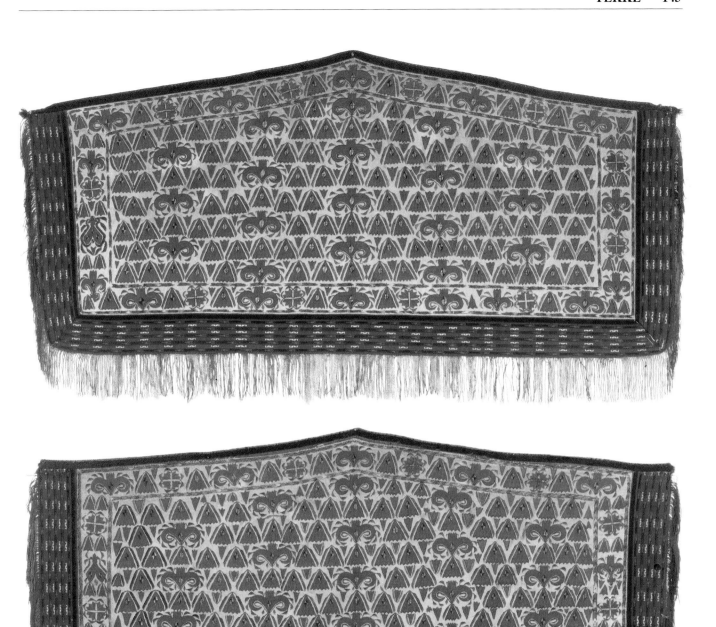

PILE WEAVINGS OF THE YOMUT AND SURROUNDING REGIONS

The term 'Yomut' is very often used as a convenient label rather than as the identification of a historically accurate tribal group. Despite numerous attempts in the past, it has so far been impossible to work out a precise classification system. With some types of Yomut weavings it is not even certain whether they are Yomut at all. This is made more difficult by an unusually broad range of shapes, design types and very different technical characteristics.

Numerous more or less definable sub-tribes and related groups of the largely settled Yomut have been mentioned in the literature: the Atabai, the Jaffarbai, the Imreli and the Ogurjali, to name only a few. It seems more sensible to restrict oneself to the definition of clearly distinct groups of pile weavings without making tribal attributions; this has, for example, been attempted with the 'Eagle gul' groups (nos. 113 etc.).

98

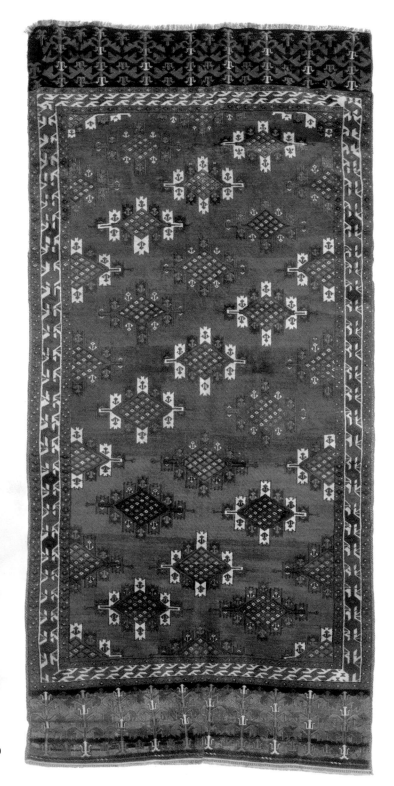

99

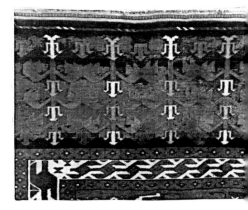

Detail 99a

99. Yomut - Main Carpet. 1st half of the 19th century

Size: 304 x 145 cm.

Condition: areas piled in brown severely corroded, worn, repiled areas.
At the centre of each *kepse* gul are mosaic-like, concentric rhombuses. This rug is impressive for its clear colours and for the very tribal nature of the design in its deep brown-ground *elem* panels; these grounds have become almost totally corroded, perhaps due to damp, but this has created a pleasing relief effect (see detail no. 99a).
Nagel, Stuttgart
Literature: Straka Collection, cat no. 1

100. Yomut - Main Carpet. 1st half of the 19th century

Size: 298 x 175 cm.

Inside each of the *kepse* guls seen here is a hooked cross motif diagonally set; as on no. 98, this motif appears in the rows at either end cut by the main white-ground border. The hooked, angular, vine-like design in the main border is often called the 'boat' pattern. However, this is a Turkoman variation on the vine patterns with palmettes or cloudbands found on Persian, Caucasian and Anatolian rugs (see no. 283a).
Galerie Ostler

100

101

101. Yomut - Main Carpet. Mid 19th century

Size: 298 x 153 cm.

Condition: worn, some repiling.
Controversy still exists about the significance of so-called 'eagles' or 'eagle' guls found on some carpets attributed by many writers in the past to the Yomut; such motifs appear here in the *elem* panels at either end of the rug. Some authors maintain their relationship to the 'double-headed eagle' motif; others consider its origin to be the Chinese *toa-tie* motif, a talismanic animal figure which usually appears in the form of an animal mask. It is worth, however, considering a derivation from palmette motifs.
Nagel, Stuttgart
Literature: Hoffmeister, no. 2

102. Yomut - Main Carpet. 19th century

Size: 250 x 159 cm.

Condition: worn through age, restorations, damage to sides.

In terms both of colour and of some elements of the composition, this is a very unusual *kepse* gul Yomut main carpet. Particularly striking are the dark blue main border and the *atanak* pattern in the flanking guards which also frame the *elem* panels. These anomalous elements of design as well as the clear, rich, colours, make it difficult to date the rug, although it is certainly early. The warps and wefts are of wool and it is quite finely knotted, with about 2,400 symmetric knots per dm^2.

Nagel, Stuttgart

Literature: McCoy Jones and Boucher, 1976, no. 119

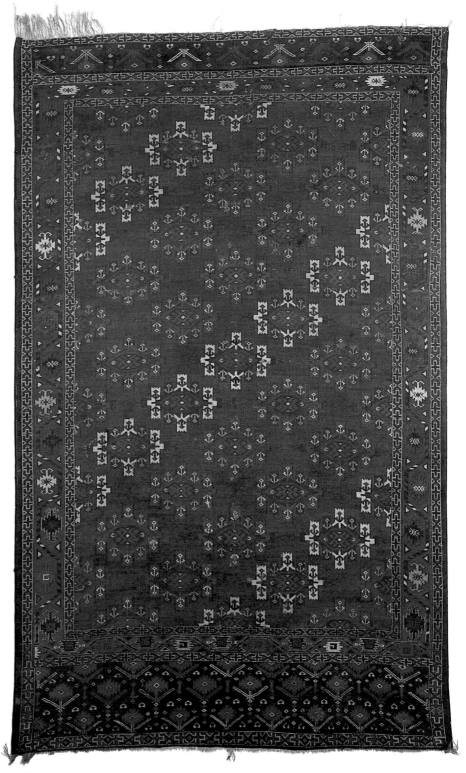

102

103

103. Yomut - Main Carpet. End of the 19th century

Size: 187 x 135 cm.

Condition: light moth damage, traces of wear, repaired and repiled areas.

From the late 19th century, the Yomut seem to have mostly used a dark ground colour and the repeated guls in the field are crowded closer together. Compared with the Yomut main carpets just illustrated, it is difficult to recognise the *kepse* guls as separate entities, despite the fact they are large and have the expected details. The so-called Yomut 'eagles' in the *elem* panels look like they have been squashed into too small an area. Small opposing triangles in the *ashik* pattern main border have been left as negative-space counterpoints to the vine pattern which runs in the opposite direction (see no. 101). Here, the flanking guards, rather than the main border, have white grounds.

Nagel, Stuttgart

104. Yomut - Main Carpet. End of the 19th century

Size: 298 x 188 cm.

Condition: traces of wear, repaired areas.

A comparable rug (Troost, pl. 61) has been dated to the second half of the 19th century. On that rug, as on this, the *dyrnak* gul appears in two variants and creates a tile-like effect on the field. In contrast to the following rug, the guls with 'anchor' motifs do not dominate those with a hooked rhombus in their centre. The meandering vine pattern in the main border is set with pronged spikes instead of the usual animal heads; this surrounds *ashik* forms with enclosed *kochanaks* with spiral hooks. In the short borders, this composition is drawn in a compartmentalised manner, as is usual.

Nagel, Stuttgart

104

105

105. Yomut - Main Carpet. Last quarter of the 19th century

Size: 315 x 190 cm.

Condition: very good.

Here the *dyrnak* gul also appears in two variants although the large ones with 'anchor' motifs predominate. An interesting feature is that the colour of the guls' hooks are not arranged diagonally opposite each other; instead, they are finely drawn in red and white and, in the upper three quarters of the field, surrounded by finely drawn contour lines (compare this rug to the *ertman* gul carpets of the Chodor). On white goat's hair warps and with a double weft of red-brown wool, it has about 1,800 knots to the dm^2. At both long sides are red flatwoven finishes and an outer red and blue chequerboard-pattern selvedge.

Nagel, Stuttgart

Literature: McCoy Jones and Boucher, 1976, no. 14

106. Yomut - Main Carpet. Last quarter of the 19th century

Size: 321 x 187 cm.

Condition: very good.

The concentrically drawn *dyrnak* guls with the centres chromatically quartered, are the principal motifs in the field; they are arranged in tile-like alternate rows and are diagonally arranged according to the variations in colour. On pieces previously illustrated, this version appears as a minor gul. The typically white-ground main border has *ashik* motifs, with double hooks at either end on the vertical axis. The broad *elem* panels have the Yomut 'eagle' motif. The carpet retains its original flatwoven edge at the top and it has the remains of hanging cords.

Nagel, Stuttgart

Literature: Danker Collection, cat. no. 104

106

107

107. Yomut Group - Main Carpet. 1st half of the 19th century or earlier

Size: 275 x 171 cm.

Condition: worn, repiled areas.
Of all the carpets with the *dyrnak* gul which are illustrated here, this is undoubtedly the earliest. The pattern in the *elem* panels is striking; large tree-like forms such as these constitute some of the most beautiful *elem* designs of early weavings attributed to the Yomut group (see no. 152). In colour and structure, this carpet is similar to the one with *tauk nuska* guls illustrated as no. 110; both were probably made in the same period. Its warps are goat's hair; the weft shoots are of cotton alternating with goat's hair. It has about 2,400 symmetric knots per dm^2.
Nagel, Stuttgart
Literature: Mackie and Thompson, no. 42

108. Yomut - Main Carpet. 2nd third of the 19th century

Size: 268 x 169 cm.

Condition: worn, restorations, the ends a little cut.
The minor gul on this carpet looks like an amalgam of the gul centre seen on no. 99 with the hooked outlines of the *dyrnak* gul. The major gul, however, is the so-called *tauk nuska*, variations of which also appear on Arabachi weavings, as well as those of the Chodor and Ersari. Compared to other design groups of Yomut main carpets, those with the *tauk nuska* gul seem to have a greater knot density.
Nagel, Stuttgart
Literature: Hali, vol. 4, no. 4, p. 391; McCoy Jones and Boucher. 1976, no. 17

108

109. Yomut - Main Carpet. 2nd third of the 19th century

Size: 271 x 159 cm.

Condition: worn very thin in places, repaired areas, damage to edges.

The main guls, of *tauk nuska* design, have chromatically quartered, hooked cross centres. The minor gul is a *chemche*. The main border contains the so-called 'boat' vine pattern. The *gapyrga* pattern is used in the *elem* panels, this being sometimes referred to colloquially as the Yomut 'fir tree'; the small stylised human figure in one of the upper corners is unusual.

Nagel, Stuttgart

Literature: Martin, 1984, no. 31; Schürmann, no. 19

109

**110. Yomut Group - Main Carpet.
19th century**

Size: 244 x 171 cm.

A very early and extremely rare carpet from
the Yomut 'family'. It has above average
knotting for a rug with symmetric knots,
having about 2,450 per dm^2; because of this,
its colour and its mixed cotton and goat's hair
warps, it has been attributed to the Ogurjali,
apparently a sub-tribe of the Yomut. Unlike
the attributions made in respect of other
Yomut pieces, this attribution is debatable. A
very important Turkoman main carpet.
Bausback, Mannheim

110

111. Yomut Group - Main Carpet. 19th century

Size: 275 x 173 cm.

Very few carpets are known, whose fields are decorated with the octagonal gul used here. As to the question of its origin, from its structure, the style of its motifs, its colour and, also, from lack of evidence to the contrary, it seems safe to label this piece as a Yomut. It has warps of grey-brown wool, and mixed wefts of dark brown animal hair and cotton; it has about 1,800 symmetric knots per dm².
Bausback, Mannheim
Literature: Hali 32, p. 23 (Ashmolean Museum, Oxford); McMullan Collection, 1968, cat. no. 71, pl. 126.

111

112. Yomut - Main Carpet. 2nd half of the 19th century

Size: 275 x 165 cm.

In the field of this extremely rare example, the *dyrnak* gul is combined with a motif which also appears in the field of the famous old carpet in the Metropolitan Museum of Art, New York (no. 59) in a stretched variant form. Here it is chromatically quartered on the diagonal with a small double-cross motif in each section. The pattern in the *elem* panels is reminiscent of Tekke weavings, but it also belongs to the design repertoire of the Yomut. Pakzad
Literature: Schürmann, no. 25; Mackie and Thompson, nos. 62 and 38 ('Imreli')

112

113. Yomut - 'Eagle Group' Main Carpet. 19th century or earlier

Size: 218 x 165 cm.

Carpets of this design have been called by various names including 'Ogurjali' (Schürmann, pl. 24), 'Imreli' (Thompson, no. 56); 'Eagle Group' and 'Göklan' (Azadi); such attributions have been much discussed in recent years. The main motif seen here is the so-called 'eagle' gul (see fig. 88).

Bausback, Mannheim

Note to the English edition: since the German edition of this book appeared, weavings of this type have been gathered together in a monograph by Rautenstengel and Azadi, *Kultur der Turkmen*, 1990, where they are called 'Eagle Group' and divided into three distinct sub-groups by structure. This example is described as 'Eagle Group III' and appears as pl. 19. There seems to be no consistent structure for weavings included in 'Eagle Group III' other than the fact that they are all asymmetrically knotted.

114. Yomut - 'Eagle Group' Main Carpet. Around 1800

Size: 312 x 189 cm.

The two forms of *dyrnak* gul appear in the field of this carpet, together with the so-called 'Eagle' gul. A comparable piece with this combination of field motifs and the 'boat' border was attributed by Mackie and Thompson to the Imreli because of its asymmetric knots open to the left. The 'eagle' gul itself has often been compared to the 'sunburst' motif found on many Caucasian carpets.

Ostler, Munich

Literature: Loges, no. 39; McMullan Collection, 1972, cat. no. 123, pl 46; Moshkova, pl. 59 ('variation of the dyrnak gul')

Note to the English edition: see note to 113 above. Illustrated by Rautenstengel and Azadi as 'Eagle Group II', pl. 12.

114

115. Yomut - Main Carpet. 1st half of the 19th century

Size: 317 x 177 cm.

Condition: worn in places, repiled areas.
The rhomboidal gul with zig-zag outlines and octagonal centres used here has certain parallels with motifs found on early Caucasian carpets. These unusual main guls are arranged here diagonally by colour, and staggered to form a tile-like pattern. The quartered centre of each gul is surrounded by 'C'-shaped *naldag* motifs (see no. 116). The white-ground main border contains *ashik* motifs and is flanked by minor guards containing the 'running dog' pattern.
Courtesy *Hali*, London (Lefevre archive)
Literature: Mackie and Thompson, no. 66; Schürmann, no. 16

115

116. Yomut - Main Carpet. 1st half of the 19th century

Size: 294 x 167 cm.

Different versions of the gul seen on this carpet are found, in some instances the pure 'C'-gul version seen here, in other instances variations of the *kepse* gul. The name 'C'-gul is derived from the small shapes within each gul, these being known as the *naldag* motif; the dark 'frame' to each gul has a zig-zag outline on its upper and lower edges, this presumably being derived from palmettes. The main border design, with its bird or palmette extensions, is unusual, as is the small human figure in the field almost halfway down on the left.

Sailer, Salzburg

Literature: Tzareva, no. 66

117. Yomut - Main Carpet. End of the 19th century

Size: 168 x 113 cm.

Condition: good.

The main motif seen in the field of this small Yomut main carpet is obviously a simplified variant of the *kepse* gul, in which two of the zig-zag areas of the *kepse* outline are arranged in opposition and have the 'anchor' motif (see no. 103). The colour has also been arranged diagonally. The motifs in the *elem* panel are late versions of a form orginally with four arrow-like shapes at the side called the *erre* gul by Moshkova; according to Troost, it is a motif typical of weavings by the Atabai, a sub-tribe of the Yomut, which supposedly settled at the turn of the century in the neighbourhood of Serachs alongside the Tekke, Salor and Saryk.

Nagel, Stuttgart

Literature: Moshkova, pl. 68/15; Gombos, no. 13 (with small variants of the dyrnak gul)

118

118. Yomut - Small Rug. 1st half of the 19th century or earlier

Size: 109 x 169 cm.

Condition: Full pile, minimal reweaves. When sold at auction in Germany in 1986, this well-known and extremely unusual rug was catalogued as being around 1800; at that time it made DM 104,400. The pattern of the field, divided into compartments each containing a cross, is immediately reminiscent of the field of the Pazyryk carpet in the Hermitage Museum, Leningrad, datable to around the 5th century B.C. (see figs. 89-90).
Courtesy Rippon Boswell
Published: Danker Collection, cat no. 109; Schürmann, pl. 20

119. Yomut - Small Main Carpet. 1st quarter of the 20th century

Size: 176 x 109 cm.

Condition: Very good.

Pakzad noted, when writing about a comparable piece, that it was mainly the Atabai and Jaffarbai sub-tribes of the Yomut who settled in the northerly part of eastern Persia and that their principal market town was, and still is, Gombad-i-Kabus. Characteristic features of Turkoman weavings made in Persia are the glowing rich red ground colour and the extensive use of dark blue and ivory. Both the series of borders and the *elems* show very dense patterning, another typical feature. This example has a relatively high knot count of 2,800 symmetric knots per dm². There is what would appear to be an inwoven signature in the lower *elem*.
Nagel, Stuttgart
Literature: Pakzad, 1978, pp. 347 ff.; McCoy Jones and Boucher, 1976, no. 24

**120. Yomut - Small Main Carpet.
Around 1900**

Size: 169 x 127 cm.

Condition: very good.

Like both the previous example and the
following one, this rug was probably woven
in northeast Persia. The main gul is of the
'Salor gul' type, the minor gul being the
dovodov (see no.7) which is sometimes called
the 'Jaffarbai gul'. The white ground main
border contains a pattern based on a star
pattern which seems to have been very
popular with this group of weavers. The piece
is finely knotted on a goat's hair warp.
Nagel, Stuttgart
Literature: Pakzad, no. 263

120

121. Yomut - *Salachak*. End of the 19th century

Size: 109 x 75 cm.

The primary gul used on no. 120 predominates here also and is arranged in the centre of the field on the vertical axis. The minor guls of this six-sided prayer rug or cradle rug are cut by the borders and indicate an infinite repeat; above the central field is a gable embedded into a panel with a mosaic-like pattern (compare *ensis*) which also appears in the base panel.
Nagel, Stuttgart
Literature: Straka Collection, cat. no. 45 (with Göklen features)

121

122. Yomut - *Salachak*. Around 1900

Size: 144 x 123 cm.

Condition: very good.

Weavings of this type are most often
attributed to the Göklen or the Jaffarbai
Yomut. The pattern seen in the field seems
obviously derived from flatweaves and has
probably been transposed from a slit-tapestry
(kilim) into pile (see nos. 124-126).
Interestingly there is an inwoven date in the
small white-ground gable at the top; this reads
1387 AH (1967 AD). The *boteh* pattern used
at the top of the piece shows the Persian
influence; it also appears occasionally on
Yomut horse-blankets and saddle-covers.
Nagel, Stuttgart
*Literature: Tzareva, no. 103; Beresneva, pl.
16; Straka Collec*

Note to the ⌐ 　　　　　　　　　　　on to
the 　　　　　　　　　　　　　　　　ire.

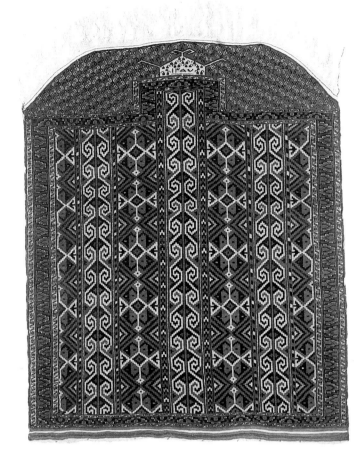

122

123. Yomut - *Eyerlik*. End of the 19th century

Size: 49 x 60 cm.

Condition: very good.

As seen on the *salachak* just illustrated, this
weaving also has a pattern consisting of
motifs with stepped outlines, an indication
that it has been borrowed from a weaving in
the kilim technique. The two main areas of
the field are considered by Moshkova to show
a pattern typical of the western Yomut; the
tree-like *ak-nagysh* pattern in the centre is
flanked by guards containing the *ak-gas*
motifs resembling vertebrae. It has a thick
velvety handle.
Nagel, Stuttgart

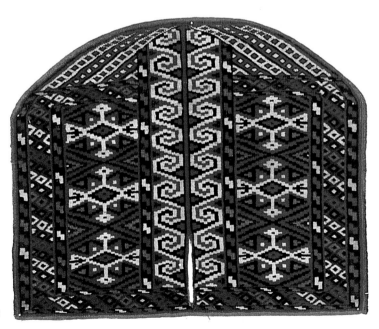

123

124

124. Yomut - Flatweave. Beginning of the 20th century

Size: 190 x 97 cm.

Condition: very good.

A characteristic flatweave in the colour palette normal to the type. Flatweaves from the second half of the 19th century are usually wider in format and are almost always in the slit-tapestry (kilim) technique with a relatively sparse use of cotton in the white areas. Towards the end of the 19th century, however, such weavings become narrower, with broader patterned bands in the kilim technique with narrower dividing bands in the so-called *oidume* technique, a form of brocading. The border is also worked in this latter technique.

Nagel, Stuttgart

Literature: Milhofer, no. 77

125. Yomut - Main Carpet. End of the 19th century

Size: 239 x 127 cm.

Condition: very good, a small amount of damage to the upper flatwoven end.

Unlike no. 124, this carpet is piled and is an example of the so-called 'banded Yomut' design. Instead of the minor bands having the *ak-nagysh* pattern, they contain a meander pattern, a form of the 'running dog' pattern; the major bands have the *ak-gas* pattern. In this piled version, all the diagonals are stepped, a feature technically necessary to examples in the kilim technique but here simply transposed as a design feature. Symmetrically knotted in quite a high density, these 'banded Yomuts' are usually attributed to the Jaffarbai.

Nagel, Stuttgart

Literature: Azadi, pl. 17

125

126. Yomut - *Oshak-bashi*. End of the 19th century

126

Size: 234 x 191 cm.

Like no. 118, this weaving is exceptionally rare; indeed, very few examples of these so-called 'hearth surround' rugs are known in any pattern. The *ak-nagysh* ornament, in contrast to the previous two pieces, is the only motif used in the field. It made DM 8,600 at auction in Germany in 1979 but in the light of recent knowledge, it is almost certainly worth many times that today.
Nagel, Stuttgart
Orientteppich-haus, Wedel
Literature: Bennett, 1982, p. 158; Troost, no, 58 (identical); Danker Collection, cat. no. 105; Rudenko, nos. 34-5

127

127. Yomut - *Oshak-bashi*. End of the 19th century

Size: 239 x 159 cm.

Like no. 126, another example of this rare type of weaving. Its striped pattern is probably taken from weavings in the kilim technique; horse-blankets and saddle-covers were often decorated in a similar way, with supplementary piling or brocading (see nos. 128-9, 132). In some of the single colour bands there appear small four-legged zoomorphic forms.
Literature: Milhofer, no. 89a

128

128. Yomut - Horse Blanket. About 1880

Size: 138 x 111 cm.

Condition: slight wear through use, old repairs to the slit for the saddle pommel.
Together with their brown underfelt, these weavings called *tainaksha*, were considered by Franses to be by the Yomut. There is an unusual weaving technique used with pairs of supplementary two-coloured warps forming a pattern on the upper surface and laid together in groups of five. There is an appliqué band at the edges and the remains of a blue added fringe.
Nagel, Stuttgart
Literature: Franses, pl. 24

129

129. Yomut - Horse Blanket. End of the 19th century

Size: 129 x 91 cm.

Condition: very good.
Unlike the previous example, this *tainaksha* is piled. The hooked bars in the two small side panels seem to have been derived from kilims. Very lustrous, densely piled wool, symmetric knots. Leathery, tight, handle. Presumably by the Persian Yomut.
Nagel. Stuttgart
Literature: Milhofer, no. 89b; Thompson, p. 8

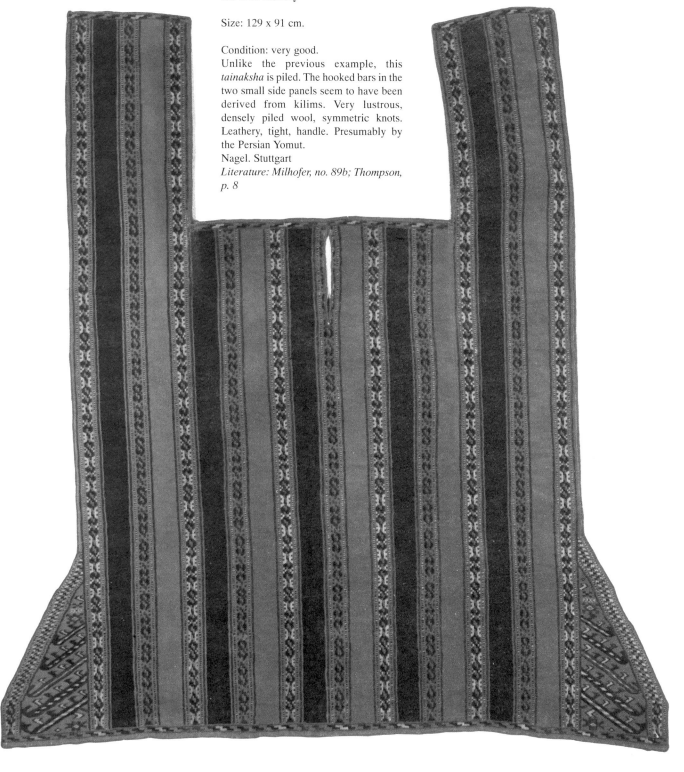

130. Yomut - *Salachak.* **Last quarter of the 19th century**

Size: 120 x 90 cm.

Condition: traces of wear, repiled areas.
The oldest of the weavings, perhaps prayer rugs, from western Turkmenistan and northeast Persia, an area inhabited by the Göklan, the Jaffarbai and the Atabai, have a six-sided format. As here, their designs are sometimes taken directly from flatweaves (see no. 55) or are influenced by them. Typically strong wool and firm knotting; the pile, however, is velvety to the touch. It has its original side finishes all round.

**131. Yomut -*Salachak*.
Last quarter of the
19th century**

Size: 140 x 107 cm.

Condition: Fairly
good, small areas of
repair.
Compared with its
frequent appearance on
the weavings of other
Turkoman tribes, the
ashik pattern was used
only rarely by the
Yomut; even more
unusual is to find it
covering the field of a
salachak. Various
theories have been
advanced about the use
of such weavings but
they remain unproven;
suggestions include
prayer rugs, children's
rugs and cradle rugs.
This example has a
narrow white-ground
main border with the
syrga motif.
Nagel, Stuttgart
*Literature: Bennett,
1982, p. 159
(described as a saddle-
cover); Moshkova,
pl. 64/22 (for the
border pattern)*

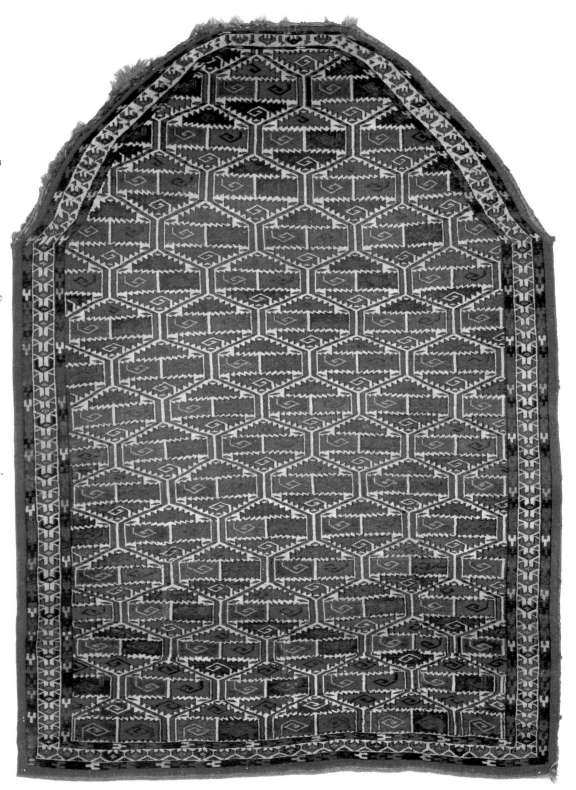

131

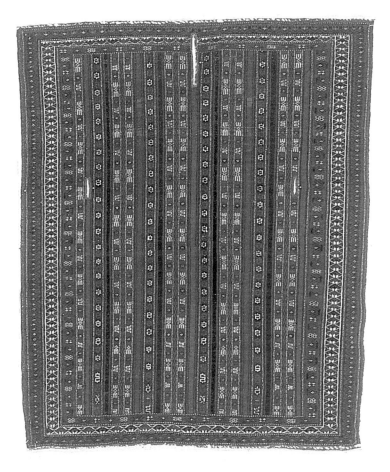

132

132. Yomut - *Cherlik.* **Beginning of the 20th century**

Size: 92 x 77 cm.

Condition: very good.
Relatively rare Turkoman saddle blanket in a rectangular format, with a slit for the pommel and two further slits for the girth. Apart from the patterned bands, with designs taken from the supplementary warp decorated flatweaves (see no. 127) and the usual single colour undecorated bands, this example has other motifs, including what Moshkova called the *Parsi* gul (the 'Persian' gul) in the white-ground borders.
Nagel, Stuttgart
Literature: Moshkova, pl. 54

133. Yomut - Small Rug. 19th century

Size: 135 x 142 cm.

One is often surprised by the wealth of design ideas shown by Yomut weavers, in spite of the traditional and conservative nature of many of their patterns. Looking at the picture, one might think that, like no. 135, this is a rug made for hanging and made from sections of a tent-band. In fact it is made in one piece and piled throughout in the symmetric knot; perhaps it is a so-called 'hearth' rug. This great rarity made SF 11,200 at an auction in Switzerland in 1988.
Ghigo, Turin

133

134

135

134. Tent

Size: 530 x 350 cm.

Complete with outer 'scissor' fencing, 64 roof slats, mats, felts and tent bands. Called a *yurt* by the Turkoman (Russian *kibitka*), this example appears to be of the type attributed to the Khirgiz of Central Asia.
Nagel, Stuttgart

135. Yomut - *Jolami* fragment. End of the 19th century

Size: 196 x 140 cm.

Condition: some age damage, exceptional colours.
Sections of two different Yomut tent-bands have been sewn together to form a hanging piece with a long interwoven fringe. It has interesting ornamental details which are piled on a white plain-weave ground.
Nagel, Stuttgart
Literature: Tzareva, no. 126 ('Karakalpak wedding hanging')

136. Yomut - *Jolami*. 1st half of the 19th century

Size: 1,500 x 24 cm.

Condition: very good.
Of all white-ground Turkoman tent-bands, those of the Yomut are among the most wonderful. Their designs are produced by a specific knotting technique over three warps which is hardly visible from the back. Supposedly they were made for weddings and only used on such special occasions. The sparse ornamentation of this example is a rare feature and indicates that it is early.
Nagel, Stuttgart
Literature: Eiland and Shockley, Tent Bands of the Steppes, exhib. cat.; Moshkova, no. 65

137

137. Yomut - *Jolami*. 2nd half of the 19th century

Size: 1,410 x 42 cm.

Condition: complete, including its attractive knotted and wrapped warp ends.
Only a section of this typically Yomut white-ground tent band is shown. A very attractive design feature, which can be seen here, is the inclusion of two figurative elements, one of which is a camel with a howdah-like chair on top possibly for a bride and an equestrian figure, presumably the bridegroom (see nos. 192-4).
Nagel, Stuttgart
Literature: Milhofer, nos. 91-2, 94

138

138. Yomut - *Ensi*. 2nd half of the 19th century

Size: 150 x 144 cm.

Condition: worn thin in places, edge damage, small repair.

The designs of Yomut *ensis* can be similar to those used by other tribes; however, Yomut versions can usually be recognised easily, even without a knowledge of their structure. The field patterns are richly varied and apart from the classic *insikush* pattern shown here and others seen in the following illustrations, there are constant surprises among this group. On this example, the vertical beam cuts across the horizontal one, and has an arch-like top end with hooked outline. The *elem* panel at the base is divided into two, with archaic looking 'Yomut eagles' at the top at the *gapyrga* tree pattern below.
Nagel, Stuttgart
Literature: Franses, no. 42

139. Yomut - *Ensi*. End of the 19th century

Size: 160 x 125 cm.

Condition: slight signs of age.
The horizontal dividing beam and the inner guard border both contain the *ashik* pattern; the vertical beam has the tekbent pattern. The outer *sainak* pattern does not frame three sides, as is more usual, but all four. The *elem* contains the so-called 'Yomut firs' pattern.
Nagel, Stuttgart
Literature: Lefevre, pl. 9

139

140

140. Yomut - *Ensi*. 3rd quarter of the 19th century

Size: 161 x 134 cm.

Condition: worn thin in places, slight edge damage.

The usual *ensi* field arrangement is followed here but in each of the four panels are diagonally arranged motifs which one writer has called *pekvesh;* it is certainly one of the rarest patterns found on Yomut *ensis.* Another remarkable feature are the nine motifs arranged next to each other in the upper part of the *elem* panel; each has arrow-like extensions on the vertical axis and contains an *ashik* motif.

Nagel, Stuttgart

Literature: Troost, pl. 57; Straka Collection, cat. no. 5; Tzareva, no. 73

141. Yomut - *Ensi*. Beginning of the 20th century

Size: 177 x 138 cm.

Condition: good, with original flatwoven ends and hanging cords.

Both in structure and in design, this is reminiscent of Tekke *ensis,* although it would be unusual to find a continuous vertical bar on an example of the latter tribal type; nor would one be likely to find the outer white-ground *syrga*-pattern guard border. Unusually, this example has an *elem* panel at both top and bottom.

Nagel, Stuttgart

141

142

142. Yomut - *Ensi.* **Late 19th century**

Size: 178 x 151 cm.

Condition: signs of wear, some repiling.
An unusual example, both the colour and
structure of which suggest an origin among
the western Yomut. A very strange but most
attractive feature is the pair of *elem*-like
panels at top and bottom (see the previous
piece) which here contain multiple running
animals, which are placed 'upside down' at
the top end. Also note the many human
figures in the four field quarters. Neither of
these two latter design features are normal for
the Turkoman but demonstrate the wide
repertoire of motifs available to them.
Nagel, Stuttgart

143. Yomut - *Ensi.* **Last quarter of the
19th century**

Size: 152 x 150 cm.

Condition; pile worn thin in places; the sides
and the base cut.
The motifs in the inner and outer white-
ground side guards appear to be stylised
versions of a double-headed animal or bird
motif and this may be true also of the motifs
used in the four fields. Like the *shemle* gul,
however, they could be interpreted as
palmettes or with the forms found on some
early Anatolian carpets (cf. no. 12). Soft,
velvety wool pile of great lustre.
Nagel, Stuttgart
Literature: Hoffmeister, no. 18; Reed, no. 33

143

144

144. Yomut - *Ensi.* **Late 19th century**

Size: 168 x 148 cm.

Condition: Signs of age but good overall.
A fine example of a Yomut-*Ensi,* with richly
varied field patterns and divided into the
characteristic four panels but without a
pentagonal *kejebe* motif. The distinctive *elem*
panel at the base contains the *gapyrga*
ornament, sometimes called the 'Yomut-firs'
design. The unbroken horizontal centre band
and the main borders contain the familiar
sainak ornament.
Brian MacDonald, Samarkand Galleries

145. Yomut - *Ensi.* **3rd quarter of the
19th century or earlier**

Size: 168 x 149 cm.

Condition: Signs of age, some restoration,
otherwise good.
An especially impressive feature is the
totemic-like crowning of the vertical bar by a
so-called 'Yomut eagle' motif. The
rhomboidal motifs seen in the upper part of
the *elem* in no. 143 are here used in the four
quarters of the field. Here, the white-ground
syrga-pattern outer guard is on only three
sides.
Nagel, Stuttgart
*Literature: Franses, nos. 5 and 42; Troost,
pl. 55*

145

146

146. Yomut - *Ensi*. End of the 19th century

Size: 172 x 142 cm.

Condition: worn thin in places, repaired areas, remains of the original selvedges.
A small motif is closely arranged in the top two fields in an overall upward-pointing chevron pattern; in the bottom two it forms a series of diagonal stripes. In one of the lower *elem* panels there is an anchor-like motif similar to that found in *kepse* guls. The main border contains an archaic-looking 'curled leaf' pattern and it has outer white-ground *syrga*- pattern guards.
Nagel, Stuttgart

147. Yomut - *Ensi*. Last quarter of the 19th century

Size: 167 x 149 cm.

Condition: slight damage to edges.
Like nos. 144-5, this example also has a double *elem* panel with 'Yomut eagles' at the top and the *gapyrga* motif or 'Yomut firs' at the base, the latter on a dark brown ground. The four quarters of the field have the *ashik* motif in alternate bands of blue and red forming an all-over upward-pointing chevron.
Nagel, Stuttgart
Literature: Tzareva, no. 72

147

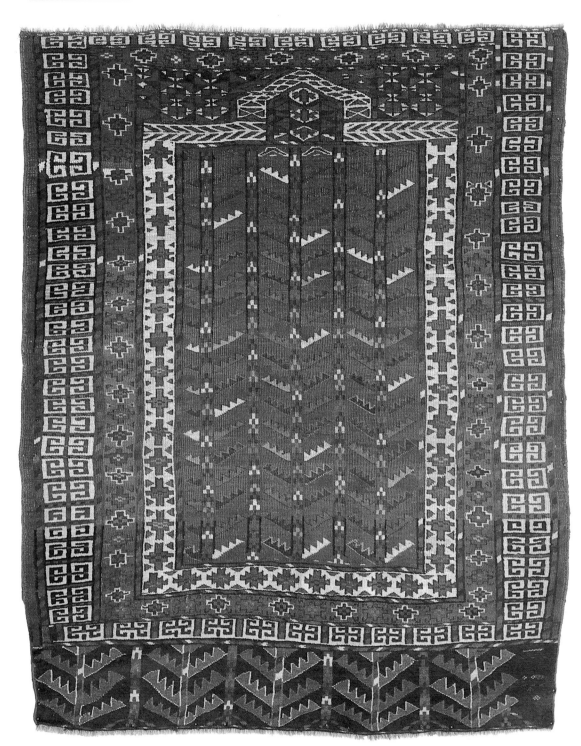

148

148. Yomut - *Ensi*. 2nd half of the 19th century

Size: 152 x 119 cm.

Condition: Worn, some repiling.

Old Yomut *ensis* without the crossbeams quartering the field are very unusual. Because of this, and the arch at the top, this example looks as if it has the *mihrab* arch found on prayer rugs. The three vertical *gapyrga* trees in the warm red-ground field are surrounded by borders with stepped pattern and the *ashik* motif.

Nagel, Stuttgart

Literature: Hali, vol. 4, no. 4, p. 395, no. 5

149

149. Yomut - *Ensi*. Mid 19th century or earlier

Size: 153 x 134 cm.

Condition: worn thin in places; some areas of repair.

An early and very rare example of a design group of Yomut *ensis* with an undivided field. The tree-like motifs, unlike those on the previous example, are arranged here in diagonal rows. The infinite repeat this creates is framed by the usual arrangement of three borders of almost equal weight. The palette of this rug is very striking, in particular the use of a light turquoise.

Nagel, Stuttgart

Literature: Tzareva, no. 35 (attributed to the Tekke); Loges, no. 41

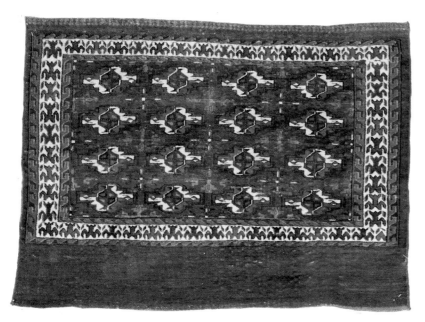

150

150. Yomut - *Chuval*. 3rd quarter of the 19th century

Size: 81 x 111 cm.

Condition: worn thin in places.

This Yomut *chuval* has the the so-called *chuval* gul as the main motif in its field. In its 'small' variant, as on no. 155, the hooks on the vertical axis within the gul are reduced to small triangular extensions. The main guls on this piece are acccompanied by a comparatively rare minor gul. A remarkable feature of many Yomut *chuvals* is the broad piled *elem* left free of all decoration; this continues round the sides to form a frame. Fine symmetric knotting.

Nagel, Stuttgart

Literature: Lefevre, no. 14; Straka Collection, cat. no. 6

151

152

151. Yomut - *Chuval.* **2nd third of the 19th century**

Size: 75 x 108 cm.

Condition: some wear, considerable repairing, patched with a piece from a Tekke *torba.*

On most Yomut *chuvals,* the *chuval* guls are arranged either 4 x 4, as here and on the previous example, or 3 x 3 as on the next one; weavings with similar arrangements of *chuval* guls by the Saryk and Tekke have already been shown. This example has a beautiful and unusual main border pattern, flanked by typical continuous 'running dog' guards. The *pekvesh* motif arranged diagonally in the *elem* also constitutes a rare feature.

Nagel, Stuttgart
Literature: Gombos, no. 44

152. Yomut - *Chuval.* **Mid 19th century**

Size: 81 x 124 cm.

Condition: damage to upper edge, minimal moth damage, otherwise very good.
Large and clearly drawn *chuval* guls in a 3 x 3 arrangement, with well-defined hooked extensions in the guls which are diagonally quartered by colour, with tiny dice-like flowers in each quarter; the minor gul is the *chemche.* Perhaps the most outstanding design feature is to be found in the *elem:* five large forms whose significance is now unknown but which at the time of weaving may have hearkened back to faintly remembered ancestral patterns.

Rippon Boswell
Literature: Smith Collection, cat. no. 64; Hali 25, p. 50, no. 2
Note to the English Edition*: a chuval of very similar design was illustrated by Rautenstengel and Azadi, pl. 24, as 'Eagle Group II'.*

153

153. Yomut - *Chuval*. 4th quarter of the 19th century

Size: 72 x 128 (face)

Condition: good.
This example comes complete with its red plainweave back. The piled field has 4 x 4 guls accompanied by a cruciform minor gul called the *ara-gul.* An attractive feature is the depiction of a horse, as well as small 'dice'

flowers, on the the otherwise undecorated reddish brown *elem*. Probably made by the western Yomut.
Nagel, Stuttgart
Literature: Troost, pl. 21 (identical); Andrews, no. 6; Mackie and Thompson, no. 145

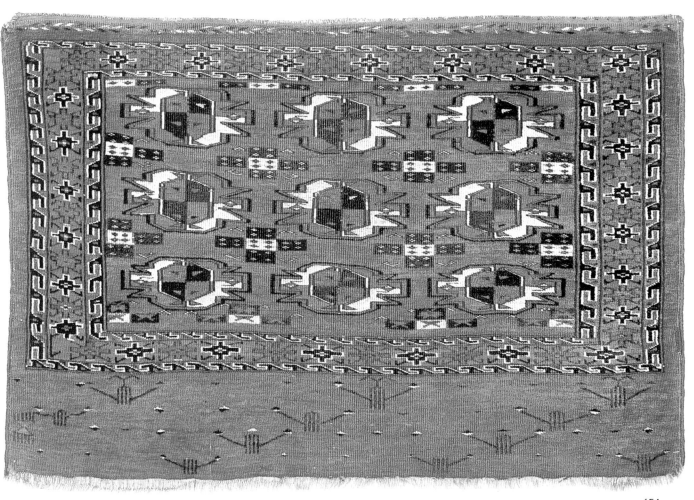

154

154. Yomut - *Chuval*. 19th century

Size: 76 x 118 cm.

Condition: slight wear, otherwise very good. Unquestionably an early *chuval* with interesting design characteristics. The main gul is itself unusual, like the large version of the *chuval* gul, but with a pointed extension at each diagonal axis; also it has no hooks on the vertical in the centre. The half row of minor guls visible along the base have different internal ornaments to the rest. The imaginative *elem* has one *muska* amulet to the left.

Nagel, Stuttgart

Literature: Gombos, no. 45; Troost, pl 16

155

155. Yomut - *Chuval*. 3rd quarter of the 19th century

Size: 77 x 101 cm.

Condition: worn a little thin in places.
Rounded guls in a 3 x 3 arrangement, accompanied by minor guls composed of rectangles containing stars - the *sharch palak* gul (see nos. 6 and 63-5). As on the previous piece, the lowest part row of minor guls are different in design to those on the remainder of the field. 'Running dog' guards flank the blue-ground main border.
Nagel, Stuttgart
Literature: Loges, no. 61

156

157

156. Yomut - Pair of *Chuvals*. Last quarter of the 19th century

Size: about 70 x 130 cm. each.

Condition: very good.
So that pack animals could be loaded on both flanks, *chuvals* were probably always made in pairs, although they have rarely been preserved as such. The field and borders of this pair are similar to those on no. 155. The aubergine-ground *elems* have been folded over to give added strength to the plainwoven backs. The extra narrow decorated pile panel at the upper end of the back is a rare additional feature of each bag.
Nagel, Stuttgart

157. Yomut - *Chuval*. 2nd third of the 19th century

Size: 80 x 102 cm.

Condition: repiling, cut all round, especially to the left.
The minor guls of this rare and beautiful example are similar to the *sharch palak* gul but here have four hooked extensions and each rectangle is decorated with a stylised flower. The white-ground main border has the *ashik* motif flanked by guards with reciprocal 'arrow-head' motifs (*medachyl*); this changes at the top and bottom to a *kochak* motif. The design in the beautiful *elem* is one also found in this position on Yomut main carpets.
Nagel, Stuttgart
Literature: Cassin/Hoffmeister, pl. 25; Straka Collection, cat. no. 8

158

158. Yomut - *Chuval.* **3rd quarter of the 19th century**

Size: 71 x 114 cm.

Condition: signs of wear.
Instead of the large *chuval* guls seen on some of the pieces just illustrated, here the simplified small version has been used. This, however, should not be considered a sign of a later period of manufacture; the minor gul consists of an arrangement of four free-standing diamonds in a rhomboidal arrangement. The variant 'tree' pattern in the *elem* is reminiscent of that found on some Chodor *ensis.*
Nagel, Stuttgart
Literature: Troost, pl. 22; Tzareva, no. 78.

159

159. Yomut - *Chuval.* **End of the 19th century**

Size: 73 x 119 cm.

As on the previous piece, note the two blue piled 'arrow-head' motifs in the upper otherwise plain 'frame'. According to Troost, who called it the *gyjak* 'bird track', this ornament may appear in this upper 'frame' two, three or even more times close to the sides where the closing cords appear, if they have been preserved. One can speculate that they may have had an amuletic significance, protecting the contents of the closed bag. This motif is also discussed by Julian Homer.
Nagel, Stuttgart
Literature: Julian Homer, Hali, nol. 3, no. 4, pp. 310 ff.; Troost, plates. 23, 29; Dovodov, pl. 83 (described as a chuval with chamak-gul, wool pile, mixture of natural and synthetic dyes

160

160 Yomut - *Chuval*. 3rd quarter of the 19th century

Size: 74 x 122 cm.

Condition: complete with natural white wool flat-weave back.

An important minor gul often found on Yomut *chuvals* is the *erre-gul* (see fig. 87). However, a specific attribution of this motif to the Atabai remains unproven. As on the previous two pieces the upper plain frame bears two blue 'arrow head' motifs. A very attractive feature is the clear drawing of the shrub-like motifs in the *elem*.

Nagel, Stuttgart
Literature: McCoy Jones and Boucher, 1976, no. 28; Azadi, pl. 21c

161

161. Yomut - *Chuval*. Mid 19th century

Size: 77 x 114 cm.

Condition: minimal repiling.
The large guls in a 3 x 3 arrangement are accompanied by minor guls with ray-like extensions on the diagonals. The piece has a very effective use of colour, including different shades of blue, yellow and a large amount of ivory in the guls; also note the white-ground main border with its *syrga* pattern. The design in the *elem* is also very imaginative, consisting of details from the *kepse* gul arranged diagonally both by form and colour. A very attractive *chuval*.
Nagel, Stuttgart

162

162. Yomut - *Chuval*. 1st quarter of the 20th century

Size: 73 x 121 cm.

Various designs are found on Yomut *chuvals,* both piled and flatwoven examples. No. 162a shows a detail from a flatwoven *chuval,* the field of which, like that of the piled example illustrated here, has stepped and hooked major guls (the *sekis-kochak* gul). The diamond shaped minor guls are also very similar on both pieces. The pattern in the *elem* of 162, however, is only found in piled examples.

Detail 162a

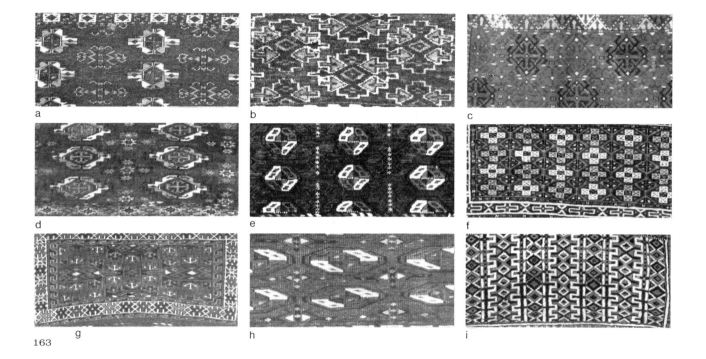

163

163. Yomut Group - Selection of *Torba* and *Mafrash* Designs

Small Yomut bag faces exhibit an astonishing range of designs and our knowledge of this is constantly being enriched as more pieces come on to the market. Readers seeking a comprehensive account dedicated to these delightful items should refer to the 1981 editorial feature 'Small is Beautiful. The Yomut Mafrash' in HALI Vol. 4, No. 1 and, of course, to Troost's 1983 'Die Yomut.'

a). *Torba* with *chuval* major guls and *chemche* minor guls. 46 x 109 cm.

b). *Torba* with *chuval* major guls and *sharch-palak* minor guls. 44 x 118 cm.

c). Pair of *mafrashes* with *kepse* guls. 19th/20th century. About 40 x 75 cm. each.

d). *Mafrash* with *erre-guls*. 19th century. 39 x 90 cm.

e). *Mafrash* with diamond-shaped guls. 19th century. 39 x 93 cm.

f). *Mafrash* with diamond-shaped guls. 19th century. 36 x 64 cm.

g). *Mafrash* with hooked cruciform guls. 19th century.

h). *Mafrash.* 19th/20th century. 36 x 37 cm.

i). *Mafrash* with striped pattern. 19th/20th century. 33 x 62 cm.

Nagel, Stuttgart

164. Yomut - *Mafrash*. 2nd half of the 19th century

Size: 47 x 97 cm.

Condition: slight signs of age.
In the *mafrash* article referred to in the caption to no.163, this extraordinary piece is published as fig.13. The article mentions that the format of this beautiful tent bag is between that of a *mafrash* and a *torba*. The formats of *mafrashes* can vary and seem to be less uniform than those of *chuvals*. The *erre gul* is the best known of the three field motifs. The symmetrically knotted wool is of good quality with a fleshy, velvet-like handle.
Nagel, Stuttgart

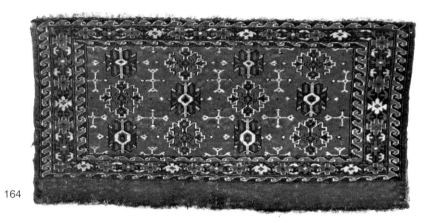

164

165. Yomut - *Mafrash*. Last quarter of the 19th century

Size: 37 x 75 cm.

Like no. 163d, this small piled bag-face has the *erre-gul* in diagonal rows. On 163d it appears in its most usual form, with four arrow-like intrusions, two on each horizontal side; here, however, the gul appears in a simplified variant form. An especially attractive design feature of this well-preserved weaving are the four quadrupeds which surround each gul. Velvety wool, remains of an added fringe.
Nagel, Stuttgart
Literature, Hali, op. cit., p. 13, no. 12; Dovodov, no. 45

165

166. Yomut - *Torba*. 3rd quarter of the 19th century

Size: 41 x 105 cm.

166

Condition: minimal traces of wear.
The *kepse* gul was a popular main motif for Yomut weavers; it was used not only on main carpets, but can also appear on *mafrashes*, *khorjins*, *chuvals* and *kapunuks*. On *torbas*, there are usually two or three complete guls in the field, with part guls at top and bottom giving the impression of a section from an endless repeat. Here, the design of the main border is unusual, as is that of the *elem* (not seen in this illustration).
Literature: Straka Collection, cat. no. 8; Pinner and Franses, no. 417; Iten-Maritz, p. 313; McCoy Jones and Boucher, 1976, no. 44

167

168

169

167. Yomut - *Khalyk*. 19th/20th century

Size: 30 x 94 cm.

Condition: very good.
This form of piled hanging is typical of the Yomut. In the Pinner and Franses essay mentioned in the caption to no. 90, other designs of Yomut *khalyks* are illustrated, for instance one with compartments containing stars, another with six vertical stripes and a third with the *kepse* gul. The pattern of stepped diamond seen here can also be found on small bags. Symmetrically knotted.
Nagel, Stuttgart
Literature: Pinner and Franses, p. 200; Landreau, no. 81

168. Yomut - *Mafrash*. 19th century

Size: 48 x 81 cm.

The piled field of this remarkable Yomut bag has a lattice pattern made up of hexagons and diamonds, a repeat pattern which reminds one of the large cargo bags (also called *mafrashes*) made by the Shahsavan tribe in northwest Persia. The latter, though sometimes with similar designs, are always flatwoven in the sumakh technique which is usually finished, along the bottom fold of the bag, with a broad band of pile work to prevent the loaded sack from chafing the sides of the pack horse.
Arditti, Christchurch (England)
Literature: Hali, vol. 4, no. 1, p. 12, no. 9

169. Yomut (?) - *Torba*. 19th century

Size: 40 x 100 cm.

An arrangement of 5 x 3 hooked diamond guls enclosing eight pointed stars are the main motifs used in the field (the so-called 'Memling' gul - see also the Salor *torba*, no. 9); the minor guls consist of diamond containing four hooks arranged diagonally by colour; these represent a hooked cruciform in negative space. The field design, although rare, can be found on the weavings of various Turkoman groups. This example has approximately 2,800 aysmmetric knots per dm^2 open to the right, which suggests that it is either not Yomut or a member of the 'Eagle group'.
Courtesy Hali
Literature: Hali, ibid., no. 8

170

171

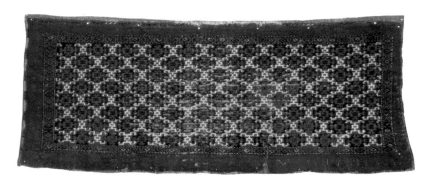

172

**170. Yomut - *Mafrash*. End of the
19th century**

Size: 40 x 96 cm.

Condition: full silky pile.
The *ashik* field pattern appears in many
variations on Yomut *mafrashes;* here it is
arranged in a diamond-lattice, as on some of
the *asmalyks* illustrated later. An unusual
feature is the fact that the field has a white
ground and so do the main border and the
elem panel.
Nagel, Stuttgart
*Literature: Hali, ibid., p. 14, nos. 16, 26;
Troost, pl. 10*

171. Yomut - *Torba*. 19th century

Size: 30 x 99 cm.

In contrast to the previous piece, the *ashik*
motif is here used in its rectangular 'curled
leaf' form, as often found on Tekke *kapunuks*
(see also no. 131). The warps and wefts are of
undyed brown wool; it has unusually fine
knotting, about 4,000 per dm².
Bausback, Mannheim

172. Yomut - *Torba*. 19th century or earlier

Size: 44 x 114 cm.

Condition: slight wear, several areas of
restoration.
This *ak-su* pattern has already been seen in
the work of three other Turkoman tribes and
will also be found on others illustrated later.
Because of the structure and colour of some
of these so-called 'Yomut' examples, Mackie
and Thompson suggested an attribution to the
Imreli, although this is no longer accepted. It
is difficult to suggest an exact dating for this
finely knotted example, but it is undoubtedly
both early and rare.
Rippon Boswell, Frankfurt
*Literature: Mackie and Thompson, no. 58;
Grote-Hasenbalg, second box, pl. 91 (almost
identical)*
Note to the English Edition: the implication
of this caption is that this *torba* is
asymmetrically knotted, in which case it
would now be included with the 'Eagle
Group'. See Rautenstengel and Azadi, p. 93,
nos. 21a and b for two *torbas* of this design
placed in 'Eagle Group 1', attributed to the
Göklen. They have the same diamond pattern
guard border as no.172.

173. Yomut - *Mafrash*. Second half of the 19th century

Size: 30 x 68 cm.

Condition: exceptionally good.
This *mafrash*, like the one below, is believed to have been woven by the Igdir, one of several Yomut sub-tribes. The field is divided into two, with small rectangles containing stars overlaid on two large star-like forms. Velvety pile; complete with its flatwoven back, hanging cords and added fringe.
Nagel, Stuttgart
Literature: Moshkova, pl. 68/16

173

174. Yomut Group - *Mafrash*. Mid 19th century

Size: 38 x 76 cm.

Condition: pile a little low, selvedges loose. The German dealer Peter Bausback wrote of weavings attributed to the Igdir sub-group: "Main carpets are almost unknown. The handle of these weavings is firm and hard and the density of the symmetric knotting is between 2,000 and 3,000 per dm². They usually have goats' hair warps and dark brown wool wefts. The geometric pattern stands out as a series of interlocking rectangular forms". An important piece with excellent colours.
Rippon Boswell, Frankfurt
Literature: Bausback, Antike Orientteppiche, p. 468; Hali, vol. 4, no. 1, p. 17, no. 2

174

175

176

177

175. Yomut Group - *Mafrash*. 1st half of the 19th century

Size: 43 x 71 cm.

Few would quarrel with *Hali's* description of this *mafrash,* believed to be an Igdir, as 'exceptionally beautiful' nor with the assertion that its white field makes it somewhat of a rarity. Because of the hook forms of the trees' branches, and the 'tuning fork' in their trunks, that same article related it to a rare group of Yomut *asmalyks* with white fields. The main border has a section of an infinitely repeating star pattern.
Bausback, Mannheim
Literature: Hali, vol. 4, no. 1, p. 16, no. 20

176. Yomut Group - *Torba*. 2nd half of the 19th century

Size: 34 x 96 cm.

Condition: good.
Like the previous bag, this also has tree-like motifs arranged next to each other on an ivory-ground field, these main motifs being separated by series of vertically linked diamonds. Similar palette to no. 177. It is known that several smaller tribal groups became absorbed into the main Yomut tribe during the nineteenth century so that, in the absence of documentary evidence, it is imprudent to be dogmatic about this *torba* being from the Igdir or from the Shlichen.
Nagel, Stuttgart
Literature: Moshkova, pl. 74/2 ('field design of a Shlichen torba*')*

177. Yomut - *Mafrash*. 19th century

Size: 28 x 81 cm.

Condition: traces of wear.
As can be seen from no. 88, this is a variant of a pattern to be found on Tekke weavings. However, the example shown here is in both structure and colour definitely Yomut in character and may well be the work of a group commonly identified as the Igdir. The *aiyly* design here is, according to Moshkova, typical of weavings made by the Igdir of the Amu-Darya region, specifically the Porsy Settlement. Quite a rare piece.
Nagel, Stuttgart
Literature: Moshkova, p. 299; Gombos, no. 56 (Museum of Applied Arts, Budapest); Tzareva, no. 61 (as Tekke)

178

178. Yomut - *Mafrash*. **19th/20th century**

Size: 39 x 79 cm.

A third variant of the Yomut 'tree' design with
minor diamond motifs; the ground colour of
this example is a deep brown-red. Linked
motifs form the 'branches', which, when
compared to other examples such as no. 181,
have a strong avian character - in which case
the field pattern should perhaps be interpreted
as a stylised version of the 'bird' or 'animal-
tree' design. The back of this *mafrash* is of
plain weave.
Nagel, Stuttgart
Literature: McMullan, 1972, no. 73

179

179. Yomut - *Torba*. **Mid 19th century**

Size: 42 x 123 cm.

Condition: very good.
An important essay by Leslie Pinner, 'A
Group of Ertmen Torba: Chodor or Yomut?'
concluded that *torbas* with the *ertmen* gul, a
motif thought to be specific to the Chodor,
could not always be so attributed. The *torba*
shown here, although very similar in design
to the Chodor pair illustrated as no. 228, have
wool wefts and regular symmetric knotting, a
structure which indicates a Yomut origin.
Rippon Boswell, Frankfurt
*Literature: L. Pinner, Hali, vol. 2, no. 4,
pp. 286 ff.; Hoffmeister, nos. 27, 55*

180   181   182

180. Yomut - Bag. Last quarter of the 19th century

Size: 25 x 51 cm.

Similar in format, the use of tassels and border design to the following example, this bag, however, has a field pattern associated with the Yomut *ok-bash*. In this form, it has a tree-like character but it can be interpreted as a section of the *ashik* motif. Complete with its undyed white flatwoven back, two-coloured selvedges and hanging cords and an opening edge bound in 'herringbone' pattern.
Nagel, Stuttgart
Literature: Tzareva, no. 81

181. Yomut - Bag. 3rd quarter of the 19th century

Size: 25 x 40 cm.

Condition: well preserved pile.
Like the *mafrash* no. 175, this bag has a tree-like motif on an ivory ground, a motif also found in somewhat similar form in the *elems* of no. 118 and which may be a version of the 'animal-tree'. The weaving is technically unusual; the warps of the face run horizontally. On both the long sides, the pile gives way to flatweave, which is folded back and sewn together on the reverse. Bags with this design are rarely found on the market.
Nagel, Stuttgart
Literature: Azadi, pl. 25c

182. Yomut - *Ok-bash*. End of the 19th century

Size: length 62 cm. (inc. tassels).

Condition: good.
Probably used to cover the ends of bundles of tent struts during migrations; these weavings were always made in pairs, so that camels could be packed evenly on both flanks. The openings are in undyed flatweave folded over with red and blue stitching at the edges; the lower ends are similarly stitched, the upper end consisting of four pairs of warps wrapped. The piece retains its original tassels and two-coloured plaited wool cords. The tassels are in six colours although only five are used for the pile.
Nagel, Stuttgart
Literature: Hubel, pl. 125 (Völkerkundemuseum, Munich); Mackie and Thompson, nos, 3, 82-3

183

184

**184. Yomut - Bagface. End of the
19th century**

Size: 40 x 63 cm.

Condition: slight corner damage.
This is one piled face from what was
originally a *khorjin*, possibly made by a
western Yomut group such as the Jaffarbai or
Göklen. The *hash-gul* pattern of the field was
used in somewhat similar form on Seljuk rugs
from Anatolia. It may also appear as a field
pattern on some Yomut small rugs, as well as
on flatwoven *chuvals* of the type shown in no.
162a. The fine weaving is responsible for the
delicacy of the pattern at the sides and along
the top.
Nagel, Stuttgart
*Literature: Andrews, no. 8b; Straka
Collection, cat. no. 46*

**183. Yomut - *Khorjin*. 2nd half of the
19th century**

Size: 98 x 48 cm.

A piled double bag with unusual decoration.
Both the fields and the central dividing panel
have a compartment design made up of
interlocking triangles; this should be
compared with weavings by the Ersari (no.
288), where there is also a diagonal zig-zag
effect created by the use of colour. Although
apparently purely abstract, the triangles retain
a bird-like appearance, which is why the
design has sometimes been called the 'bird
triangle'. The *elem*-like panels have motifs
which remind one of the 'animal-tree' theme.
About 3,500 symmetric knots per dm².
Bausback, Mannheim
*Literature: McCoy Jones and Boucher, 1975,
no. 51*

185. Yomut - Bag Front. 3rd quarter of the 19th century

Size: 31 x 46 cm.

Condition: slight wear, small rewoven areas. Piled bag-face in an unusual rectangular format (compare nos. 180-1). The striped pattern in the field is derived from flatweaves such as no. 186, as can be seen by the stepped outlines to the individual motifs. A similar field pattern can be seen on a *khorjin* attributed by Tzareva to the Ersari and on a *mafrash* illustrated by Gombos. Beautiful clear colour, good drawing and a rare design. Christie's, New York
Literature: Tzareva, no. 106; Gombos; no. 57; Hali, vol. 6, no. 2; Dovodov, no. 84

185

186. Yomut - *Chuval*. End of the 19th century

Size: 78 x 125 cm.

Condition: very good.
In contrast to the previous piece, this is flatwoven in the slit-tapestry (kilim) technique. In the main bands, there are *kochanak* motifs with small diamond centres and hooked extensions on either side; in the minor bands are opposing pairs of hooks; in Moshkova, this is referred to as the *kyrk syrga* ornament, although it may have an avian origin.
Nagel, Stuttgart
Literature: Moshkova, pl. 69,5,6; Milhofer, frontispiece (as Beshir); Kalter, no. 35

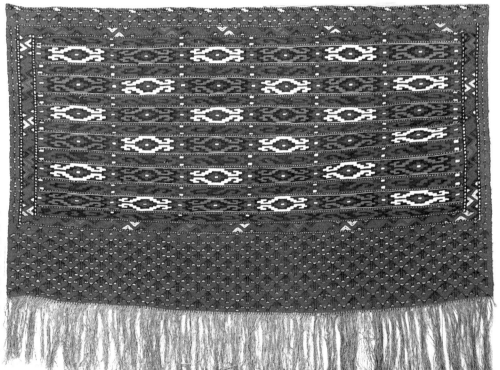

186

187

187. Yomut - *Bokche*. 2nd half of the 19th century

Size: 60 x 68 cm.

Condition: good.
A piled Yomut *bokche* is one of the most highly regarded weavings in any Turkoman collection It is woven in one piece with a piled front and a plain weave 'back', being then folded inwards like an envelope and sewn, the latter often being very attractively executed. These weavings were used, apparently, during wedding ceremonies to keep flat loaves warm and were subsequently used by the bride as a form of handbag for small personal belongings. The design of this example, with a combination of the *kyrk syrga* and *syrga* motifs, is unusual. Completely preserved with two coloured cords for added strength at the edges and a broad surrounding band with a long row of tassels.
Nagel, Stuttgart
Literature: Mackie and Thompson, nos. 80-1; Tzareva, no. 84; Azadi, pl. 23e

188. Yomut - *Bokche*. 2nd half of the 9th century

Size: 84 x 83 cm.

Condition: very good, almost as new.
The second *bokche* has a pattern often found on this type of bag; the continuous diamond pattern of the main border, each diamond containing a cross, is flanked by white ground guards. The design in the four white ground panels is interesting; a similar hooked red motif can be seen on the Yomut *khorjin* illustrated earlier. Very finely knotted with good, clear details.
Rippon Boswell
Literature: Grote-Hasenbalg, second box, pl. 90

188

189

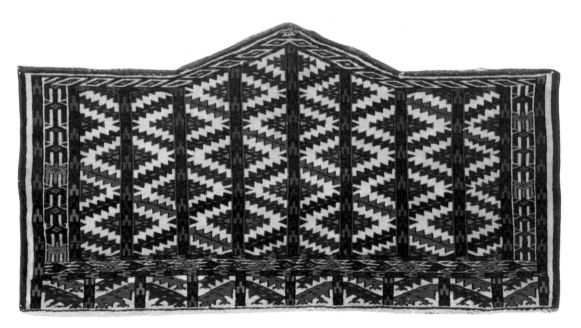

190

191

189. Yomut - *Asmalyk*. 3rd quarter of the 19th century

Size: 65 x 126 cm.

Condition: well preserved.
As can be seen from the group of Yomut examples shown here and on the following pages, *asmalyks* constitute a large, varied and important chapter in the history of Turkoman weaving. The most common field pattern is the *ashik*, which can have different motifs in its centre. Most examples have white-ground main borders; the beautiful mid-blue used here is rarer and also contains further variants of the *ashik* motif. It is flanked by 'running dog' minor guards.
Nagel, Stuttgart
Literature: Troost, pl. 39, 41, 47; Mackie and Thompson, no. 75

190. Yomut - *Asmalyk*. 3rd quarter of the 19th century

Size: 59 x 115 cm.

Condition: trimmed at the lower edge, otherwise very well preserved.
This is a rare seven-sided *asmalyk*, although with a typical *ashik* pattern field; as on the following example, each *ashik* is enclosed and connected vertically. This 'tree trunk' system continues into the lower *elem* panel, where the somewhat more spiky nature of the drawing suggests branches (see no. 196). Velvety wool, symmetric knotting.
Nagel, Stuttgart
Literature: Loges, no. 46; Straka Collection, cat. no. 9 (now Textile Museum, Washington)

191. Yomut - *Asmalyk*. 3rd quarter of the 19th century

Size: 80 x 125 cm.

Condition: slightly worn.
This is a more unusual example than the five-sided *asmalyk* illustrated as no. 189. The field is surrounded on three sides by a broad frame of border and guards, while the upper edge has a narrow guard with diagonal stripes. In the white ground guards, the pattern changes in places to a two-directional variant of the *syrga* motif. The field lattice contains *erreguls* with 'six arrow' centres; these main medallions are connected vertically by bars crowned with double hooks; this is an unusual variant of the motif which, again, suggests a stylised tree-like pattern, as on nos. 198-9.
Nagel, Stuttgart
Literature: Schürmann, 1969, no. 33; Troost, pl. 46

192

193

194

192. Yomut - *Asmalyk*. 2nd half of the 19th century

Size: 70 x 123 cm.

Condition: worn, areas of repair, damage to edges.
What makes this piece of interest is the depiction of a wedding procession at the top. In the centre is the bride's camel with her howdah, which also depicts a five-sided *asmalyk* in use. In front of her is an equestrian figure, probably the bridegroom - compare the depiction on the tent band no. 137. *Asmalyks* with *ashik* fields and the depiction of a bridal procession are known to have been woven in the 20th century; this example, however, is earlier.
Literature: Heinz E.R. Martin, 1983, pl. 64 (this example); Azadi, 1980, no. 375; Moshkova, no. 60

193. Yomut - *Asmalyk*. 1st half of the 19th century

Size: 76 x 130 cm.

Compared to the design of the felt *asmalyk* shown in fig. 1, this example has huge branches ending in spirals. When sold at auction in Germany, the cataloguers suggested that these motifs could be interpreted as stylised antlers rather than trees. In contrast to the following example, this piece has five large pieces of pectoral jewellery (*tumars*) in the top frieze, as well as two pieces for the side of the head (*adamlyks*) and a pair of earrings, the headpieces being of typical anthropomorphic form; there is also a small water-pitcher in the left corner and various small amuletic motifs. When sold at auction on 3 May, 1986, this extremely important weaving made DM 104, 400.
Rippon Boswell, Frankfurt
Literature: Herrmann, 1979, no.91 (almost identical)

194. Yomut - *Asmalyk*. 19th century

Size: 89 x 127 cm.

The second of three spectacular *asmalyks* shown here with the related field patterns. Again, the bridal caravan appears at the top, the camel behind that bearing the bride's howdah having an *asmalyk* on its flank; there are also cattle, possibly a sign of fertility or wealth and at the top a pectoral jewel (*tumar,* see fig. 95). Dating this and nos. 193 and 195 is not without problems; other examples of this group have been dated from the end of the 18th to the beginning of the 19th centuries.
Bausback, Mannheim

195

195. Yomut - *Asmalyk*. 19th century

Size: 64 x 124 cm.

This *asmalyk* made the extraordinary price of
DM 139,200 when sold at auction in
Germany in May 1985. The field design of
this pieces is related to the two just discussed
but note the *ashik* pattern main border with its
blue-green ground; this main border design is
more usually associated with later *asmalyks*.
The white ground frieze at the top is
considerably narrower than on the other two
and has a row of triangular motifs, perhaps
representing an encampment. The incomplete
human figures seen at either side, missing
their heads, are found on many different
Turkoman weavings.
Rippon Boswell, Frankfurt

196. Yomut - *Asmalyk*. 19th century

Size: 81 x 115 cm.

Condition: signs of wear, expertly restored.
An interesting variant of the 'tree' pattern,
with two different versions alternating in five
vertical rows; one is a fir-like tree with
downward pointing 'branches'. Camels also
appear on this piece, but as small 'filler'
motifs (see details nos. 196a and b). A
remarkable design feature is the wide main
border on three sides containing a version of the
'curled leaf' pattern.
Nagel, Stuttgart

196

Detail 196a & b

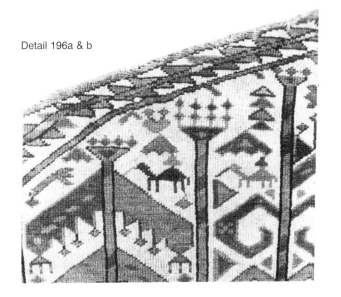

197

197. Yomut - *Asmalyk*. **3rd quarter of the 19th century**

Size: 62 x 107 cm.

Condition: slightly worn, repiled areas.
This design type of Yomut *asmalyk* with its particular version of the 'tree' pattern appears frequently in the literature. The *gapyrga* or 'Yomut fir' has already been seen in similar form on no. 196 but on an ivory ground; compare also the Yomut *ensi* no. 148. Tzareva illustrates a rare example, also with five trees but on a white ground and with an extra panel below, as on no. 190. The white-ground *syrga* pattern border seems almost obligatory for this design type; usually, however, it appears on three sides linked together as in the side borders here.
Nagel, Stuttgart
Literature: Troost, pl. 49; Tzareva, no. 75-6

198. Yomut - *Asmalyk*. **Late 18th/early 19th century**

Size: 77 x 133 cm.

Few *asmalyk* of this seven-sided design type are known. Three are in the Russian Museum in St. Petersburg. One white one was sold by Sotheby's in New York (and was published by Mackie and Thompson). Two white ones were sold by Christie's in London in 1986 and one of these (which sold for £16,200) appears to be the pair of this piece which was offered by Rippon Boswell of Wiesbaden in 1987 (sold for DM. 75,400).

199. Yomut - *Asmalyk*. **19th century**

Size: 79 x 137 cm.

Though Tzareva dated the only other published example of such a piece as being 'not later than the first half of the 19th century', and despite the considerable coincidence of design between the two, there are some who believe that this piece might be from the late 18th century. To all appearances this is the pair of Tzareva's piece for, though there are slightly different motifs in the arch of the field, this is of no great significance. Variations of this order regularly occur between pairs of all sorts of rugs and bags, even *asmalyks*. This is an important piece, impressive in colour and design, woven on wollen warps and having a knot count of about 2,800 symmetric knots per dm². Bausback, Mannheim
Literature: Tzareva, 1984, no. 74

198

199

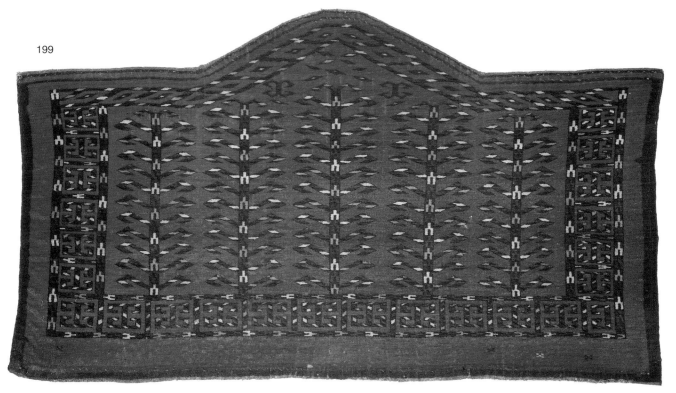

200

200. Yomut - Pair of *Diah Dizlugh*. 19th/20th century

Size: 29 x 17 cm. each.

The name given above to these ornaments for the foreknees of camels was used by Azadi; other writers have referred to them as *sanuband-e-shotor*. The most usual format is pentagonal and the most usual decoration the *ashik*, making them appear like miniature *asmalyks*. Azadi also illustrates two three-sides weavings which he describes as 'pan-holders'. It is interesting to compare the design of these weavings with that on the following pair of *asmalyks*.
Nagel, Stuttgart

201. Yomut - Pair of *Asmalyks*. 19th century

Size: 84 x 127 and 80 x 125 cm.

Among the most beautiful white-ground *asmalyks* to have been published. At the time of the German edition, no directly analogous examples were known, although another damaged pair has surfaced since then. The 'snowflake'-like appearance of each motif is reminiscent of the designs found in the *elems* of some Yomut main carpets and some *chuvals;* the strange pendants on the four branches of each motif have a definite zoomorphic quality, although less strongly defined here than on other Yomut weavings.
Bausback, Mannheim

201

202. Arabachi - Main Carpet. 1st half of the 19th century

Size: 250 x 224 cm.

Condition: fragmented, cut and rejoined across at the sixth row of guls.
Writing in 1978, the German Turkoman specialist Werner Loges suggested that only four Arabachi main carpets were known, of which no. 203 in this book is one. There is some difficulty in distinguishing between the main carpets of the Arabachi and Kizil Ayak (see no. 238) tribes by design, although they can be distinguished structurally; they both have asymmetric knots but the knots of the former are open to the left and those of the latter to the right. Structurally this example is Arabachi; it has the *tauk-nuska* main gul and a diamond shaped minor gul; the wefts are a mixture of wool and cotton.
Nagel, Stuttgart
Literature: Loges, pp. 175 ff.

ARABACHI PILE WEAVINGS

It is possible to give a more accurate definition of Arabachi pile weavings than of the four groups discussed previously. In comparison with the uncommonly broad range which can be attributed to the Tekke or Yomut, only a few types of pile weavings can be described as Arabachi.

These normally very distinctive weavings are distinguished in terms of structure by the use of asymmetric knots open to the left, and piled wefts of wool and cotton mixed. The backs of these weavings are ribbed and display scattered flecks of white cotton.

Although these characteristics make attributions appear unproblematic, it is nevertheless not always easy. Loges (1978, p. 176) refers to the difficulty in differentiating between Arabachi and the Kizil Ayak weavings identified by him. The latter, however, can be distinguished by the use of asymmetric knots open to the right. The Kizil Ayak tend to be described, erroneously, as a sub-group of the Ersari. It is worth noting that Elena Tsareva describes the Arabachi as also being a sub-group of the Ersari.

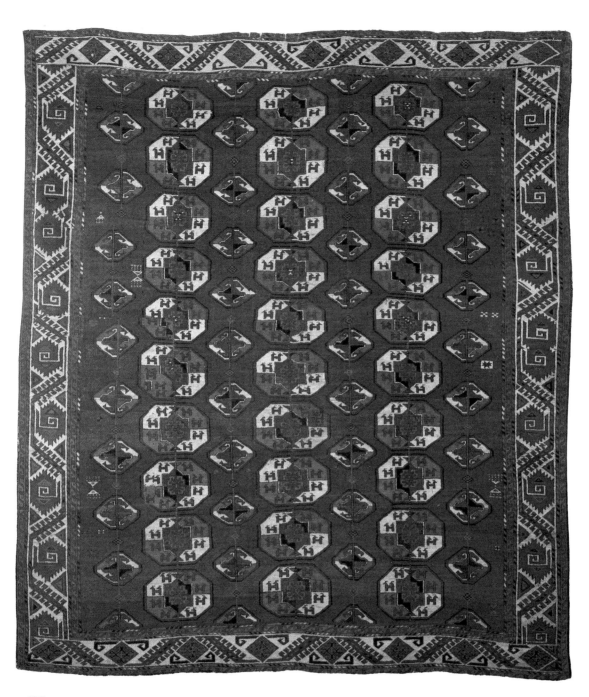

202

203

203. Arabachi - Main Carpet. 2nd half of the 19th century

Size: 277 x 224 cm.

Condition: very good.
The ground colour of this carpet is chestnut-brown with a hint of aubergine. The decoration in the minor guards, as well as the selvedges, remind one of Saryk carpets attributed to the Pendeh Oasis (see nos. 17 ff.). Exceptionally long and silky pile. An important documentary piece; note the striped flatwoven ends. The rug has a firm handle, a ribbed back and it uses eight colours.
Nagel, Stuttgart
Literature: Loges, 1978, no. 108 (this carpet)

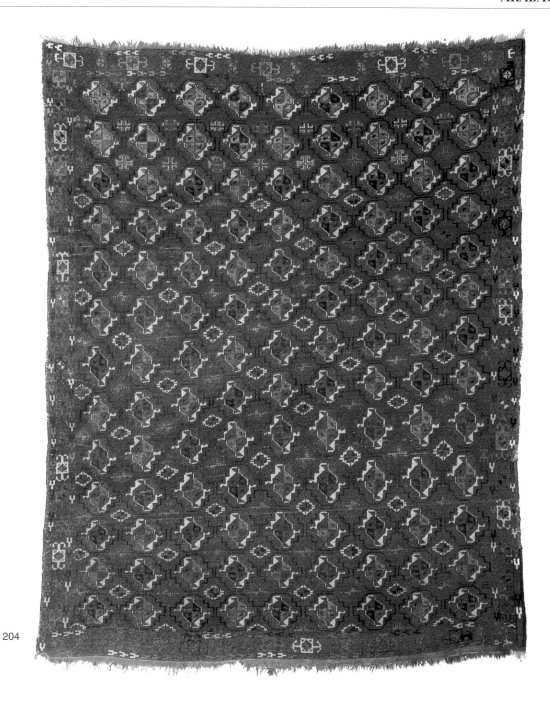

204

204. Arabachi - Main Carpet. 2nd half of the 19th century

Size: 196 x 160 cm.

Condition: slight signs of wear, edges damaged.
An unusual carpet, although structurally it can be identified with the Arabachi. In both the major and minor guls, there is a similarity to guls found on some Saryk main carpets (see no. 18) in colour and border design, however, it reminds one of weavings by the Ersari (see no. 267). The overall density with which the guls cover the field is an unusual design feature, giving it an almost tiled appearance. In the upper part of the field are two rows of cruciform minor guls.
Nagel, Stuttgart
Literature: Cassin and Hoffmeister, pl. 16 (chuval)

205

205. Arabachi - *Ensi*. 2nd half of the 19th century

Size: 159 x 135 cm.

Condition: slightly worn.
Occasionally, the *ensis* of the Arabachi can have a surprising range of colours, the strong tones of which are not to everyone's taste. Several of the motifs used on such pieces are also found on the weavings of other tribes. Particularly interesting, apart from the colour, are the *gapyrga* trees in the main borders and these also appear in the dividing beams; also note the camel train in the *elem*. The two-coloured 'chequerboard' selvedges have been partly preserved; brown warps, possibly of goats' hair, mixed wool and cotton wefts, asymmetric knots open to the left.
Nagel, Stuttgart

206

206. Arabachi - *Ensi*. 19th century

Size: 126 x 132 cm.

Condition: wear, restorations.
Only two design types of Arabachi *ensi* have been published to date. This type, with the classic 'four field' arrangement and with four *kejebe* gables at the top, is rarely seen in so attractive a form. The design of this type has many features in common with the weavings of other Turkoman groups. However, the compartment design of the main border, also seen in the vertical beam seems to be specific to the Arabachi. Somewhat similar weavings, however, although with different colouring, are known with Ersari structure, the latter tribe possibly having absorbed some small Arabachi groups. The *elem* with its depiction of a camel-train is a typical Arabachi design feature. Undoubtedly an early example of its type.
Nagel, Stuttgart
Literature: Bausback, pp. 496-7; Hali 37, p. 91; Hali 41, p. 89

207

207. Turkoman (?) - Animal Cover (?). 1st half of the 19th century

Size: 297 x 97 cm.

Condition: worn, corroded in places, minor restorations.

Placed here because of the similarity of some of its motifs to those found on Arabachi weavings, this long rug is difficult to attribute. Its field is obviously based on a Turkoman *ensi* with *elem*-like panels at either end with camel-trains resembling those on the Arabachi *ensis* we have illustrated. The placement of the horizontal beam exactly in the centre suggests that this rug might have been woven as an animal blanket. Another interesting design relationship is with Salor *ensis*, of which very few are known. Both the palette and structure of this rug are atypical of Turkoman weavings. The wefts are of undyed cotton and it is symmetrically knotted. It has been suggested that it was made by Turkoman weavers in the Shirvan area of the eastern Caucasus. This might explain the unexpected pattern in the inner border.
Nagel, Stuttgart

208. Arabachi - *Ensi*. 1st half of the 19th century

Size: 142 x 147 cm.

This is the second well-known design type of Arabachi *ensis;* these have an overall field design, with saw-edged diamond motifs arranged diagonally but joined by vertical bars. The border patterns and the camel-train *elem* are typical. Examples of this design type are almost always dated to the first half of the 19th century.
Bausback, Mannheim
Literature: Bennett, 1978 (as second half of the 19th century)

209

210

Detail 210a

209. Arabachi - *Chuval*. 2nd third of the 19th century

Size: 75 x 150 cm.

Condition: slightly worn.

Arabachi *chuvals* with lobed guls are among the most beautiful of all Turkoman large bags. This gul, similar to that used by the Tekke, has, however, a different and very distinctive outline which can be related to medallions seen on some early Anatolian carpets; there may also be a relationship with the ancient Chinese cloud-collar motif. The minor gul also seems to have Anatolian antecedents. The main border design is similar to those seen on other examples illustrated in the literature; the motifs in the *elem* seem almost obligatory, as are the T-shaped *kochak* motifs in the upper guard. An unusual feature is that the centres of the main guls are partly piled in silk.

Nagel, Stuttgart

Literature: Hali, vol. 5, no. 3; Loges, no. 110; Mackie and Thompson, no. 54 (Metropolitan Museum of Art, New York).

211

210. Arabachi - *Chuval*. 19th century

Size: 83 x 157 cm.

Condition: signs of wear, some repiled areas. Arabachi *chuvals* of similar colour are usually dated to the first half of the 19th century in the literature; this dating is given to an example with *chuval* guls illustrated by Tzareva, which also has the same main border design as this one. It is also worth mentioning a bag of similar design illustrated by Bogolyubov, which Jon Thompson at that time placed in what he called the 'S Group'; other patterns used by the Arabachi which are found on the weavings of other Turkoman groups include the *kejebe* pattern, *chuval* guls and star medallions similar to those seen on no. 269. This bag has a wide palette which includes five distinct shades of red.

Nagel, Stuttgart

Literature: Tzareva, no. 112; Bogolyubov, ed. Thompson, no. 10

211. Arabachi - *Chuval*. 19th century

Size: 91 x 135 cm.

Condition: signs of wear, areas of repiling. Loges dates an example of similar design to the beginning of the 19th century 'or earlier'. On both pieces, the main motif in the field is the *chuval* gul in a 4 x 4 arrangement, accompanied by the minor *chemche* gul. The main border is divided into compartments and is flanked by narrow guards. The form of flower or shrub seen in the left and top main border of this example is found all the way round on the Loges piece; here, however, the right and bottom borders have only the flower 'heads'. Interestingly, on this same Loges piece, the motifs in the *elem* have stems just as can be seen on no. 209.

Nagel, Stuttgart

Literature: Loges, no. 109; Tzareva, no. 112 (Russian Museum, St. Petersburg); Cassin and Hoffmeister, plates. 11 (as Chodor) and 15

212. Chodor - Main Carpet. Mid 19th century or earlier

Size: 468 x 273 cm.

Condition: slightly worn; some restorations, selvedges replaced.
The *ertmen* gul and its variations has been thought of as the tribal emblem of the Chodor Turkomans and is found on both their carpets and bags. They are laid closely together on the field in tile-like fashion and are usually enclosed, as here, by a fine, ribbon-like diamond lattice. The unusually large size of this example makes it difficult to believe that it is a nomadic weaving and it has guls arranged diagonally in two alternating colours. A stem in the centre of each gul is flanked by four flower-heads with bird-like hooks (*kochaks*). At the edges of the long sides of the field, small 'filler' motifs suggest the possibility of an endless repeat. The warps are a mixture of wool and animal hair, the wefts cotton and the knots asymmetric open to the right.
Nagel, Stuttgart
Literature: Bennett, 1982, p. 167

CHODOR PILE WEAVINGS

As with pile weavings which have been labelled Arabachi, Chodor weavings are also relatively easily identified, even though in both groups it is not enough to base a classification purely on decorative elements.

It may nevertheless be difficult to distinguish these weavings from some Yomut and Ersari examples. Technical characteristics, such as the use of the asymmetric knot or cotton wefts - according to Loges (*Hali* 26), the latter are never found in really early Chodor pieces - may not be enough for unambiguous classifications, as they are also found in pieces that are generally known as Yomut. The provenance of certain design types which have long been described as Chodor, can also be called into question, as is the case with *mafrashes* with Ertmen guls (see nos. 179 and 228). Furthermore, variants of the Ertmen gul design can be found in Ersari weavings (see nos. 251 and 264).

212

213. Chodor - Main Carpet. 3rd quarter of the 19th century

Size: 301 x 177 cm.

Condition: very good for its age.
It is interesting to compare this example with the previous one; here the *ertmen* guls have four alternating ground colours (the colour reproduction makes it difficult to distinguish between those piled in dark blue and blue-green). In the upper half of the field, the blue ground guls have a variant interior design, an eight-pointed star motif with two flowers. The guls are less crowded than on the previous examples and are surrounded on the vertical axis by 'star-studded' zig-zag lines. The design in the long white-ground main borders is similar to that found on many Yomut carpets. The ground colour is a distinct dark violet-brown and the *ashik* pattern in the *elems* is typical. Original flatwoven ends and selvedges.

213

214. Chodor - Main Carpet. Last quarter of the 19th century

Size: 353 x 215 cm.

Condition: slight damage, areas of repiling. Similar in field design to no. 212, but with a stronger red, a pale green and a petrol blue typical of late Chodor rugs; the ground colour is liver-brown. Unusual features of this example, are the patterns used in the main borders and *elems*. The white-ground main border contains a continuous series of hooked diamonds with quartered centres. The *elems* have a version of the *ak-su* pattern, which can be seen in the field of the main carpet no. 219 and the prayer rug no. 220. Original selvedges in two colours.
Nagel, Stuttgart
Literature: Schürmann, no. 12; Bogolyubov, ed. Thompson, no. 23

214

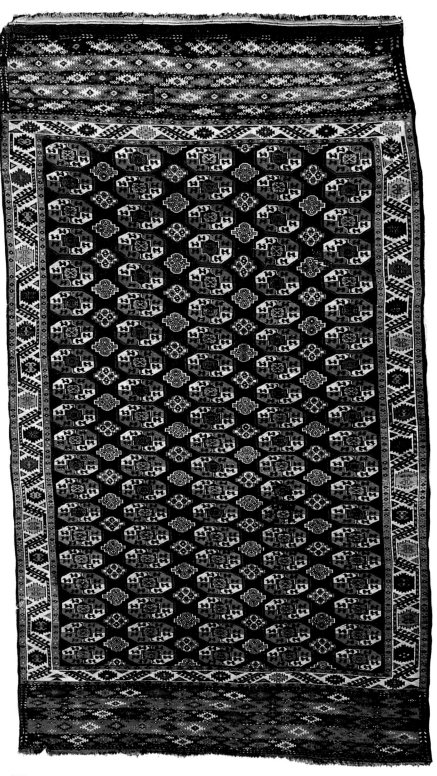

215. Chodor - Main Carpet. 2nd half of the 19th century

Size: 370 x 221 cm.

Condition: good for its age.
Chodor main carpets with dark chocolate-brown grounds have been said to have come specifically from Khiva. The major gul, here the *tauk-nuska*, is sometimes accompanied by what has been interpreted as a small and simplified *ertmen* minor gul. The five vertical rows of main guls are, as usual, quartered chromatically, each quarter containing two small stylised animals; the minor guls typically contain four flowers with *kochak* extensions. This carpet has a surprising palette, especially in the main borders and *elems*, where deep blue and turquoise are used. Relatively fine knotting.
Nagel, Stuttgart
Literature: Tschebull, Hali, vol. 3, no. 2, pp. 91 ff.; Tzareva, no. 115 (analogous border and elem patterns); Nagel auction catalogue no. 273, lot 98 (tauk-nuska main guls with erre minor guls)

215

216. Chodor - Main Carpet. 19th century

Size: 360 x 225 cm.

Condition: slightly worn, some repiling.

Werner Loges was unsure of this carpet's provenance when he came to publish it in 1978. It appears in his chapter of 'Other Central Asian Carpets' as plate 111, where he describes it as an early 19th century piece, possibly a Yomut. Hoffmeister, whose understanding of Central Asian weaves is comparable to Loges', has since been convinced that the piece is a Chodor (cf. his *Turkoman Carpets in Franconia*, 1980, in which he discusses this piece on p.58) and the piece is now confidently attributed to weavers from that tribe.

The knot density of the lustrous wool pile lies somewhere between carpets of the so-called Khiva group (1,200 to 1,500 per dm^2) and those which Tschebull (op. cit.) called 'Group 4'(about 2,000 per dm^2). The beautiful *elem* pattern is noteworthy, with the main motifs joined by a net-like lattice.

Nagel, Stuttgart

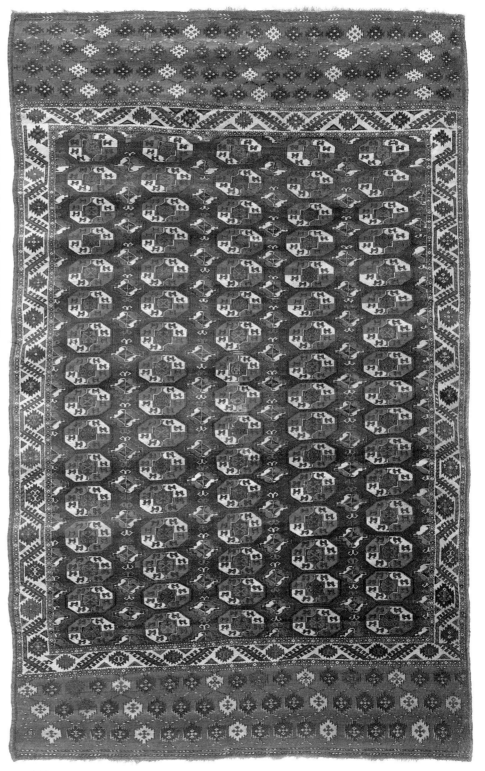

216

217. Chodor - Main Carpet. 2nd half of the 19th century

Size: 293 x 164 cm.

As has been noted several times, it is often difficult to make specific attributions for Turkoman weavings, a problem which arises with this main carpet. In colour and structure, it fits into what we consider to be the Chodor group. Moshkova notes that similar field patterns are used by the Chodor, the Igdyr and the Shlichen. The typically Yomut main border design does not not necessarily mitigate against a Chodor attribution. The *gul-aidi* pattern in the narrow *elems* can be found on at least one Chodor *ensi* and on a prayer rug which Loges attributed to the Ersari.

Nagel, Stuttgart

Literature: Moshkova, no. 74/8; Mackie and Thompson, no. 53 (ensi); Loges, no. 90 (prayer rug); Hali, vol. 4, no. 2, p. 21; Bausback Catalogue, 1975, p. 305 (Chodor prayer rug with stepped top)

218. Chodor - Main Carpet. Last quarter of the 19th century

Size: 299 x 190 cm.

Condition: signs of wear, the added flatwoven ends damaged.

As the field pattern of a main carpet, the stepped grid-like design seen here has no close analogies, although it is found in variant form on some rare Chodor prayer rugs with stepped tops and on at least two Yomut *ok-bash*. In some respects, it is reminiscent of the *dyrnak* gul of Yomut main carpets, especially when adapted for use as a minor gul (see no. 108). There is some camel hair in the foundations, the knots are asymmetric open to the right, and it has broad, five-cord goats' hair selvedges.

Nagel, Stuttgart

Literature: Loges, Hali 26, pp. 30 ff, no. 1 (prayer rug)

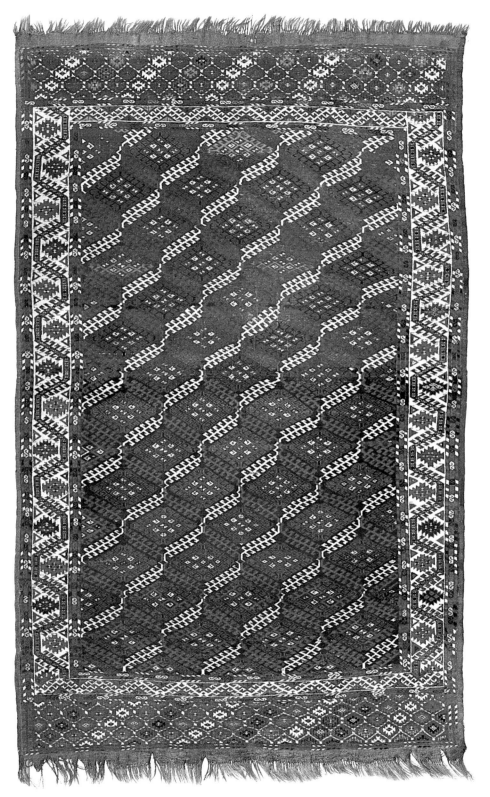

218

219. Chodor - Main Carpet. 19th century

Size: 405 x 253 cm.

Condition: areas of damage and repair.
In general, Turkoman main carpets with the
ak-su pattern in their fields are quite rare; few
Chodor weavings with it are known, although
the prayer rug illustrated next is another
example. The German auction house which
sold this piece dated it to the beginning of the
19th century; given its colour, crowded field
and main border pattern, it could be from the
same time and place as no. 212. The *elems*
have the *ashik* motif arranged diagonally by
colour. Complete with original selvedges.
Rippon Boswell
Literature: Loges, no. 67]

220. Chodor - Prayer Rug. 19th century

Size: 183 x 124 cm.

Condition: worn in places but good generally.
It is even more unusual to find the *ak-su* field
pattern on a prayer rug than on a main carpet.
The designs in the borders and *elems* of this
example are almost identical to those on
another Chodor prayer rug with *ertmen* guls
in its field, formerly in the Straka Collection,
and often published. Another example of this
latter design type was published by Loges. In
colour and structure, including six-cord
selvedges wrapped in dark brown goats' hair,
this piece is analogous to no. 218. A rarity
*Literature: Loges, Hali 26, p. 32, no. 2;
Volkmann, 1985, p. 217; Hali 45, p. 47
(identical, Völkerkunde Museum, Munich);
Straka Collection, cat. no. 10*

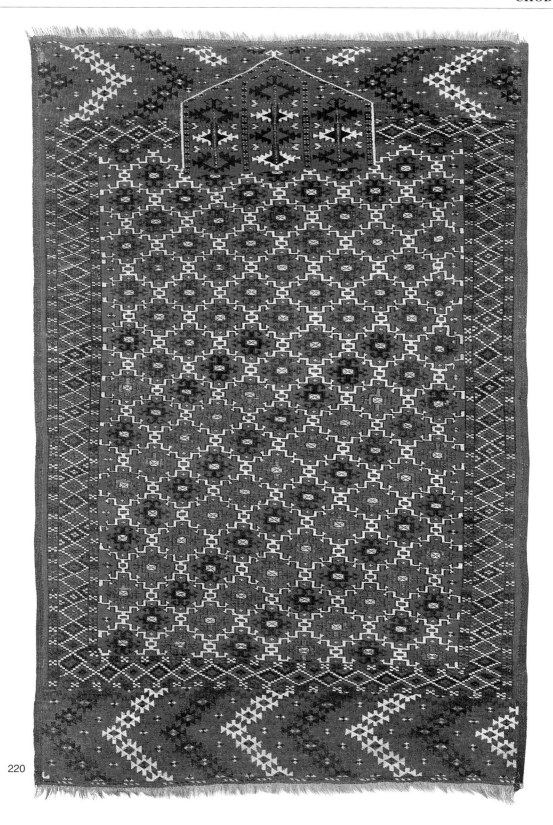

220

221

221. Chodor - *Ensi*. Last quarter of the 19th century

Size: 165 x 130 cm.

Condition: good for its age; areas of repiling. As on the following example, this *ensi* has stemmed *ashik* motifs in its four aubergine-ground field compartments; each *ashik* contains a shrub-like motif with three 'shoots'. There is an obvious similarity in both colour and design to some Yomut *ensis;* no. 139, for example, has the *ashik* motif in the horizontal beam and the inner white-ground guards, as well as the *gapyrga* pattern in its dark brown ground *elem*.
Christie's East, New York

222. Chodor - *Ensi*. 19th century

Size: 147 x 125 cm.

Condition: worn, partly rewoven.
Loges suggested, in an article he wrote in 1985, that few Chodor *ensis* were known. He then listed seven pieces, one of which is this rug. *Ensis* with a frieze of animals in their base *elem* panel are usually associated with the Arabachi (see nos. 205-6, 208) and very occasionally, with Salor *ensis*, (as we discussed in relation to no. 207), though there is some controversy about whether the Salor continued to weave their own designs independently after they were defeated and absorbed by the Tekke in the 19th century. It is interesting to compare the animals on this piece with those depicted on a rug in a painting by the 14th century Florentine Niccolo di Buonacorso (see fig. 100, page 249). A very similar *ensi* was dated by Mackie and Thompson to the middle of the 19th century.
Nagel, Stuttgart
Literature: Mackie and Thompson, no. 37; Loges, Hali 26, pp. 30 ff., no. 6 (this ensi)

Detail 222a

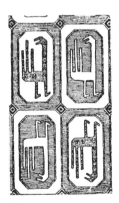

Fig. 100

222

223

223. Chodor - Piled Panel. 19th century

Size: 35 x 145 cm.

A very unusual early Chodor weaving. The rare ivory field has a series of barred diamonds arranged so as to suggest an endless repeat. This toothed outlining indicates that the design was taken from a kilim, on which this type of outlining is a technical necessity. However, patterns of this type are not typical of Turkoman flatweaves which is why, as with no. 224, it is possible to suggest an attribution to some other Central Asian group rather than the Chodor specifically. Goats' hair warps, cotton and wool wefts, about 1,800 asymmetric knots per dm^2.
Bausback, Mannheim

224. Chodor - *Ensi*. Mid 19th century

Size: 152 x 122 cm.

Condition: slight wear, some areas repiled or repaired.
Like no. 222, this *ensi* was also illustrated by Loges in 1985. Here, however, the field was not divided into four but had an overall design; another Chodor *ensi* with an all-over field design, using the *ashik* motif, was also illustrated by Loges (see our nos. 221-2). The vertical rhomboidal pattern does not seem to be part of a strictly Turkoman design tradition and may by based on textiles in the ikat technique, as are a number of other carpet designs. (Ikat weaving was undertaken mainly by the other peoples of Central Asia – most notably by the Uzbekis – and had a city-based tradition). Structurally, however, this is typically Chodor, with alternate wefts in wool and cotton.
Christie's East, New York
Literature: Loges, Hali 26, pp. 30 ff., nos. 4 and 5 (this ensi)

224

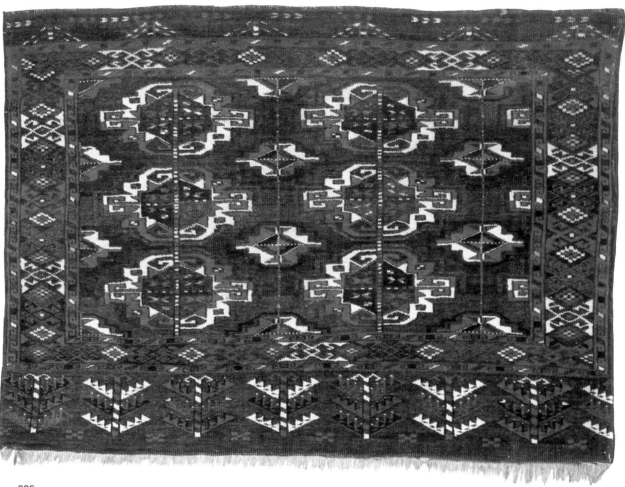

225

225. Chodor - *Chuval*. End of the 19th century

Size: 83 x 118 cm.

Condition: good for its age, some repiling. Rugs featuring these guls can be found amongst both Yomut and Chodor weavings but, more frequently, the former. As with *torbas* with *ertmen* guls (cf. nos. 179 and 228) their origin can easily be determined by reference to their colour palette and their structure. An unusual feature is the presence of part minor guls at the top and bottom of the field and to the left and small sections of the major guls down the right side; this suggests once again an infinite repeat. The design in

the main borders at the sides makes an interesting comparison with the motifs found on some early Anatolian animal carpets (see fig. 101).
Nagel, Stuttgart
Literature: Loges, no. 71; Cassin and Hoffmeister, pl. 11; Hoffmeister, no. 30

Fig. 101

226. Chodor - *Chuval*. Mid 19th century

Size: 76 x 112 cm.

Condition: wear, edge damage, repiled areas.
The *ertmen* gul is the motif most often used
by the Chodor, not only on their carpets and
rugs but also on their bag faces. Despite this,
examples which can be confidently dated to
before about 1870-80 are rare and much
sought after by collectors. They constitute a
fairly homogenous group, with the guls
usually in four different colours and with a
tall, 'stretched', shape, especially on *chuvals*.
In most instances, there are five horizontal
rows of guls, surrounded by a fine zig-zag
lattice often with small floral inclusions. A
kochanak compartment main border pattern is
the norm (see no. 72), as well as *ashik* or
gapyrga variants in the *elem* (no 225).
Nagel, Stuttgart
Literature: Hoffmeister, no. 29; Loges, no. 72

226

**227. Chodor - *Torba*. Last quarter of the
19th century**

Size: 45 x 122 cm.

Condition: worn, edges damaged.
In contrast to the following example, we are
fairly confident in attributing this weaving to
the Chodor; however, arguments over which
examples are Chodor and which Yomut will
probably continue (see no. 179). Typical is
the use of two variants of the *ertmen* gul. One
contains the usual dice-like flowers with
diagonal protrusions at the top and bottom,
the other blue-ground gul having a central
kochak is surrounded by what could be
described as small variants of the same
hooked bird's head motifs.
Nagel, Stuttgart
Literature: Beresneva, no. 20; Loges, no. 70

227

228

229

228. Chodor or Yomut - Pair of *torbas*. 19th/20th century

Size: about 45 x 105cm. each.

In 1980, Leslie Pinner illustrated a single *torba* which is very similar to these; this pair, however, is in a remarkable state of preservation. In concluding her essay on the difficulties involved in attributing *torbas* with the *ertmen* gul, Mrs Pinner wrote: "It is unlikely that we shall ever be able to decide for certain whether the *ertmen* torbas of this group were made by Chodor women who adopted Yomut techniques or by Yomut weavers who had taken over Chodor designs. What can be said is that the torbas belong to a group which must stem from an area where, and from a period when, the opportunity was given for the interaction of Chodor design and Yomut techniques."

Nagel, Stuttgart

Literature: L. Pinner, Hali, vol. 2, no. 4, pp. 286 ff.

229. Chodor - *Torba*. 3rd quarter of the 19th century

Size: 45 x 125 cm.

Condition: traces of wear, repiling to upper edge.

The *kejebe* pattern is also part of the design repertoire of the Chodor. In a rare Chodor *kapunuk* illustrated by Loges, four *kejebe* 'gables' adjoin along the top of the three-sided weaving and have the usual inner motifs. Here there are only the upper parts of the 'gables', a variant of the usual *kejebe* design also found in the *elem* of a remarkable Chodor prayer rug with stepped upper outline. The variations on the present piece include the use of *ashik* motifs and the use of starred octagons in the centre of each dark area. A very rare piece.

Nagel, Stuttgart

Literature: Hali 25, p. 70, no. 11 (very similar panel, an animal trapping); Vienna, 1986, no. 117; Loges, no. 69 (kapunuk); Hali vol. 4, no. 4, p. 395, no. 6 (prayer rug)

ERSARI PILE WEAVINGS

There are distinct differences in design, palette and structure between the many pile weavings that are generally identified with the Ersari or several Ersari sub-tribes. A subdivision seems therefore essential but it is no less problematic than that of the Yomut groups. The difficulties begin with the definition of a nomenclature. Many authors, therefore, do not even attempt to explain the meaning of the frequently used term 'Beshir'. Does this describe a sub-tribe of the Ersari, or were these carpets woven in the settlement of that name? The term may also apply to the surrounding region or even its population. On the other hand, pile weavings made in the Bukhara Emirate are frequently described as 'Beshir', even though it is not certain whether they were woven by Turkomans at all.

There have been several interesting contributions to the problematic subject of Ersari weavings: Hans König, for example, attempted to divide 'Ersari' carpets into four design groups (*Hali* 4/2 and *Turkmen,* Thompson 1980). Robert Pinner in 'The Beshir Carpets of the Bukhara Emirate - A Review' (*Hali* 3/4) further adds to the problematic nature of this classification and presents the available evidence.

Despite all efforts, it has not yet been possible to make a confident definition of those groups which are generally described as Ersari or Beshir. It has also proved impossible to put forward such a concept in this catalogue. Those carpets, whose characteristics suggest that they may have been made in the Bukhara Emirate, will be illustrated as one group in the plate section, despite the fact that the definitions 'Ersari group' and 'Bukhara Emirate' are merely compromise solutions.

230. Ersari - Main Carpet. End of the 19th century

Size: 319 x 260 cm.

Condition: traces of wear, some repiling.
Like the principal guls of Salor main carpets, the octagonal major guls often found on Ersari main carpets have floral forms resembling clover-leaves in their interiors, with a star-like motif in the centre; this latter motif is used as the minor gul on no. 232. The design of the main border of continuous linked diamonds is typical and is complemented by the *shudur* design in the flanking guards; there is also an outer guard with a zig-zag pattern. Unusually, this example has *elems,* in the top half of which are stylised shrubs. Flatwoven *elems,* in sumakh or similar techniques, and with related designs, are, according to O'Bannon, typically found on rugs woven in the Mazar-i-Sharif and Kunduz areas of northeast Afghanistan. Most amusing is the tiny camel with an eight pointed star piled in silk almost two-thirds down the left side of the field; a generally well-preserved carpet, mostly in full pile.
Nagel, Stuttgart
Literature: O'Bannon, p. 125; Loges, no. 79

230

231

232. Ersari - Main Carpet. End of the 19th century

Size: 316 x 216 cm.

Condition: slightly worn.
The great similarity between this carpet and no. 230 indicates that they both come from the same area of northeast Afghanistan. According to Gans-Ruedin, carpets with this variant of the *gulli-gul* are particularly associated with the Ghazan sub-tribe which lives in the area of Akcha, northwest of Mazar-i-Sharif; each gul has a 'plaited diamond' outline which is echoed by its central motif, which is also known from weavings with the *kejebe* design (see nos. 2ff.). The guards flanking the main border have the *shudur* pattern, although the pattern in the outer guard is reminiscent of that found on some Saryk weavings. The carpet has beautiful flatwoven *elems* in six colours and its original goats' hair selvedges.
Nagel, Stuttgart
Literature: Gans-Ruedin, 1971, p. 361; McCoy Jones and Boucher, 1975, no. 30

231. Ersari - Small Rug. End of the 19th century

Size: 75 x 71 cm.

Condition: obvious signs of wear.
Carpets with the so-called *gulli-gul*, like the one just illustrated and the one following, have been made in various formats, some of them having only three medallions or, like here, one. Such small weavings have occasionally been described as *germeches,* used for the base of the tent entrance, although this description is usually applied to small weavings in a landscape format such as no. 34. The central gul is surrounded by a diamond lattice drawn in a manner somewhat reminiscent of a design group of early Chinese carpets.
Nagel, Stuttgart

233

233. Ersari - Main Carpet. 19th century

Size: 273 x 213 cm.

Condition: worn.

Robert Pinner, discussing a rare Saryk carpet in the Museum of Islamic Art, Berlin, noted that there was a rare group of Saryk examples with either the *gulli-gul* or the *temirjen* gul used as the main motif, but that these were found more often on Ersari carpets. Considering both the ethnographic relationship of these two tribes and their common use of some motifs, Pinner concluded that such guls were used on carpets from the middle Amu-Darya region and were used there both by the Ersari and the Saryk during the early 19th century before the latter migrated westwards towards Merv. Compared to other symmetrically knotted carpets with this gul, the present example differs only in the motif at the centre of each gul and in the use of the minor gul seen here.

Nagel, Stuttgart

Literature: Pinner (in Pinner and Denny, eds.), pp. 140 ff.; Loges, no. 24 (Saryk): Milhofer, no. 36 ('Ersari gul')

234. Ersari - Small Carpet. End of the 19th century

Size: 194 x 167 cm.

As on the last piece, there are three rows of guls framed by a main border with a compartment pattern and an outer zig-zag guard on the long sides. However, in contrast to those we have seen so far, this carpet has a very rustic quality: loose knotting, vitality of colour and unconventional playfulness of design. When published previously it was described as being from the Amu-Darya region. According to Thompson, however, such colourful rugs were made by the Ersari in the late 19th century after they had fled from Turkestan to north Afghanistan, where they lived as semi-nomads.

Galerie Sailer, Salzburg

Literature: Vienna, cat. no. 120 (this rug); Thompson, p. 37

234

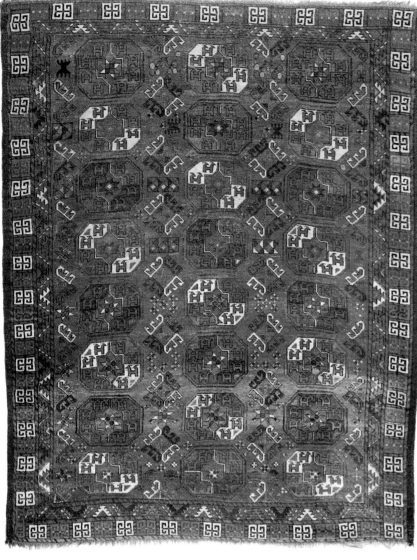

235

235. Ersari Group - Small Carpet. End of the 19th century

Size: 200 x 156 cm.

Condition: slight signs of wear.
This small carpet with the *tauk-nuska* main gul originates from the Amu-Darya area. Such weavings are clearly less colourful than some Ersari carpets we have seen which have had a reddish-brown hue. A section of *ashik* lattice is usually found in the main border but the outer *sainak* pattern border is unusual, and reminds one of *ensis,* as indeed does the format of this piece. In addition, all the animals in the guls are in one direction.
Nagel, Stuttgart
Literature: Hofmeister, no. 13

236 Ersari - Main Carpet. End of the 19th century

Size: 254 x 168 cm.

Condition: very good.
19th century Ersari carpets with *chuval* guls from the Amu-Darya region are quite rare. Here, they retain their old clarity of detail and rounded form and are arranged in rows of three; the motif in the centre of each one is the same as one of the minor guls. The other minor gul is the *pudak*, and is highlighted by small areas piled in yellow with the main border containing a version of the 'curled leaf' design.
Nagel, Stuttgart
Literature: Milhofer, no. 44; Gans-Ruedin, 1971, p. 350

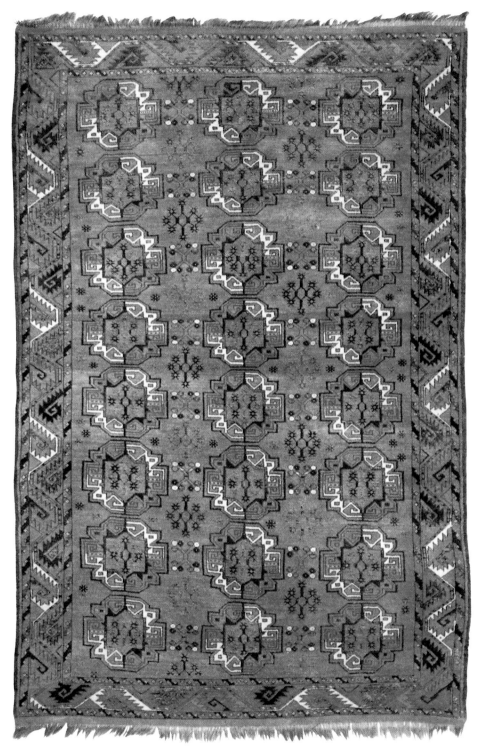

236

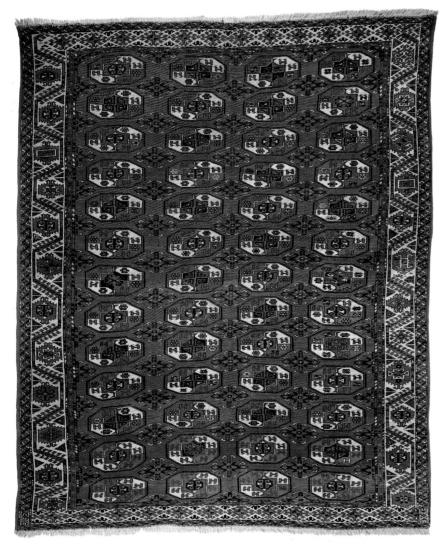

237

237. Ersari Group - Main Carpet. 19th-20th century

Size: 234 x 199 cm.
Weavings by the Chob-Bash and Kizil Ayak tribes were made in areas adjacent to those of the Ersari. From its palette and various aspects of its design, this piece is most likely to be from the Chob-Bash. It is not clear what the ethnic composition might have been of various weaving settlements in Central Asia, but certainly the Kizil Ayak and, especially the Chob-Bash borrowed or copied motifs used by the Yomut and the Chodor. In this carpet the stylised animals in the variant *tauk-nuska* guls have been partly replaced by flowers, a phenomenon also encountered with some *ertmen* gul variants (Nos. 212 ff.). Original selvedges.
Nagel, Stuttgart
Literature: Hali 32, p. 24 (as Kizil Ayak or Chob-Bash, in the Ashmolean Museum, Oxford); Danker Collection, cat. no. 112

238. Kizil Ayak (?) - Main Carpet. 2nd half of the 19th century

Size: 287 x 224 cm.

Condition: signs of wear, minimal damage, some restoration.
Although at first sight this would appear to be a Kizil Ayak main carpet, one of the principal structural characteristics of such weavings, asymmetric knotting open to the right, is not present here, the piece being symmetrically knotted. It has the *tauk-nuska* main gul and the *chemche* minor gul. The common use of designs and designs by different Turkoman tribes living adjacent to each other often makes exact attributions difficult.
Nagel, Stuttgart
Literature: Loges, no. 73; Azadi, pl. 10

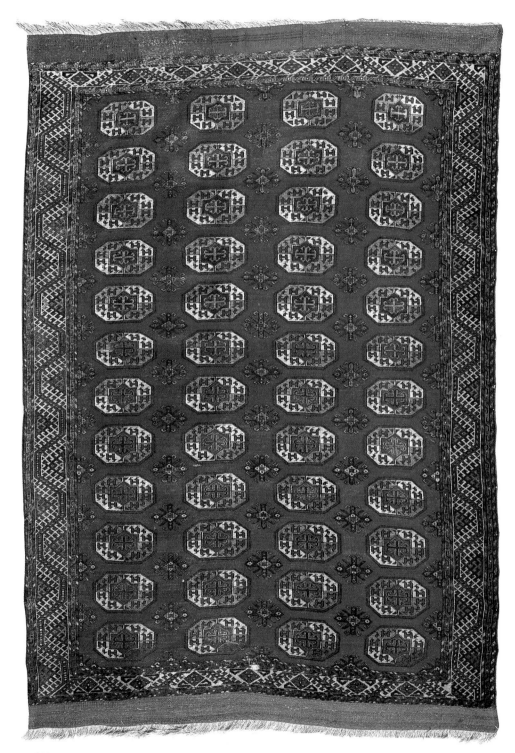

238

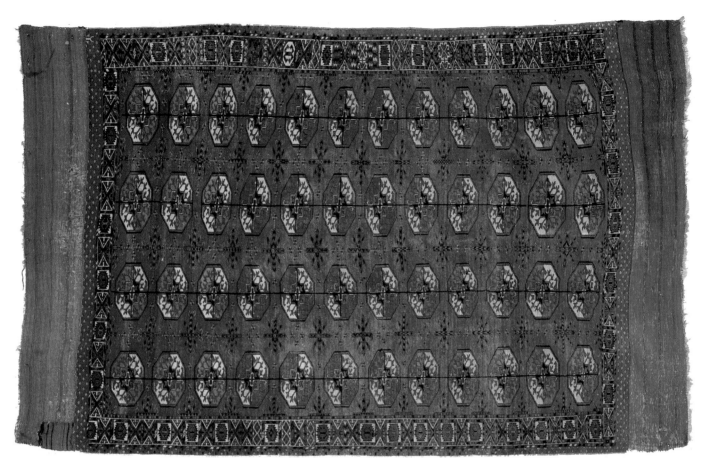

239

239. Ersari Group (?) - Main Carpet. 19th century

Size: 238 x 178 cm.

Condition: some damage, repair to flatwoven ends, pile good.

Although looking very like Tekke work, the octagonal form of the Tekke main guls would not normally be found on a Tekke carpet of this age. The design in the white-ground main borders is interesting and no close analogies can be found on any of the Tekke main carpets illustrated earlier (see Literature below). Pinner and Franses, however, discussed three Tekke main carpets with white-ground borders containing the 'curled leaf' design. In this version seen here, it is stylised and reminds one of the version of the design seen on some Yomut and Kizil Ayak carpets. In the upper left corner of the piled outer guard there is a headless human figure and there are some brocaded amuletic motifs in the upper flatwoven end.

Nagel, Stuttgart

Literature: Pinner and Franses, pp. 102 ff., nos. 173-5, col. plates IV-V; Hali 25, p. 70, fig. 10 (Tekke main carpet with closely related main border design)

240. Kizil Ayak - Main Carpet. 3rd quarter of the 19th century

Size: 256 x 207 cm.

Condition: signs of wear, some repiling.
Reminiscent of the Arabachi main carpet illustrated as no. 202, the structure of this example allows it to be identified as Kizil Ayak, a tribe associated with northern Afghanistan. Loges described a typical Kizil Ayak carpet as having a silky and tightly woven pile about 4-6 mm. in height, with a light brown wool weft and between 1,800 and 2,100 asymmetric knots open to the right per dm². The field has four rows of *tauk-nuska* main guls and *chemche* minor guls; both the inner and outer parts of the main guls are quartered diagonally by colour. The form of 'curled leaf' design in the main border is almost the same as that on the Arabachi carpet mentioned above.

Nagel, Stuttgart

Literature: Neff and Maggs, pl. 44; Loges, no. 73

Note to the English Edition: It is no longer considered correct to describe the Kizil Ayak as a sub-group of the Ersari; they were an independent weaving tribe. For some of the latest research on this and other complex questions of Turkoman attributions, see Robert Pinner, *The Rickmers Collection - Turkoman Rugs*, 1993.

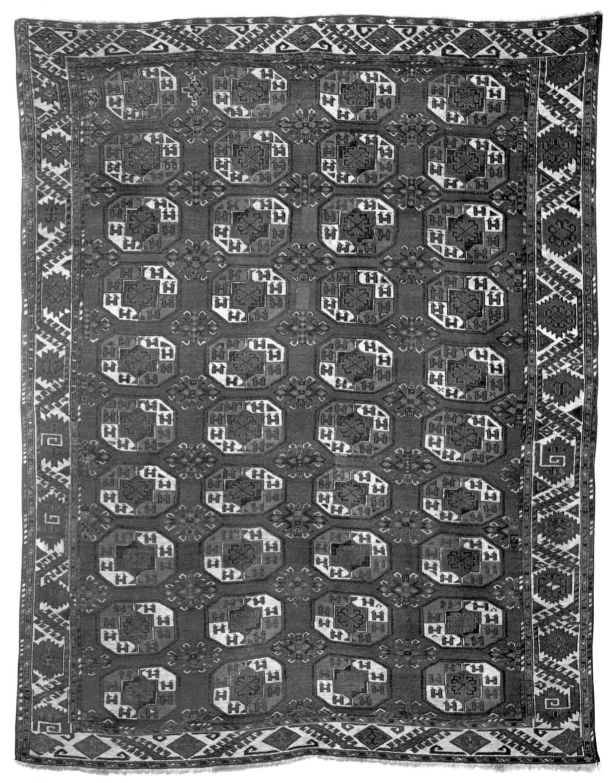

241

241. Ersari Group - Main Carpet. 2nd half of the 19th century

Size: 374 x 268 cm.

Condition: partly worn, repiling, lower outer guard missing.

Weavings with this field design are relatively unusual and the majority are smaller and of 20th century workmanship; as a 19th century main carpet, therefore, this example is quite a rarity. The palette is reminiscent of weavings attributed to the Charshangho area of Afghanistan; the shrub-like motifs seen in each of the squares into which the field is divided and also in the main border are found on *chuvals* (see no. 266), which Loges attributed to the Kizil Ayak. It is worth mentioning that the division of the field into squares, the vertical orientation of the design and the framing of each square *shudur* pattern inner guards, all make this piece reminiscent of the general design of *ensis*.
Nagel, Stuttgart

242. Ersari Group - Small Rug. End of the 19th century

Size: 134 x 106 cm.

Condition: worn overall.

The design and use of colour is close to that of some Ersari Beshir prayer rugs; it should be remembered also that many *ensis* have design features in common with prayer rugs and some authors have suggested that they may have been used as such, as well as for covering the entrance to a tent. As on the last piece, the field is divided into rectangles framed by inner guards with the *shudur* pattern (note the variation in the use of these guards round the two rectangles at the base of the field, which gives this part of the rug an *elem*-like appearance). On related prayer rugs, supposedly from the Kerki area, a 'trunk' appears in the centre of the field, representing a tree, with the small triangles, arranged chromatically into diagonal rows, forming the 'branches' (see the variant no. 299). Note the attractive pattern in the kilim ends.
Nagel, Stuttgart
Literature: Schürmann, no. 64; O'Bannon, p. 121, fig. E

242

243. Ersari Group - Main Carpet.
19th century

Size: 228 x 143 cm.

Condition: partly worn, some repiling.
Compared to the Ersari Group of carpets
illustrated so far, this example has a very un-
Turkoman field design but its main border
design is known from Ersari carpets and from
the weavings of other Turkoman tribes. The
design in the field may have been derived
either from kilims or ikats. According to
O'Bannon, rugs with similar border designs
were made in the Dalautabad region of
northwest Afghanistan. This is a rare weaving
with very lively colours and an unusual
amount of white.
Nagel, Stuttgart
*Literature: Cassin and Hoffmeister, pl. 29
(chuval)*

244. Ersari Group - Small Rug.
19th/20th century

Size: 137 x 104 cm.

Condition: slightly worn.
The arrangement of the field, with interior
shudur pattern guards - the latter probably
derived from Persian floral designs - reminds
one of the two carpets illustrated as nos.
241-2; here, however, the design in the two
vertical field panels has been transferred from
ikat textiles to a pile weaving (see fig. 102 for
a detail of an ikat prayer textile). This
tranferrence from the ikat dyed medium into
pile knotting is a frequently enountered
phenomenon (see also no. 255).
Nagel, Stuttgart
*Literature: Bennett. 1982, p. 172 (as 'early
20th century'); O'Bannon, p. 152, fig. A*

243

Fig. 102

244

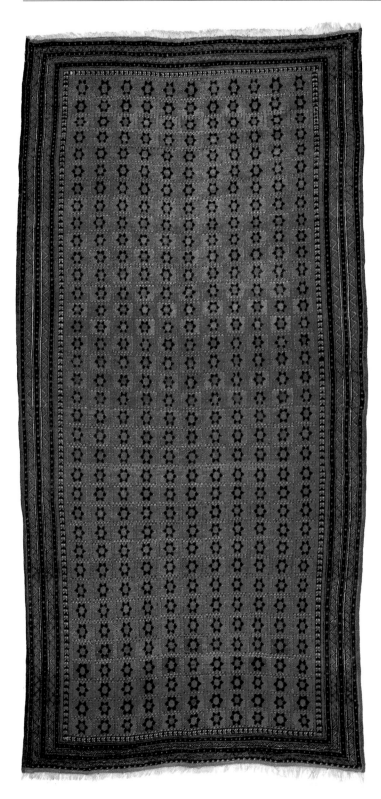

245. Ersari Group - Main Carpet.
Late 19th/early 20th century

Size: 253 x 128 cm.

Condition: good for its age.
This carpet belongs to a design group
distinguished by the strictly geometrical
nature of its designs. During the last few
years, a few related bags have come onto the
market, variously described as Ersari, Beshir
and Uzbek, and have created considerable
interest. Their fields are often quartered and
are framed by borders containing rows of
triangles. Here, each compartment of the
rectangular grid in the field contains a star, an
overall design sometimes encountered on the
weavings of other Turkoman tribes (see no.
11). Presumably this and related weavings
come from areas in the border region of
Tajikistan inhabited by the Beshir.
Nagel, Stuttgart

245

**246. Ersari Group - Prayer Rug.
End of the 19th century**

Size: 172 x 199 cm.

Condition: signs of wear, expert restoration.
An extremely interesting prayer rug from the
Amu-Darya region, although one which it is
difficult to attribute to a specific tribe. The
hooked hexagon which fills the whole field is
an example of design tranference from felt to
pile. The arch-like forms of the hooks, here
arranged in opposition on the vertical axis, as
well as the echoing design within the
hexagon, with its large hooked 'crown' at the
top, are all features found on felts (see figs.
57ff.) In the bottom corners of the field are
two triangular 'bird's head' motifs and in the
top corners half guls containing crested birds'
heads. An extraordinary and important piece
which in itself makes a contribution to our
knowledge of Turkoman designs.
Nagel, Stuttgart
Literature: Basilov, vol. VIII, pp. 141 ff., no. 4

246

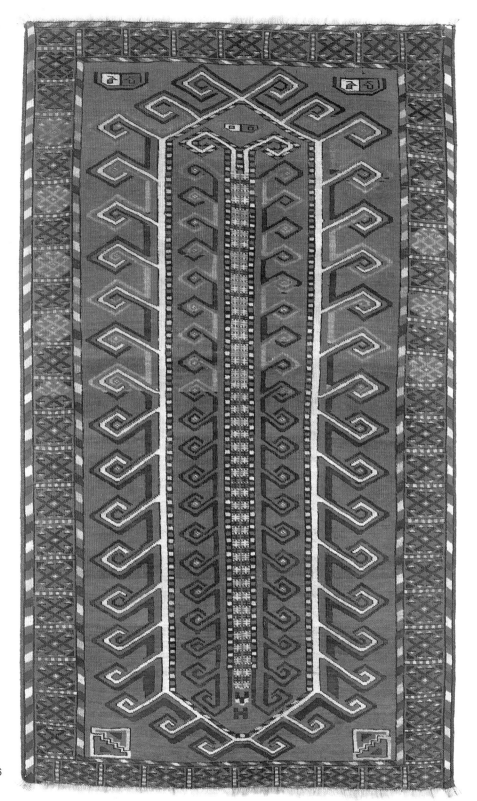

247

247. Ersari Group - *Ensi.* **19th century**

Size: 127 x 101 cm.

Condition: worn, flatwoven ends damaged.
A very individualistic handling of the *ensi*
design, with the four fields not, as is usual,
framed by common main borders, but by two
main border systems which separate the
upper two panels from the bottom two.
Outlined in white, the motifs in the two
central dividing bars remind one of stylised
birds arranged in facing pairs on either side of
the middle sections of these bars. The latter
contains the same pattern of linked hexagons
containing 'S' forms as is used in the white
ground main borders; this pattern is found on
the weavings of many Turkoman tribes.
Nagel, Stuttgart
*Literature: Tzareva, no. 102 (Ethnographic
Museum, St. Petersburg)*

248. Ersari Group - *Ensi.* **19th/20th century**

Size: 170 x 143 cm.

Condition: good.
The brilliant colour of this piece reminds one
of no. 233 and thus of certain Saryk
weavings. This relationship is strengthened
by the two-colour brocading at the top edge
(see no. 22). The broad flatwoven woven
bottom end, however, contains rows of
amulets, as on no. 252. Very typical of Afghan
weaving.
Nagel, Stuttgart

248

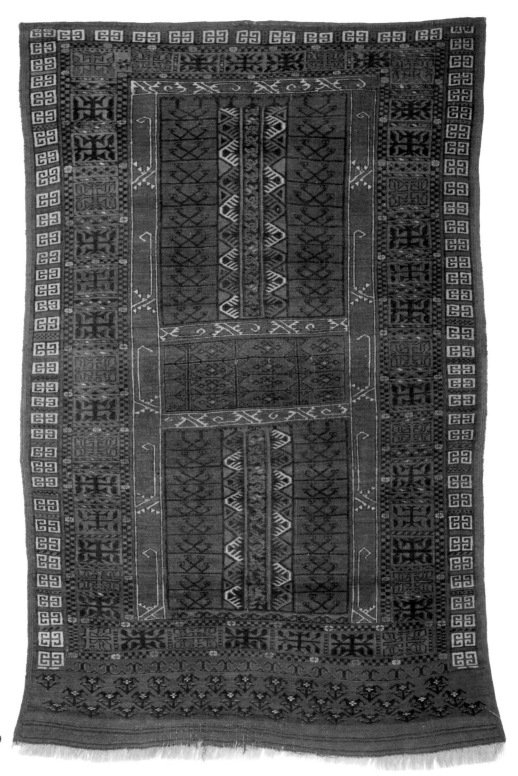

249

249. Ersari Group - *Ensi*. 19th/20th century

Size: 183 x 123 cm.

Condition: slight signs of wear.
A remarkable feature of this example is the stretched and simplified version of the 'curled leaf' design in the inner frame, especially on the long sides; the compartment main border, with its motif reminiscent of the Pazyryk carpet, is also noteworthy.
Nagel, Stuttgart
Literature: Bennett, 1982, p. 171

250. Ersari Group - *Ensi*. 2nd half of the 19th century

Size: 154 x 123 cm.

Condition: worn.
This design type of *ensi* is perhaps the most individualistic of the several variations attributed to the Ersari. The relatively small format of this design type is emphasised by the two powerful arch forms, one above the other in the centre, each of which, as is usual, contains three stylised trees; these arches take up much more room than the four fields, with their *insikush* pattern, which have been reduced to narrow vertical strips. The ornamentation of the horizontal dividing bar is very simple and instead of an outer *sainak* pattern outer guard, here there is one containing an ikat-derived design of phylomorphic character. A typical feature is the narrow brown-ground piled *elem* at the base, decorated with *pudak* motifs.
Nagel, Stuttgart
Literature: Moshkova, pl. 78/1 (for the pudak pattern); Ettinghausen, no. 37; Hoffmeister, nos. 15-16

250

251

251. Ersari Group - *Ensi*. 1st quarter of the 20th century

Size: 185 x 137 cm.

Condition: good.
The inner extra frieze along the bottom of the lower two field compartments is unusual; it contains pairs of part motifs arranged diagonally. 20th century *ensis* woven by Ersari groups in Afghanistan, where they are called *pardahs* ('curtains'), are often considerably larger than older examples, suggesting that they were no longer used as tent entrance covers. Typical features found here are the robust structure and silky wool.
Nagel, Stuttgart
Literature: Gombos, no. 29 (Museum of Applied Art, Budapest)

252. Ersari Group - *Ensi*. End of the 19th century

Size: 176 x 144 cm.

Condition: slight signs of wear.
The great arch forms of this *ensi* relate it immediately to no. 250; here they seem embedded into a tight, mosaic-like diamond lattice. The paired motifs in the middle border on the long sides are interesting and have an obvious zoomorphic character. The frieze panel immediately below the lower arch has similar motifs to those seen on the Yomut *ensi* no. 140. The piece retains its original broad goats' hair selvedges and flatwoven ends, which at the lower end have tiny brocaded amulets.
Nagel, Stuttgart

252

253

Detail 254a

254. Ersari Group - *Ensi*. End of the 19th century

Size: 202 x 146 cm.

Condition: very good.

The detail 254a shows the structure of the mosaic-like chequerboard pattern flatwoven lower end. Dovodov illustrated an almost identical piece from the State Museum of Turkmenia with the caption: "Ersari ensi with edresi pattern; wool, natural and synthetic dyes. Burdaly-Beshiz, late 19th century". Like no. 255, the field pattern, not divided into four panels as usual on *ensis*, has what seems to be motifs derived from ikats, arranged diagonally by colour.

Nagel, Stuttgart

Literature: Dovodov, vol. XII

253. Ersari Group - *Ensi*. 19th/20th century

Size: 213 x 155 cm.

Condition: good.

A number of factors help in determining the origin of this piece. The chequerboard pattern of the flatwoven end is similar to that seen on the Ersari carpet with *gulli-guls*, no. 230, a feature which O'Bannon associated with Afghan weavings from the area between Mazar-i-Sahrif and Kunduz. There are also 'dice' flowers and a *kejebe* pattern frieze, motifs which, like the part *ertmen* guls in the frieze of no. 251, are probably borrowed from the Chodor.

Nagel, Stuttgart

Literature: O'Bannon, p. 124, figs. C, F (as Beshir and Ersari respectively); Landreau, no. 94 (as "Chakish yürt door rug")

255

255a

255. Ersari Group - Saddle Cover. Early 20th century

Size: 54 x 66 cm.

Condition: good.

A very similar example illustrated in *Hali* is described as a Beshir saddle blanket from the upper Amu-Darya region, on the border of Turkmenistan, Uzbekistan and Afghanistan and probably made around the turn of the century; both examples have patterns derived from ikat silks and velvets (see the ikat velvet coat in no. 255a), patterns which contain motifs which Cammann related to 'double' eagles and phoenix motifs.

Nagel, Stuttgart

Literature: Hali, vol. 3 no. 4, p. 351, fig. 11; Cammann, p. 32, fig. 5; Dovodov, no, 54 (Beshir Ersari torba)

256. Ersari Group - *Ensi*. 19th/20th century

Size: 162 x 138 cm.

Condition: partly worn.

Continuous series of conjoined diamonds form a vertically orientated lattice in the field, both this design and the palette being suggestive of ikat influence; see also the rare Chodor *ensi* illustrated as no. 224. The nine totemic shrubs seen in the dark brown ground *elem* are similar to those found on some Saryk examples (see nos. 21 ff.). The palette is somewhat similar to that of no. 234 and both might have been woven in the same area. The *sainak* pattern main border on three sides is typical; there is a zig-zag pattern outer guard and the piece retains its broad dark brown goats' hair selvedges.

Nagel, Stuttgart

Literature: Mackie and Thompson, no 59 ("square carpet for tent"); Loges, no 104 ("Ersari Beshir torba"); Hali 27, p. 22, no. 16 (Charshango torba)

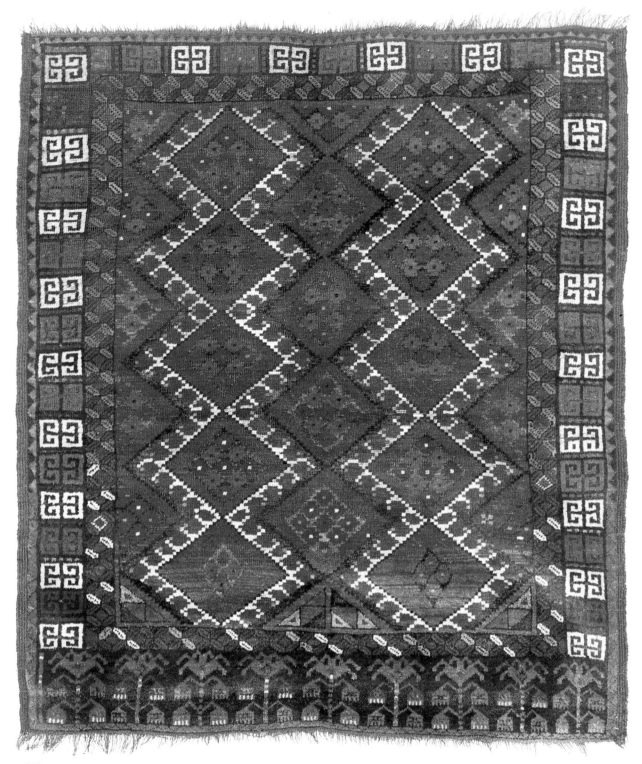

256

257

257. Ersari Group - *Torba*. 19th/20th century

Size: 40 x 143 cm.

Condition: very good, complete.
Both in structure and, to some extent, in ornament, this piece can be related to the saddle-cover illustrated as no. 255; Dovodov describes this pattern as *edresi*. The three large main medallions on this bag are sometimes called the 'Beshir gul', although its description as a gul is open to doubt. It also appears in halved form on some *torbas* (see the following *chuval*) and on some Beshir carpets as a border motif (see no. 281). It is rare to find a *torba* so well preserved, with a tightly woven pile and original fringes with 'netting'.
Nagel, Stuttgart
Literature: Franses, no. 16; Bausback, catalogue 1987-88, p. 189

258

259

258. Ersari Group - *Chuval*. 18th century

Size: 113 x 123 cm.

Condition: worn, areas of repair.
Certainly one of the earliest Ersari bags shown here, orginally catalogued by Nagel as 18th century. This strange repeated design in the ikat style is more often found on *torbas* of a later date and seems influenced by Beshir weavings. Variants of the motifs in the *elem* can be seen on nos. 259 and 263.
Nagel, Stuttgart
Literature: Schürmann, no. 45

259. Ersari Group - *Chuval*. 2nd third of the 19th century

Size: 123 x 162 cm.

Condition: worn.
An unusually large bag face from a quite well documented design group. The field lattice, placed so as to indicate an infinite repeat, is often found on different types of Ersari bags and main carpets (see no. 293). Moshkova asserted that *torbas* and *chuvals* of this design were woven in the settlements of Beshir and Burdalyk and she called the two variants seen in the pattern the *gaimak* gul and the *ak gaimak*. The design of the two main side borders is typical, each containing what could be interpreted as a stylised tree. According to Thacher, the design in the *elem* is 'borrowed' from East Turkestan weavings. Goats' hair warps, brown wool wefts; it has about 900 asymmetric knots per dm^2.
Nagel, Stuttgart
Literature: Moshkova, plates 97/7-8; Cassin and Hoffmeister, pl. 31; Thacher, pl. 36; Landreau, no. 83 (as Beshir chuval, early 19th century)

261

260

260. Ersari Group - *Torba*. Last quarter of the 19th century

Size: 45 x 107 cm.

Condition: very slight pile damage, otherwise good.

The *ak gaimak* pattern seen on the previous piece appears here in a single row and has hooked diamonds as interior decoration. The main border design is typical, as is the appearance of stylised floral motifs in the otherwise plain outer frame. Examples of this type are often described as Beshir, although it is not certain that all pieces so described were actually made in that settlement.
Nagel, Stuttgart
Literature: Hali 27, pp. 20 ff., no. 2; Milhofer, no. 48; Loges, no. 105

261. Ersari Group - *Chuval*. End of the 19th century

Size: 94 x 177 cm.

Condition: worn, repiled areas.
Here the *ak gaimak* field pattern is accompanied by its diamond shaped secondary motifs. This design type often has the *kochanak* main border pattern, as here. Chuvals such as this one with *elem* panels at both top and bottom are often found and a similar example to this, in both design and colour, formerly in the Straka Collection, was described as early 19th century. Some examples, however, can be dated much later because of their colours, showing that the design itself survived almost unchanged over a fairly long period. Small details of this example are piled in pale green silk.
Nagel, Stuttgart
Literature: Straka Collection, cat. no. 34

262

262. Ersari Group - *Chuval*. 2nd half of the 19th century

Size: 105 x 148 cm.

Condition: good, minimal repairs.

Given the number of examples that have survived, this well-known design must have been very popular for quite a long period of time. The three main motifs in the centre of the field can be related to those on the *ensi*, no. 254; here they are surrounded by zig-zag bands in the ikat style, giving an effect somewhat similar to that of the pieces with *ak gaimak* patterns just discussed. Examples are known on which the entire field is covered with such bands.

Nagel, Stuttgart

Literature: Loges, no. 101; Straka Collection, cat. no. 36; Bausback, no 503 (ensi with all over 'ikat band' design field)

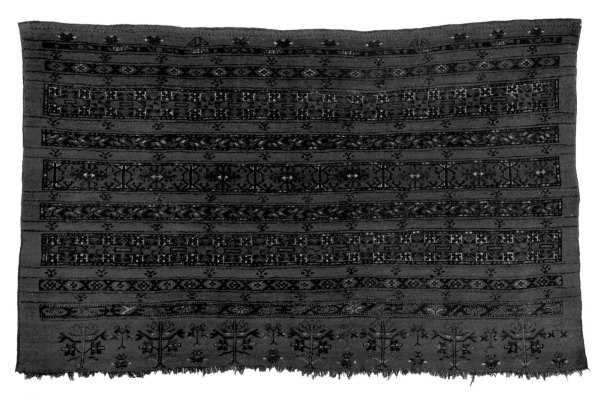

263

263. Ersari Group - *Chuval.* **3rd quarter of the 19th century**

Size: 93 x 162 cm.

Condition: very good.

This striped *chuval* belongs to a very specific design group. Although the *shudur* pattern seen in some of the stripes and the motifs in the *elem* are typically Ersari, other motifs are more usually associated with the Yomut while the banded *chuval* type in general is usually associated with the Tekke (see no. 81). It is interesting that, like Tekke *chuvals* of this design type, early Ersari examples also have unusually fine knotting, something which lends weight to the idea of design transference.

Nagel, Stuttgart

Literature: Reed, no. 44; Straka Collection, cat. no. 38; Gombos, no. 52

264

264. Ersari Group - *Chuval*. End of the 19th century

Size: 95 x 134 cm.

As on no. 262, the medallions of the field are framed by zig-zag bands. This bag, which has been called Chob-Bash, has medallions which might be related to the Chodor *ertmen* gul (see no. 251). Here, the medallions have hooks, resembling those of the Yomut *dyrnak* gul, although the palette is wider.
Nagel, Stuttgart
Literature: Cassin and Hoffmeister, pl.30 (as Ersari); Hali, vol. 3, no. 4, p. 317 (as Beshir)

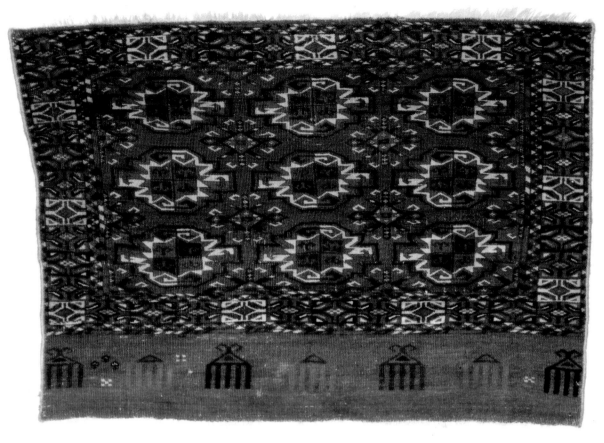

265

265. Kizil Ayak (?) - *Chuval*. 3rd quarter of the 19th century

Size: 85 x 123 cm.

Condition: worn, slightly trimmed at the sides.
In both field and border, this is very similar to an example illustrated by Loges as Kizil Ayak and to another in the Victoria and Albert Museum, London (inv. no. T.197-1922). Both the motifs and the palette also remind one of Tekke weavings (see no. 72). The seven large brocaded *muska* motifs in the flatwoven *elem* are worth mentioning; they are based on Turkoman jewelled breast pieces (see fig. 95).
Nagel, Stuttgart
Literature: Loges, no. 74

266. Kizil Ayak (?) - *Chuval*. End of the 19th century

Size: 72 x 169 cm.

Condition: very good.
Authors' opinions of largely similar pieces are mixed, with Azadi and Loges attributing them to Kizil Ayak whilst others hold different views. According to Loges, the principal motif used on most Kizil Ayak *chuvals* is the *chuval* gul with a quartered centre containing a repeated 'ram's horn' motif. The typical *elem* pattern has already been seen in very similar form on no. 241.
Nagel, Stuttgart
Literature: Loges, no. 75; Azadi, pl. 13b

267. Ersari Group - *Chuval*. End of the 19th century

Size: 96 x 124 cm.

Condition: wear, damage to corners.
The small but rounded main *chuval* guls are quartered with an 'X'-shaped motif in each quarter. These main guls are crowded together all over the field with no minor guls. The field is framed by a main border containing repeated *kochanak* motifs, and this is flanked by guards containing a mosaic-like continuous 'ribbon' pattern. The diagonal rows of shrubs in the *elem* remind one strongly of certain Saryk weavings. A largely similar piece was advertised by a U.S. dealer who described it as '...possibly affiliated with Saryk tribe, West Turkestan, 19th century.' (*Hali* Vol.5, No.2. San Francisco *Bay Area Supplement*, p.12).
Nagel, Stuttgart
Literature: Straka Collection, cat. no. 39

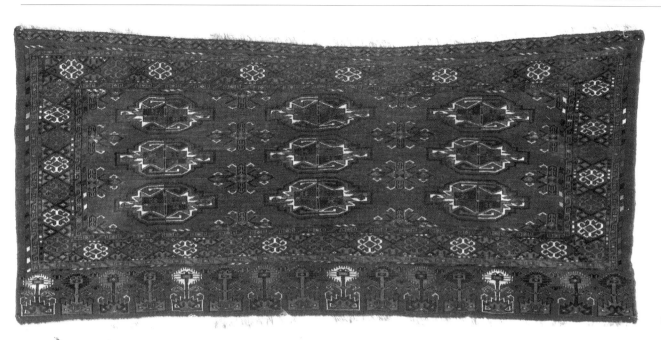

266

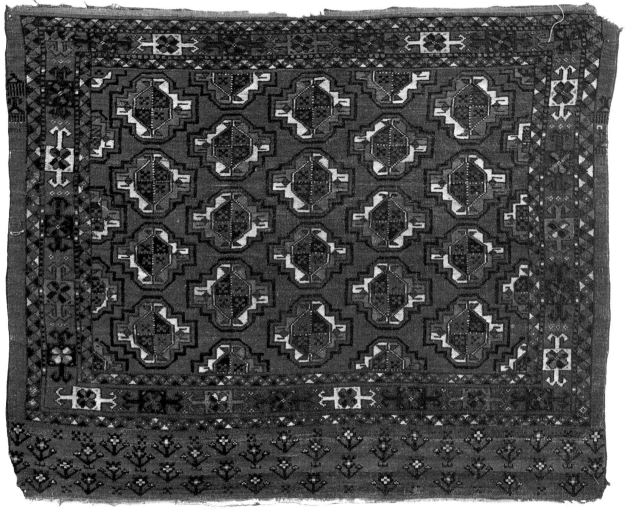

267

268

269

**268. Ersari Group - Piled Panel.
18th/19th century**

Size: 61 x 204 cm.

Condition: good for its age.
A remarkable panel, the design and large format relating to the *kejebe* design panels of the Salor (nos. 2 ff.); the latter are often described as *asmalyks* and like this example, can be considered as dating possibly to the 18th century. An example illustrated by Azadi even has the 'T'-shaped side borders typical of Salor pieces in this format, although this design feature has been dropped here in favour of the more usual four-sided border. It is interesting to note how the interior decoration of the main guls in the field relate to one of the 'Small Pattern Holbein' medallions found on early Anatolian rugs (see fig. 61).

**269. Ersari Group - Piled Panel.
19th century**

Size: 38 x 143 cm.

Condition: good generally, selvedges replaced.
There are two complete and one three-quarter medallions in the field of this *kejebe* design panel, thus implying an infinite lateral repeat; in the centre of each medallion there is an octagon with an eight-pointed star. The *kejebe* arches themselves, pointing inwards from top to bottom as on the previous example, have been simplified and contain small medallions, possibly amulets. Weavings of similar design were made by the Arabachi.
Nagel, Stuttgart
Literature: Azadi, pl.28b (torba); Tzareva, nos. 108 and 110 (Arabachi torba, Ersari group); Hali 28, p. 91, fig. 5

270

271

270. Ersari Group - Piled Panel.
Last quarter of the 19th century

Size: 59 x 169 cm.

Condition: slightly worn.
At first sight this does not seem part of the
same design group seen on the last two panels
or on the variant seen on the next example.
However, a form of 'star' medallion can still
be seen in the centre of the field of this
weaving, the field itself being defined by
hooked stripes doubled at the sides. At each
side of the field there are interesting motifs of
considerable antiquity; flanking this inner
field area, but still within the frame created by
the borders are remarkable bush-like motifs.
Nagel, Stuttgart
*Literature: Hali 27, p. 21, no. 10; Landreau,
no. 88*

271. Ersari Group - Piled Panel.
Mid 19th century

Size: 45 x 145 cm.

Condition: worn, repiled areas.
Though an analogous example has actually
been attributed to Beshir, this panel is part of
a homogeneous design group whose
weavings typically have either the outer
shudur pattern border – as in this piece – or a
star filled border. The main field motif seems
to be a version of the *kejebe* gul horizontally
stretched. Interestingly, the 'arch' forms
usually associated with the *kejebe* pattern
seem here to have been transformed into
kochak motifs.
Nagel, Stuttgart
*Literature: McMullan Collection, pl. 74; Hali
27, p. 22, fig. 11 (Hermitage Museum, St.
Petersburg); Hali 32, p. 22 (Ashmolean
Museum, Oxford); Loges, nos. 93-95*

272

272. Ersari Group - Piled Panel. 2nd half of the 19th century

Size: 37 x 130 cm.

As with Saryk and Tekke bag-faces and other panels, there is a large group of Ersari weavings with designs based on the *kejebe* pattern, usually with arched areas which oppose each other on either side of the field on the long side (see no. 5). Here there are four arches arranged side by side in one direction only, each surmounted by a double hook and filled with *sekme-guls* in a compartment-like arrangement. Individually, each arch is reminiscent of those found on *ensis*. The warps and wefts are of goats' hair and with about 1,800 asymmetric knots per dm²; original selvedges partly preserved and original added multi-coloured fringe.
Bausback, Mannheim
Literature: Loges, no. 96

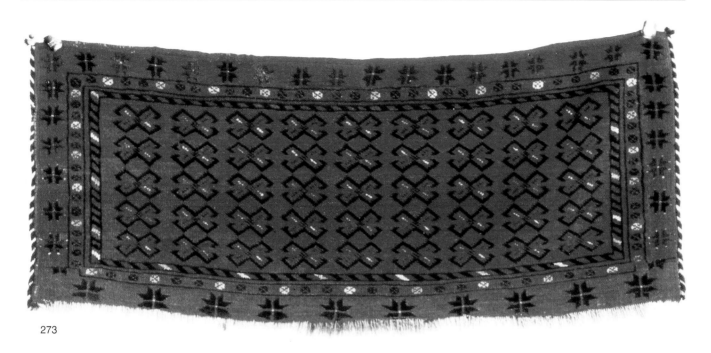

273

273. Ersari Group - *Torba*. 3rd quarter of the 19th century

Size: 40 x 100 cm.

Condition: signs of wear, repiling.
In style and palette, this bag-face seems related to no. 272, although the field pattern, consisting of quadrupled hooks arranged in rows, seems to be derived from flatweaves. No. 273a, for example, a Turkoman flatwoven *torba,* belongs to a very homogeneous group of weavings in a sumakh-like technique and can be compared to the large-scale flatweaves of the Yomut and Tekke (see no. 162a).
Christie's East, New York
Literature: Gombos, in Turkmenenforschung, vol. XIII, p. 120, no. 66; Straka Collection, cat. no. 40

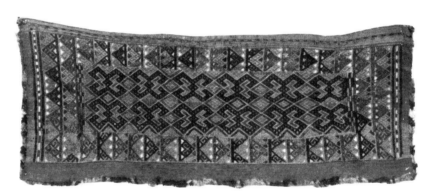

Detail 273a

274

275

274. Kizil Ayak (?) - Piled Panel. End of the 19th century

Size: 38 x 148 cm.

Condition: very good.

The *ashik* field pattern seen here is similar in style to that used by the Salor, Saryk, Tekke and Yomut. A comparable piece to this has been identified as Charshango, while other similarly decorated weavings have been variously identified in the literature, demonstrating the problems inherent in making firm attributions to tribes or regions.
Nagel, Stuttgart
Literature: Hali 27, p. 21, no. 5 (Charshango); Straka Collection, cat. no. 28 (as Yomut or Tekke); Dovodov, no. 57 (as a Chodor porsi, early 20th century)

276

275. Ersari Group - *Kapunuk*. End of the 19th century

Size: 53 x 120 cm.

Condition: slight moth damage.
Among the *kapunuks* woven by the various Turkoman tribes (see nos. 35 and 93), this example can be placed with weavings of the Ersari group because of its *shudur* border. Several Ersari group *kapunuks* are known, some with variants of the *kejebe* pattern and others in ikat style. Tiny parts of this example are piled in silk.
Nagel, Stuttgart
Literature: Azadi, in Pinner and Denny (eds.), nos. 1-5

276. Ersari Group - *Khalyk*. End (?) of the 19th century

Size: 61 x 95 cm.

Condition: good.
Such weavings - used as either decoration for the bridal carriage or for the breast of the bride's camel in the wedding procession - with the field decoration consisting of diagonally placed *kochaks*, were, until the appearance of this example, thought to be exclusively Tekke work; even the way the tassels are worked is the same as those on Tekke *khalyks*. This example, however, is clearly Ersari and is slightly larger than comparable Tekke weavings; an Ersari

kapunuk is also known with a white-ground *syrga* pattern border.
Nagel, Stuttgart
Literature: Azadi, pl. 29b (kapunuk)

277

278

**277. Beshir Ersari Group - *Chuval*.
19th century**

Size: 97 x 183 cm.

Condition: damaged, areas of repiling.
The *mina-khani* field pattern seen here,
together with the so-called Herati pattern (see
280 ff.), is more usually associated with 18th
and 19th century Persian carpets.
Nevertheless it seems to have pleased
weavers both in Amu-Darya and in the
Emirate of Bokhara for it has been found on
many types of weavings from bags to main
carpets. The use of cochineal-dyed silk for
small areas of the pile, as well as the *muska*
amulets in the upper outer frame, reminds one
of Salor weavings; a solitary rider appears in
the lower right corner of the *elem*.
Nagel, Stuttgart
*Literature: Mackie and Thompson, no. 89;
Dovodov, nos. 88-89 (as Ersari chuval with
charaty pattern, Beshir, late 19th century)*

278. Ersari Group - Piled Panel. End of the 19th century

Size: 33 x 145 cm.

Condition: very good.
Torbas with the *mina-khani* design are much rarer than *chuvals* with this design which the Turkomans call *zerbaf*. This piece, like the one illustrated in *Hali* (details below) may be by the Charshango, though it is believed to be an Ersari. The *Hali* piece has a velvety woollen pile, as does this one which also has some work piled with silk.
Nagel, Stuttgart
Literature: Hali 27, p. 21, fig. 8

279. Beshir Ersari - Large Main Carpet. 19th century

Size: 493 x 210 cm.

Condition: worn in places, a few small repairs. Here the *mina-khani* pattern is used for the field of a very large carpet whose size makes it unlikely to be the product of a nomadic loom. Such carpets are usually described as Beshir. Until 1918, the Emirate of Bukhara, bordered to the south and west by the Amu-Darya River, was a melting pot of various ethnic groups; thus it is difficult to assign weavings to any particular one of them.
Nagel, Stuttgart
Literature: Loges, no. 87; Schürmann, no. 55

279

280

280. Beshir Ersari - Large Carpet. End of the 19th century

Size: 848 x 340 cm.

Condition: worn, areas of repair.

Examples of this truly monumental size were, apparently, known as 'palace carpets' in Bukhara; a photograph taken in about 1909 shows an eminent citizen of the town with a similar carpet with the Herati pattern at his feet; this pattern is of Persian origin although the addition of octagons is a Turkoman feature (see also no. 286). Indeed, these octagons remind one of those found on 'Large Pattern Holbein' carpets made in Anatolia in the 15th century and of Mamluk Egyptian carpets of the 15th-16th centuries. The grid-like structure of the Herati pattern is not easily seen from this reproduction. Note the upward-pointing motifs in the middle border.
Nagel, Stuttgart
Literature: Straka Collection, cat. no. 31; Mackie and Thompson, p. 193, fig. 51 (photograph referred to above)

281. Beshir Ersari - Main Carpet.
3rd quarter of the 19th century

Size: 332 x 168 cm.

Condition: worn.
The underlying design framework of the
Herati pattern shows much more clearly here
than in the previous piece. It is arranged
around a diamond lattice with four fan-
shaped leaves to each diamond and four small
flower-heads at the corner. The motifs of the
main border at the long sides have a
compartment-like arrangement and the outer
guard has a version of the 'curled leaf'
pattern.
Nagel, Stuttgart
Literature: Thacher, pl. 40; Mackie and
Thompson, pl. 94

281

282

**282. Beshir Ersari - Piled Panel.
3rd quarter of the 19th century**

Size: 42 x 155 cm.

Condition: worn.

As with other Beshir weavings illustrated
here, this example has a pattern which is not
of Turkoman origin. Here there is a section of
the Herati pattern; this, as we have seen, is
often encountered on large or medium sized
Beshir carpets but rarely on small weavings.
The grid system of the design has disappeared
and at the sides, the pattern is divided by
vertical 'star' borders. Nevertheless, the
individual elements remain quite closely
crowded together. This weaving has a knot
density of about 1,200 per dm^2.

Nagel, Stuttgart

*Literature: Tzareva, no, 25 (Beshir Ersari
torba); Hali no. 27, p. 22, no. 12 (as Kerki);
Thacher, pl. 23*

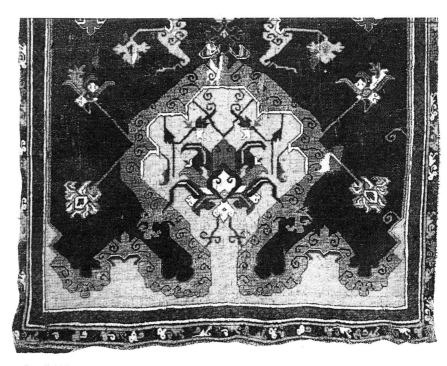

Detail 283a

283. Beshir Ersari - Main Carpet. 2nd half of the 19th century

Size: 323 x 157 cm.

Condition: slightly worn, repaired.
Like the field pattern of previously illustrated examples, the border pattern seen here is known as the 'Herati' and is found on many 19th century Persian carpets. Looking for the origin of this palmette motif leads us to Safavid and Ottoman art. No. 283a shows a detail of the Von Angeli prayer rug, made in 16th/17th century Ushak in western Anatolia, and now in the Islamic Museum, Berlin; at that time artists in Persia and Turkey were influenced by Chinese art, and the palmette we are discussing may be derived from the 'cloudband'. The use of such palmettes in both the border and, in variant style, in the field, is an unusual feature.
Nagel, Stuttgart
Literature: Tzareva, no. 97 (Ethnographic Museum, St. Peterburg); Hali vol. 3, no. 3, p. 2 (torba)

283

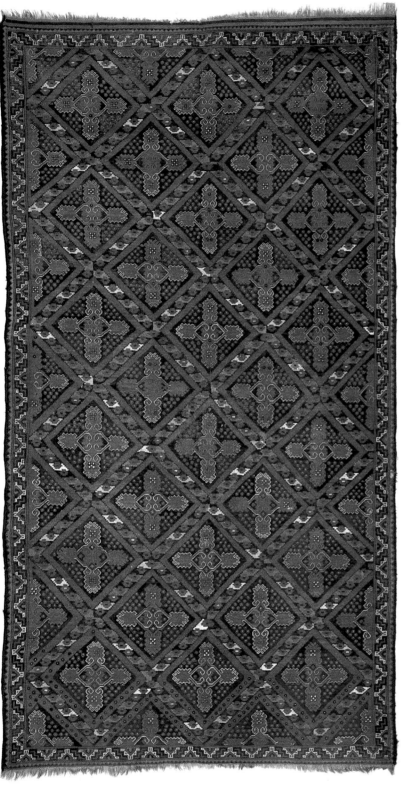

284. Beshir Ersari - Main Carpet. 2nd half of the 19th century

Size: 359 x 192 cm.

Condition: worn, repaired.
The cruciform motifs in the field of this carpet have often been said to have been derived from the Herati pattern; Thacher, writing about a *torba* with this design, remarked that the Persian rosettes and leaves had been stylised into more geometric forms appropriate to the Turkomans. Moshkova shows the design as being found on weavings by the Khirgiz from the Fergana Valley in Uzbekistan and Bogolyubov called it the "Jagal-Bayli-Göl" (the 'flying falcon' gul). Here, the interiors of the diamond grid have a pattern based on ikats. The main border has a pattern analogous to no. 293.
Nagel, Stuttgart
Literature: Thacher, pl. 43; Moshkova, plates 23/2 and 25/9; O'Bannon, p. 124 (more modern variant); Bennett, p. 168

285. Beshir Ersari - Main Carpet. Mid 19th century

Size: 279 x 204 cm.

Condition: a few areas of repiling, otherwise good.
The field pattern used here also shows the absorption of Persian patterns by weavers working in the environs of Bukhara. The main motif is a geometricised boteh, the precise origin of which is a matter of argument; its formal, curvilinear, form may have originated among shawl weavers in Kashmir in India, from whence it travelled to Persia, probably in the 18th century; no. 285a (p.306) shows how it appears on a typical Persian carpet, this one from Saruk.
Nagel, Stuttgart
Literature: Tzareva, no. 92; Mackie and Thompson, no. 93; Loges, no. 92

284

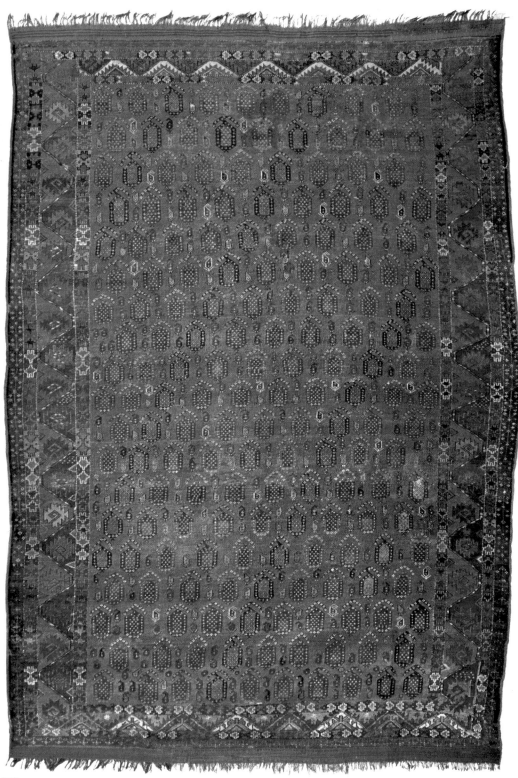

285

286. Beshir Ersari - Large Carpet. 2nd half of the 19th century

Size: 371 x 197 cm.

Condition: minimal repiling, otherwise good. At first glance, the plant-like motifs in the field of this large Beshir carpet also seem derived from botehs. Like the motifs on the following carpet, however, they may well be variants of a shield-like palmette which appears on some early, predominantly 18th century, Caucasian carpets (see no. 286a). The two principal field motifs are arranged diagonally and 'overlaid' with five octagons. Piled with very firm, lustrous wool.

Nagel, Stuttgart

Literature: König, 'Ersari Carpets', in Mackie and Thompson, no. 61, and 'Ersari Rug Names and Attributions', in Hali vol. 4, no. 2, p. 140, fig. 23

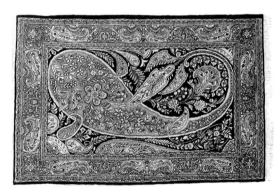

Detail 285a

287. Beshir Ersari - Main Carpet.
19th century

Size: 389 x 179 cm.

Condition: slightly worn, repaired.
Despite their rarity, carpets of this design type
are well-known through their powerful and
arresting field motifs; unfortunately, they
became known in the international carpet
trade as 'Tarantula Beshirs', although this
description is unlikely to have anything to do
with the meaning or derivation of the
principal motif. It may be more useful to
consider the motif as relating to the stylised
shield-like palmettes found on a very specific
design group of Caucasian rugs (see no.
286a). In the hexagonal centres of each motif
on this Beshir carpet there are tiny boteh-like
motifs while between the branches there are
equally tiny bird-like forms. Unfortunately,
this reproduction does not do justice to the
beautiful light blues and petrol blues which
are evident to the naked eye.
Nagel, Stuttgart
Literature: Schürmann, no. 43; Hali, vol. 3,
no. 4, pp. 296 ff.

Detail 286a

287

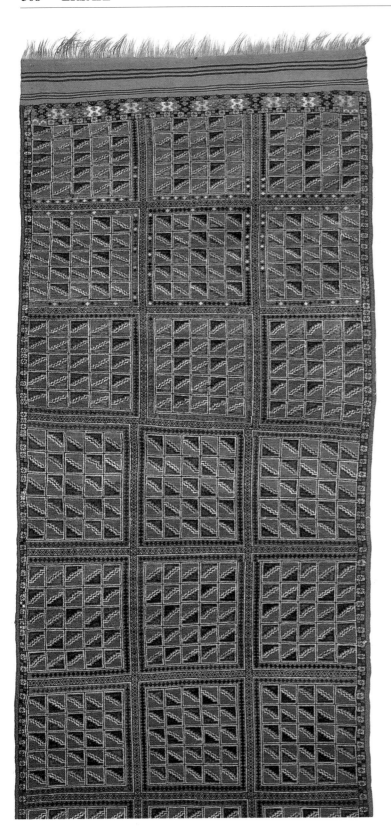

288

288. Beshir Ersari - Main Carpet (detail).
2nd half of the 19th century

Size: 393 x 147 cm.

Condition: good.

Like no. 287, the field is divided into
rectangles in a 3 x 8 arangement; the entire
field system is framed by a single and
unusually narrow border (although this
becomes wider and is flanked by guards at the
top and bottom). Each rectangle is covered
with a mosaic-like pattern made of pairs of
interlocking triangles, each with a zig-zag
hypotenuse. This type of field decoration is
also found on carpets with no division of the
field into rectangles and is sometimes created
by four interlocking triangles with a
diamond-shaped space at the centre. There
are also various bags, horse covers and *ensis*
known with similar designs. In fig. 103 below
we can see a variant in which the triangles
take the form of opposed pairs of stylised
birds seen in silhouette. Carpets of this design
type are often dated to before 1800 in the
literature.

Nagel, Stuttgart

*Literature: Gombos no. 18 (as Beshir or Kizil
Ayak, 18th/19th century); Rippon Boswell,
auction cat. no. 15, lot 69 (as Kizil Ayak,
around 1800 or earlier); Bausback, p. 525
(torba, as Khirgiz)*

Fig. 103

289. Beshir Ersari - Main Carpet. 2nd half of the 19th century

Size: 255 x 139 cm.

Condition: partly worn.

Carpets with variants of an overall diamond pattern, such as this and the following carpets, form an homogeneous group and are almost always described as Beshir in the literature. The principal variants are those with tile-like rows of diamonds or the one shown here, in which the field is divided into rectangles, each of which contains one huge diamond quartered diagonally by colour so as to create a vertical zig-zag effect. However, it is usual to find the *kochanak* motif repeated in the main and dividing borders (see the following example). The usual scheme of the field of carpets such as the one shown here is to have rectangles arranged vertically in two rows; all over the surface of each diamond and rectangle are tiny stylised floral motifs.

Nagel, Stuttgart

Literature: Azadi, pl. 7 (dated to the middle of the 18th century); Tzareva, nos. 95-96; Hali vol. 4, no. 2, , p. 139, nos. 15-16; Landreau, no. 78 (seven-sided Ersari asmalyk)

289

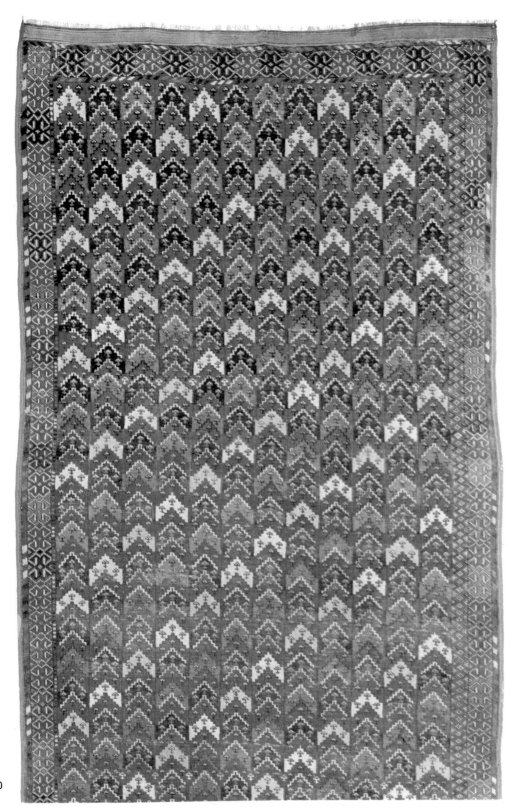

290

**290. Beshir Ersari - Main Carpet (detail).
19th century**

Size: 332 x 130 cm.

Condition: partly worn, repaired.

The rare field pattern of this carpet is related
both to the previous piece and to some Yomut
flatweaves and piled carpets (see nos. 55-56
and also no. 297). Examples with this and
with similar designs are sometimes said to
have an affinity with, or even to be, prayer
rugs. Each of the arch-like motifs contains
three flower-like motifs, a patterning similar
to that on the previous carpet. A careful look
will reveal a regulated use of colour.
Nagel, Stuttgart
*Literature: Hali no. 42, p. 4 (Beshir prayer
rug, Bausback, Mannheim); Hali no. 27, p. 90
(Kizil Ayak, Nagel, Stuttgart)*

**291. Beshir Ersari - Long Carpet.
19th century**

Size: 812 x 264 cm.

This carpet, in an unusually large and long
format, also has arched forms arranged one
above the other. As on many flat-weaves (see
no.55), these appear in several vertical panels
though not always in the same direction.
Again they are decorated with myriad small
stylised flowers. Some of the narrower white-
ground bands between the principal ones
have hooked ends, and are strongly
reminiscent of the mihrabs on the *saf* no. 297.
The design in the main borders is similar to
that on Kizil Ayak main carpets (see no. 238).
Goats' hair warps, brown wool wefts, about
900 asymmetric knots per dm^2.
Bausback, Mannheim

291

292

292. Beshir Ersari - Main Carpet. Middle of the 19th century

Size: 304 x 154 cm.

Condition: signs of wear, repairs.
As with variants of the *ertman* gul found on weavings other than Chodor (see no. 251), the presence of repeated *dyrnak* guls in the field of this carpet indicate that weavers in what may have been the context of metropolitan Bukhara were influenced by, and borrowed from, many sources. Whether or not this carpet has any other direct connection with the Yomut remains unclear, although it is worth noting that both versions of the gul appear in very pure form (see no. 104). The border design is typical for Beshir carpets and, according to Loges, the obvious use of yellow is also characteristic. In contrast to *dyrnak* gul *torbas*, Beshir main carpets with the *dyrnak* gul are very rare.
Nagel, Stuttgart
Literature: Loges, no. 83; Hali 27, p. 21, fig. 7 (torba, as either Kizil Ayak or Chob-Bash

**293. Beshir Ersari - Main Carpet.
19th century**

Size: 344 x 175 cm.

There is an obvious design relationship
between this carpet and no. 284. Some would
argue that the very different palette used for
this carpet may indicate an early origin,
possibly around 1800. The field pattern, the
gaimak-gul, was probably derived from ikats
and is more often found used on bags (see no.
259). Indeed, this carpet seems to occupy a
special place among the quite small number
of large carpets with this field design: most
other examples are far more 'rustic' both in
colour and weave. This carpet has goats' hair
warps and, surprisingly, symmetric knotting
of about 800 per dm².
Bausback, Mannheim
*Literature: Schürmann, no. 45; Gombos,
no. 19; Lefevre, pl. 19*

293

294

294. Beshir Ersari - Small Rug.
Mid 19th century

Size: 149 x 113 cm.

Condition: worn.
An unusually small example of a so-called
'cloudband' Beshir; one of the red forms
takes the shape of Chinese cloudbands (*Tchi*)
and the other is interpreted as a simplified
celestial dragon (see no. 283a). Typically, the
cloudbands have ends resembling snakes'
heads and are outlined and highlighted by tiny
white stars. The changing ground colours of
the field are usual for this design type, as are
the small red 'fillers' around the main motifs,
some like botehs, others in the form of eight-
pointed stars. This field design is also found
on *ensis* and *torbas*.
Nagel, Stuttgart
*Literature: Vienna, pl. 119; Thompson, p. 76
(ensi); Hali 27, p. 20, fig. 4 (torba, as
Charshangu)*

295. Beshir Ersari - Prayer Rug.
3rd quarter of the 19th century

Size: 165 x 100 cm.

Condition: signs of wear.
This rare prayer rug is fascinating for its
clarity of colour and design. The ivory-
ground field is dominated by a red mihrab or
prayer niche of typical form and crowned at
the top with an arch-like motif. Many
analogies can be found among early
Anatolian and other carpets of the 16th and
17th centuries. Unlike many of these early
rugs, this piece does not have two octagonal
motifs in the mihrab, the lower one touching
the upper one and thus forming the so-called
're-entry' motif. The rows of shrubs in both
the mihrab itself and the surrounding field
areas are typical features of Beshir prayer
rugs.
Nagel, Stuttgart

296

297

296. Beshir Ersari - Prayer Rug.
19th century

Size: 224 x 106 cm.

Condition: areas of repiling.
Unlike many Beshir prayer rugs, which may
have been made in urban workshops, this
example and others like it may, according to
Hoffmeister, have been made in one of the
surrounding villages or by nomads. However,
both the drawing and the motifs seen here, as
well as the colour, indicate a comparatively
late stage of development. Others, however,
have not agreed with this view and have dated
such rugs to the 18th century
Nagel, Stuttgart
*Literature: Hoffmeister, no. 21 (as 18th
century); Hubel, col. pl. 25; Hali vol. 5, no. 4,
p. 56 (Galerie Herrmann, Munich, as end of
the 18th century)*

297. Beshir Ersari - *Saf* (detail). About 1900

Size: 589 x 317 cm.

Condition: very worn, extensive damage.
Prayer rugs with multiple mihrabs, sometimes
as many as twelve, are called *safs*. 16/17th
century examples are known from Anatolia,
Persia and India and later ones from East
Turkestan. The seven white-ground prayer
niches on this rug are placed on a field
covered with a version of the so-called Herati
pattern (see nos. 280 and 281) and are
decorated internally with stylised botehs.
At auction in New York in April, 1988, this
saf, despite its rarity, fetched only $6,050, a
price which reflects both the difficulties
inherent in displaying a rug of this size and
format, and also the poor condition of this
example.
Christie's East, New York
Literature: Straka Collection, cat. no. 42

**298. Beshir Ersari - Prayer Rug.
Early 19th century**

Size: 181 x 101 cm.

Robert Pinner wrote that this piece might
almost be taken for "its famous relative from
the Dudin Collection in Leningrad" which
has been dated by Tzareva to "not later than
the beginning of the 19th century". The rug
shown here has a different border design,
apparently finer knotting and three more
colours. On the Dudin rug, the mihrab, with
its arch crowned with triple *kochanak* motifs,
is outlined by diagonally striped bands.
Because of its rarity, its value is almost
impossible to estimate.
Sailer, Salzburg
*Literature: Tzareva, no. 98 (Dudin
Collection); Martin, 1984, no. 35 (identical);
Pinner, Vienna (this rug)*

298

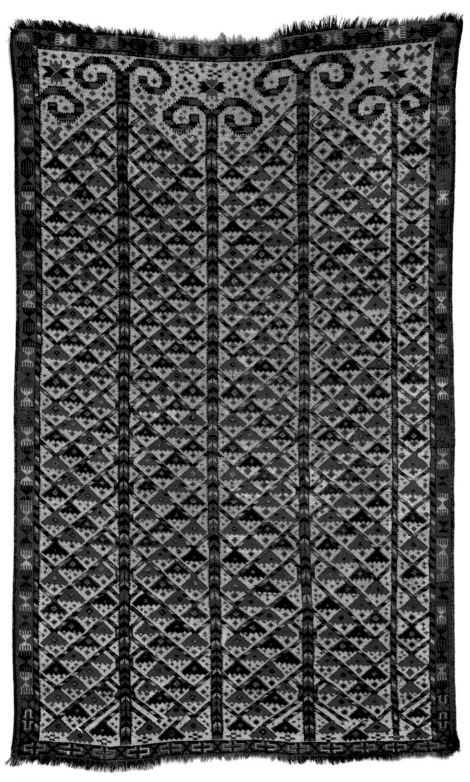

299

299. Beshir Ersari - Prayer Rug. 19th century

Size: 193 x 122 cm.

This very rare prayer rug is closely related to the one just discussed; here, however, there is not one clearly defined mihrab but four tree-like 'trunks' arranged so as to form a double mihrab, or three and a half interlocking ones of two different sizes; they all have hanging 'branches' and are surmounted by great double-hooked 'crowns'. However, these are very similar in outline to the single prayer niche seen on the previous piece; it is also possible that the triangular motifs may be stylised versions of the more curvilinear floral decoration found on no. 298 (see no. 242). Both in design and colour, this rug is quite breathtaking.
Bausback, Mannheim
Literature: Hali 32, p. 51 (Ashmolean Museum, Oxford); Oakville, Ontario (as 'Ersari Rug, Southeast Turkmenia, mid 19th century')